Dismantling the Racism Machine

While scholars have been developing valuable research on race and racism for decades, this work does not often reach the beginning college student or the general public, who rarely learn a basic history of race and racism. If we are to dismantle systemic racism and create a more just society, people need a place to begin. This accessible, introductory, and interdisciplinary guide can be one such place. Grounded in critical race theory, this book uses the metaphor of the Racism Machine to highlight that race is a social construct and that racism is a system of oppression based on invented racial categories. It debunks the false ideology that race is biological. As a manual, this book presents clear instructions for understanding the history of race, including whiteness, starting in colonial America, where the elite created a hierarchy of racial categories to maintain their power through a divide-and-conquer strategy. As a toolbox, this book provides a variety of specific action steps that readers can take once they have developed a foundational understanding of the history of white supremacy, a history that includes how the Racism Machine has been recalibrated to perpetuate racism in a supposedly "post-racial" era.

Karen Gaffney is a Professor of English at Raritan Valley Community College in New Jersey, where she teaches courses in composition, gender, and race. She focuses on antiracism activism in the community, on her blog (dividednolonger.com), and in workshops at the White Privilege Conference and Netroots Nation.

Dismantling the Racism Machine

A Manual and Toolbox

Karen Gaffney

Routledge
Taylor & Francis Group

NEW YORK AND LONDON

First published 2018
by Routledge
711 Third Avenue, New York, NY 10017

and by Routledge
2 Park Square, Milton Park, Abingdon, Oxon OX14 4RN

Routledge is an imprint of the Taylor & Francis Group, an informa business

© 2018 Karen Gaffney

Library of Congress Cataloging-in-Publication Data
A catalog record for this book has been requested

ISBN: 978-1-138-03721-2 (hbk)
ISBN: 978-1-138-03722-9 (pbk)
ISBN: 978-1-315-17800-4 (ebk)

Typeset in Adobe Caslon Pro
by Apex CoVantage, LLC

CONTENTS

PREFACE AND ACKNOWLEDGMENTS

I'd like to begin by introducing myself so readers have some context for this book and to thank those who have helped me. First and foremost, I want to acknowledge that as a white woman, I am writing from a place of privilege. I am not writing about what it means to be a person of color because I will never have that experience. I am writing as a white person who has inherited a system of privilege that I seek to dismantle because it is unjust.

I have been an English professor at Raritan Valley Community College in New Jersey since 2003, which has allowed me to establish a foundation in teaching introductory-level courses because my students are all freshmen and sophomores. I have greatly valued the opportunity to serve the community by teaching at an open-access institution. More than ten years ago, I developed an English literature elective called Race in American Literature and Popular Culture, an introductory course on race and racism. While I had no trouble finding literature and scholarship to assign, the options for an introductory and interdisciplinary textbook were limited. I hope this text can contribute to that need by connecting research from many disciplines and translating that into accessible concepts, history, and action items for readers new to this work. I've had my students in mind as I've been working on this project, and I'm especially thankful to former students Alicia Ventriglia and Rachel Dietz for providing feedback on this manuscript.

In the spring of 2017, I taught this course inside the only women's prison in New Jersey, the Edna Mahan Correctional Facility for Women, as part of my college's program to offer our liberal arts degree in several prisons in New Jersey. I'm grateful to the women inside for sharing their perspectives and insight with me. The urgency in this book's action section (Step 5) to end mass incarceration is not abstract or merely intellectual; the urgency is real for the women of Edna Mahan and for the more than two million people in our prisons, jails, and detention centers.

From October 2016 to April 2017, I facilitated a version of the course for the community that was free and open to the public. Hosted by the Unitarian Universalist Congregation of Somerset Hills (based in Somerville, NJ), I met with about twenty community members every month to discuss assigned readings that focused on the key concepts of this book: debunking the false ideology that race is biological, understanding that racism is systemic, and taking action to end systemic racism. Special thanks to Reverend Jennifer Kelleher and Social Action Committee Chair Michelle Edgar for supporting this course and for providing feedback on this manuscript. Facilitating this course outside of a traditional academic setting allowed me to engage this work in a different way, and I greatly appreciate the time and commitment of this group and how much they taught me. Many members also contributed feedback on this manuscript, and for that, I am especially grateful. Thank you especially to Jacque Drummer, Doug Anderson, Jeff Bradley, and Anne Ehrhart.

Working with the local social justice organization the Meta Theatre Company has taught me how theatre can be a path to justice in prison, at school, and in the community. I was particularly grateful to Meta to be able to participate in an ongoing discussion of the book titled *The New Jim Crow* at the Edna Mahan Correctional Facility for Women and in a corresponding weekly discussion in the community. Presenting at the White Privilege Conference with Meta members has been extremely valuable in helping me work on accountability and action. I'm especially thankful to Caroline Hann, Barbara Cannell, and Cyndie Wiggins for your leadership and your dedication to the women of Edna Mahan.

Being an active part of the Hunterdon County Anti-Racism Coalition for more than two years has allowed me to participate in discussions, events, and actions aimed at raising awareness about racism in a predominantly white and wealthy area of rural New Jersey. Special thanks to Alexa Offenhauer, Nicole Maniez, and Laura Higgins for your leadership and to the group for your work. Thank you to Filomena Hengst for your community organizing and your feedback on this manuscript. I've also been honored to participate in the planning process for the Stoutsburg Sourland African American Museum in Somerset County, New Jersey, which is teaching me a history of my local community. Also, helping create the new Central Jersey Community Coalition has been another opportunity for me to learn from and support local organizations, activists, and community members that work on a variety of social justice issues. Serving on the board of NORWESCAP (the Northwest New Jersey Community Action Partnership) has also taught me about supporting local communities. Several years ago, serving as a county meet-up leader for Democracy for America, running for local office, and working on local campaigns helped me understand the need for more people to get involved in politics at the local level, and I also learned how desperately we need to separate money from politics.

My formal educational journey in antiracism began in college at Wesleyan University in Connecticut in 1990, where I took a variety of courses that analyzed systems of power and oppression. In 2003, I received my PhD in English from the University of Delaware, where I specialized in critical race theory (CRT, a field of legal scholarship) and contemporary women's literature. Thank you to Alvina Quintana for introducing me to CRT and for encouraging me and to Jessica Schiffman for the supportive environment and opportunities in women's studies. I have been an avid reader of critical race theory ever since grad school, and I've been honored (especially as someone who did not attend law school) to present my work at recent critical race theory conferences at Yale Law School and UCLA Law School. My training in English has given me close-reading and analytical skills that I apply to all of the disciplines in which I read, including law, ethnic studies, history, American studies, cultural studies, media studies, sociology, and science.

As a self-proclaimed conference nerd, I want to acknowledge how much I've learned from listening to activists, writers, and scholars from all over the country share their work. Attending conferences is a critical part of my education, so I want to thank the following: Facing Race, the White Privilege Conference, Netroots Nation, Critical Race Studies in Education Association, the American Studies Association, the Working Class Studies Association, the Popular Culture Association, and the Modern Language Association. I've been lucky enough to see those who inspire me the most, including Kimberlé Crenshaw, Cheryl Harris, Ian Haney López, Linda Sarsour, Michelle Alexander, Rinku Sen, Ava DuVernay, and Elizabeth Warren.

This manuscript has been many years in the making. Some of its foundational ideas go back to my dissertation, and, since then, this project has taken many forms. At one time, I was focusing on a more scholarly project, but then I shifted to something that would translate that scholarship to beginners, because I realized that while so much impressive scholarship analyzing systemic racism existed, not enough was breaking through to the general reader or the beginning college student. I felt like that introduction was a contribution I could make.

Many people have helped me develop this project, in addition to those already named, and I am very grateful. The Research Writing Group at RVCC has patiently looked at many versions of my project, and their feedback has been critical. Special thanks to Michelle Brazier, Brandyn Heppard, Carl Lindskoog, Jessica Darkenwald DeCola, Jennifer Pearce Morris, and Lauren Braun-Strumfels. I also want to thank Alicia Liss, Roberta Harmon, Shay Wadher, Isabel Gutierrez, Kathy Suk, Karen Gutshall, Kevin Hinkle, Charlie Bondhus, Christine Pipitone-Herron, Sterling Bland, Carolyn Bitzer, Mike Goldberg, Christine Foster Cates, Ginger Hoffman, Ling Tjoeng, Lynn Hacker, Katrina Buchau, John Pollock, Sadiyah Seraaj, and Jenny Gleason for their ongoing support. Special thanks to Stacie McCormick for spending so much time giving me feedback over the years. I am grateful to the English department for their encouragement and to RVCC for the spring sabbatical in 2016 that allowed me to focus. Thank you so much to Routledge for this opportunity.

A very special thanks to my parents for their unconditional support and to the rest of my family and friends. Finally, I want to thank my partner, Andy Manno, for his unwavering support and encouraging feedback at every step of this ever-evolving project.

Introduction
Read This First

First and foremost, thank you for picking up this book. Engaging in racial justice is important and challenging, and I appreciate you taking time to consider this text. I am writing this introduction to several audiences, and most people are likely to belong to multiple audiences.

- To students: You may be reading this book for a course that is required, or it may be an elective. Either way, I hope you will have an open mind. There will likely be some history and concepts that you have not heard about before, and I hope reading this book will become an opportunity for you to learn, engage with your classmates, and consider how you want to take what you learn outside of the classroom.
- To readers of color: As a white educator, I appreciate that you are taking the time to read my work. I recognize that while I've studied history, laws, theories, and literature related to race and racism for a long time, I have never known and will never know what it is like to be a person of color.
- To white readers: You may have already read a lot about race and racism, or this may be your introduction. Either way, I ask that you have an open mind. This book will likely highlight aspects of

American history you have not learned and perhaps don't want to learn. I believe that we can only make progress toward racial justice if more white people learn what they are not often taught. You shouldn't feel guilty for not knowing this history. The system that I'll be describing works because many white people are not taught the inner-workings of the Racism Machine. Once we learn this history, then I strongly believe we have a responsibility to take action. (See Step 5 action #4.)

- To educators: I know the challenges of teaching, especially when it comes to a topic that many people want to avoid. I created this book with my own students in mind because I was never able to find an introductory book for beginners new to studying race and racism, something accessible, interdisciplinary, and relatively brief that could supplement other more advanced scholarship and literature. I am less focused on presenting my own original research and more interested in attempting to translate the massive amount of existing scholarship into an accessible introduction. I hope readers will then on their own turn to scholars and writers to learn more. I also hope you'll find the apparatus of this book helpful as you work with your students to engage in this work (especially the bolded key words, Reflection Questions, and Recommended Resources in every Step and the actions in Step 5). If you are new to teaching about race, I hope this book will equip you with strategies you can apply to your discipline and to the age and level of your students. If you are experienced with teaching about race, I hope this book's introductory approach helps supplement the work you're already doing. If you're a parent, then I hope the apparatus designed for educators can also guide you as well. (See Step 5 actions #1A, #3D, and #5.)

- To community groups: As with students who are reading this book together, I hope you will also find this book to be an opportunity for you to learn, grow, and take action together. It can be daunting to engage this work on your own, so reading together can be a powerful way to form community and take action.

- To individuals: You certainly don't need to be part of a group to read this book and engage in action. You need to start where you're at, and it's possible that while you may start this work on your own, you'll make connections to various groups along the way.

In order to help make sure readers are familiar with vocabulary that appears in this book, I've organized it so that the first time the term appears, it's bolded, and there is a definition. Rather than have a separate glossary where definitions are outside of the main text, I find it more effective to explain a concept in context. It will also appear in the index.

You will also see that at the end of Steps 1 through 5, there are Reflection Questions, open-ended questions that urge the reader to think about the ideas described in the chapter, to make connections, and to grow. Individuals can think about these questions during the reading process and even write about them. Educators can assign questions to students in a variety of individual and group assignments. Community groups can also use the questions as a springboard for discussion.

In addition, at the end of Steps 1 through 5, you will see Recommended Resources. These films, online videos, websites, articles, and books provide additional information about the concepts introduced in that chapter. Keep in mind that each Step barely scratches the surface of what many scholars have spent years and entire books explaining. If you want to know more about any of the events or issues discussed, I encourage you to follow up on one or more of these resources, which explore the topics in more depth and nuance.

Throughout Steps 1 through 4, you'll see references to specific actions in Step 5 that follow through on the issues and history described. All of Step 5 is devoted to action, and I've tried to identify actions that can work for a wide variety of audiences. I have assigned action items to my students, and in that context, I find that a small step of required action for a beginner helps set the stage for them to take a larger action on their own in the future. Actions can be taken individually, with other students, community members, colleagues, or other groups organized in person or online.

In order to keep this work current with new resources and to respond to questions and feedback, I will continue to update the blog I created in 2014: *Divided No Longer* (see dividednolonger.com).

I want to provide some key concepts that should establish a foundation for this book. I begin with **critical race theory (CRT)**, a legal studies field that has greatly influenced my understanding of race and racism. It developed in the 1980s when some legal scholars were dissatisfied with traditional approaches to civil rights scholarship. I find CRT valuable for three main reasons:

1. CRT scholars write in a creative and accessible way so that those of us who did not attend law school can better understand how the law contributes to racism. Rather than write very traditional law review articles, they write what they call "counter-accounts" or "oppositionist accounts" (Crenshaw et al. xiii). For example, one of the founders of this field, Derrick Bell, wrote what we might call science fiction as a way to analyze racism, as Step 3 will explore.

2. CRT scholars focus on analyzing **systemic racism**, which means that racism is embedded in our systems, including the media, criminal justice, education, healthcare, and more. When CRT scholars examine racism as systemic, they understand it as institutional and structural (built into institutions and structures) rather than focusing on racism as an individual phenomenon. Yes, individuals can certainly be racist, but if we focus solely on preventing individuals from making racist comments, we would not get to the heart of racism, which is built into our systems in ways we often don't realize. This book will explore systemic racism throughout by using the metaphor of the Racism Machine.

3. CRT scholars focus on action, not just on analysis, what one of the founding anthologies calls "a desire not merely to understand the vexed bond between law and racial power but to *change* it" (Crenshaw et al. xiii).

There is also a series of related words that can cause beginners a lot of confusion. These words include **prejudice** and **bias**, which can be very vague. While one might use a word like prejudice or bias to mean systemic racism, these words also reflect individual beliefs unrelated to systems. In other words, prejudice and bias reflect a negative view about someone or something, but the words prejudice and bias don't clarify whether that negative view replicates a larger negative view connected to systems and power. Prejudice essentially means a judgment one makes beforehand (indicated by the prefix "pre–"). Prejudice and bias are often used interchangeably. For example, a person could have a prejudice or a bias against people who wear green clothes. This prejudice or bias doesn't have anything to do with a system or with power; it's just at the personal or individual level. Yes, a person with this bias could treat someone who wears green clothes poorly or even unfairly, and that's a problem, but there is no system that oppresses people who wear green clothes. Therefore, this person's belief is only at the individual level and not systemic. Likewise, a person of color could have a prejudice against white people, but there is no system that oppresses white people. Therefore, this person's belief is individual and not systemic; this belief is not reflected, repeated, and reinforced by larger systems through oppression, which will be defined momentarily.

Implicit bias is a term that has become widely used recently, and it refers to bias we have that is not obvious or explicit to us; it is unconscious. While the vagueness of the term bias could mean the phrase "implicit bias" refers to any type of unconscious bias, systemic or not, the term "implicit bias" today generally refers to unconscious bias that reflects larger systems. Harvard University developed Project Implicit, which includes online Implicit Association Tests for a variety of issues, including race (see Step 5 action #4).

How do you know whether a bias or prejudice reflects a larger system or is just individual? Do a **power analysis**, in which you ask questions that can determine the power dynamic. Consider questions like:

- Is the bias reinforced in mainstream media, like television and film?
- Is the bias reinforced in systems like criminal justice or education?
- Is the bias something that may be encountered when applying for a job?
- Is the bias something that may limit access to resources?
- Is there a history of this bias?

Answering "yes" would likely reveal a bias or prejudice that does reflect a larger system of power, meaning that it is not merely an individual bias or prejudice but also something systemic and oppressive. For example, if you asked these questions about a bias against people who wear green clothes, the answers to all of the questions would be "no," which would reinforce that this bias is on the individual level only and not systemic. Likewise, if you asked these questions about a bias against white people, the answers to all of the questions would be "no," which would also reinforce that this bias is on the individual level only and not systemic. However, if you asked these questions about a bias against people of color, then the answers would be "yes," indicating the persistence of systemic racism, as this book will explain.

The word **oppression** is important here because it means systems of domination that relate to power. **Discrimination** is also a related term to mean oppressive actions carried out against marginalized individuals or groups. Finally, while there is some merit to the formula that "racism equals power plus prejudice," which one may encounter in a variety of social media, articles, and workshops, I'm not sure that's the most helpful way of understanding these issues. This definition doesn't encourage us to examine the history of this power, and it doesn't encourage the necessary analysis of how systems replicate this power.

Furthermore, think of the word oppression as an umbrella term that includes racism, but it also includes other systems of domination like sexism, classism, ableism, homophobia, transphobia, Islamophobia, and xenophobia. Each of these terms identifies the subjugation of marginalized people, including, respectively, women, people in poverty, people with disabilities, LGBTQ people, trans people, Muslims, and foreigners. However, many people belong to multiple marginalized categories, and their multiple marginalization, or **intersectionality**, often gets ignored. One ongoing problem has been that some activists, scholars, and other writers sometimes treat categories like race, gender, sexual orientation, and class as separate rather than as intersecting, as if people only belong to one category. When that perspective is used, then it's often the more powerful group, the dominant group, that gets the attention.

For example, a lot of scholarship about sexism has focused on straight, middle-class, white women, as if the category of women did not include women who were marginalized in other ways, like by race, LGBTQ identity, and socioeconomic class. CRT scholar Kimberlé Crenshaw uses the term intersectionality to describe an approach in which we recognize the intersections of multiple categories of oppression rather than default to the dominant group. For example, Crenshaw has helped develop a #SayHerName campaign in order to highlight how black women are killed by police violence, not just black men, who tend to get more attention.

All of these reasons contribute to why I tend to avoid identifying an individual as a "racist." I think it's much more effective to identify beliefs, comments, laws, and policies as racist because they can be tied to structure. It is only when we dismantle structures of racism that we can end racism. Focusing on a few bad apples who are overt racists will not end racism because the systems get ignored. For example, sociologist Eduardo Bonilla-Silva developed the term "racism without 'racists,'" the title of his classic text, to describe how racism operates today in a society in which most white people do not identify as racist.

As I will discuss throughout this book, I use the metaphor of the **Racism Machine** to highlight several key concepts:

1. As Step 1 will discuss, race is a social construct, and racism is a system of oppression based on invented racial categories.
2. The elite created racial categories and positioned them on a hierarchy with white at the top to protect and maintain their power through a divide-and-conquer strategy.
3. To dismantle racism, we need to understand the history and construction of race.
4. Racism is very complex, with wheels, cogs, chains, and pulleys connecting systems of education, media, law, criminal justice, housing, finance, healthcare, politics, pop culture, and more.

My title, *Dismantling the Racism Machine: A Manual and Toolbox*, identifies the Racism Machine as my primary focus, with step-by-step instructions, like a manual, for understanding the history and construction of this machine. However, this project is not only a manual, but it is also a toolbox, an approach that allows the reader to identify and select which tools can best suit the reader's context and goals. Finally, I use the word "dismantle" to emphasize the tangible nature of this project. Yes, this book is meant to raise awareness about several key theoretical concepts, but it is not intended to remain abstract. Once the reader develops a foundational understanding of how racism was built and perpetuated for centuries, there are tangible action steps that the reader can immediately turn to.

Last, a note on terms: as I will discuss in Step 1, I don't support using the word Caucasian because it makes whiteness sound like a scientific category when it isn't. As Step 1 will explain, whiteness is an invention created to protect a small, powerful elite. I also use the term people of color when discussing people who are not white. I do want to make sure that readers new to this work understand that "people of color" is usually considered a respectful, appropriate term today, though of course we must recognize that people should self-identify with the term they want used. Furthermore, beginners to this work should understand that the term "people of color" and the term "colored" are not interchangeable, a source of confusion I was surprised to notice among some of my students, including those who are learning the English language. The term "colored" is not acceptable. It was used throughout our history in an insulting and oppressive way to reinforce racism.

When speaking of groups of people, I have tried to be as inclusive as possible. I usually use the term black rather than African American because African American does not include Caribbean Americans and African immigrants. Writers and activists who focus on the importance of the political aspect of the term black have also persuaded me. I tend to avoid the term Hispanic, which came from the US government and focuses solely on Spanish speakers and excludes Latin Americans from the Portuguese-speaking country of Brazil. Instead, I use terms from the community. While I had been using Latino and Latina, more recently, I have tried to switch to **Latinx**, a more inclusive term because it does not depend on choosing one gender (the male Latino vs. the female Latina). The term Latinx also avoids using the masculine form Latinos when referring to both males and females. I also support the shift away from using a hyphen in terms like Asian American.

Thank you again for your time, and I hope you will consider emailing me with your feedback (DismantlingTheRacismMachine@gmail.com).

Reflection Questions

1. Why did you decide to read this book? Or why are you being asked to read this book?
2. What do you hope to learn from this book?
3. Does anything presented so far surprise you? If so, how?
4. What reflection question would you create, and why?

Recommended Resources

Films

Africa's Great Civilizations. PBS, 2017.
The African Americans: Many Rivers to Cross. Inkwell Films, Kunhardt McGee Productions, and THIRTEEN Productions, LLC, 2013.
Race: The Power of an Illusion. California Newsreel, 2003.
White Like Me. Media Education Foundation, 2013.

Online Videos

Decoded. Created by Franchesca Ramsey, MTV, 2015–present, YouTube.
Smooth, Jay. "Our New Video Series '#RaceAnd' Captures the Essence of Intersectionality." *Colorlines*, Race Forward, 4 May 2016, www.colorlines.com/articles/our-new-video-series-raceand-captures-essence-intersectionality.
Unequal Opportunity Race. Created by Kimberlé Crenshaw and Luke Harris, African American Policy Forum, 29 November 2010, www.youtube.com/watch?v=eBb5Tg OXgNY.

Websites

Race: Are We So Different? American Anthropological Association, 2016, www.understandingrace.org/.
Race: The Power of an Illusion. California Newsreel, www.pbs.org/race.

Articles

Gates, Henry Louis, Jr. "The History the Slaveholders Wanted Us to Forget." *New York Times*, 4 February 2017, nyti.ms/2k83fUS.
Kendi, Ibram X. "A History of Race and Racism in America, in 24 Chapters." *New York Times*, 22 February 2017, nyti.ms/2m7VVNC.
McIntosh, Peggy. "White Privilege: Unpacking the Invisible Knapsack." 1989, national seedproject.org/white-privilege-unpacking-the-invisible-knapsack.
Wise, Tim. "Hard on Systems, Soft on People: Fighting for Social Change as If People Matter." *Tim Wise*, 16 August 2014, www.timwise.org/2014/08/hard-on-systems-soft-on-people-fighting-for-social-change-as-if-people-matter/.

Books

Anderson, Carol. *White Rage: The Unspoken Truth of Our Racial Divide*. Bloomsbury, 2016.

Bonilla-Silva, Eduardo. *Racism Without Racists: Color-Blind Racism and the Persistence of Racial Inequality in America*. 4th ed., Rowman & Littlefield Publishers, 2014.

Coates, Ta-Nehisi. *Between the World and Me*. Spiegel & Grau, 2015.

Collins, Patricia Hill and Sirma Bilge. *Intersectionality*. Polity Press, 2016.

Crenshaw, Kimberlé, et al., editors. *Critical Race Theory: The Key Writings That Formed the Movement*. The New Press, 1996.

Davis, Angela Y. *Freedom Is a Constant Struggle: Ferguson, Palestine, and the Foundations of a Movement*. Haymarket Books, 2016.

Delgado, Richard and Jean Stefancic. *Critical Race Theory: An Introduction*. 3rd ed., New York University Press, 2017.

Delgado, Richard and Jean Stefancic, editors. *Critical White Studies: Looking Behind the Mirror*. Temple University Press, 1997.

———, editors. *The Latino/a Condition: A Critical Reader*. New York University Press, 1998.

———, editors. *Critical Race Theory: The Cutting Edge*. 3rd. ed. Temple University Press, 2013.

Kendi, Ibram X. *Stamped from the Beginning: The Definitive History of Racist Ideas in America*. Nation Books, 2016.

Omi, Michael and Howard Winant. *Racial Formation in the United States*. 3rd ed., Routledge, 2015.

Reilly, Kevin, Stephen Kaufman and Angela Bodino, editors. *Racism: A Global Reader*. M.E. Sharpe, 2003.

Tatum, Beverly Daniel. *"Why Are All the Black Kids Sitting Together in the Cafeteria?" and Other Conversations About Race*. Basic Books, 2003.

Wu, Jean Yu-wen Shen and Min Song, editors. *Asian American Studies: A Reader*. Rutgers University Press, 2000.

Works Cited

Bonilla-Silva, Eduardo. *Racism Without Racists: Color-Blind Racism and the Persistence of Racial Inequality in America*. 4th ed., Rowman & Littlefield Publishers, 2014.

Crenshaw, Kimberlé, et al., editors. *Critical Race Theory: The Key Writings That Formed the Movement*. The New Press, 1996.

STEP 1

CHIP AWAY AT THE FALSE IDEOLOGY THAT RACE IS BIOLOGICAL

What does it mean to say that race is a social construct?
How has science perpetuated the false ideology that race is biological over several centuries?
Why is the false ideology that race is biological so damaging?

"I'm colorblind. I don't see race." "Racism is a thing of the past." "He must have done *something* wrong to get shot by the police." "All lives matter." "The only racism today is against white people." "Some people are just lazy and don't work hard enough." "Some cultures just don't value education."

You may have heard comments like these or read them online. You may even believe some of them. These comments reflect a racialized belief system that this book will analyze, but they also reveal something that's missing. In the United States, many people are not taught a basic history of race and racism, so it's not a surprise that many people respond to the topics of race and racism with silence, discomfort, fundamental misunderstandings, and hostility. One of my reasons for engaging in racial justice has been to learn what I had not been taught, which is an ongoing process, and to come to a better understanding of how I could participate in raising awareness, starting in my classroom and community. With this book, I hope readers can develop a stronger foundation of examining race, racism, and racial justice and then build on that foundation with action. As a white educator, this approach is a contribution that I can make toward collective work on racial justice.

What exactly is race? That's a complicated question because we need to sort out the myths from the reality. I often hear college students and community members alike define race with words like "ethnicity" and "nationality." However, race, ethnicity, and nationality do not mean the same thing, and they are definitely not interchangeable. **Nationality** relates to the nation or country that one was born in or lives in. National borders often shift and can be redrawn entirely to create or eliminate nations. **Ethnicity** relates to the culture with which one identifies, which often corresponds to language, religion, and customs. The borders around ethnicities also shift from place to place and over time. One nation can include many ethnicities, and one ethnicity can cover many nations. Race, ethnicity, and nationality all relate to power, and we need to consider who has the power to define these terms, establish the borders of these terms, and patrol these borders. However, these three terms are not synonymous.

Race is a method of categorizing humans based on the false belief that human groups, "races," are biologically distinct from each other. There is a lot to unpack in this definition. One very serious problem is that we are often taught that human races are biologically distinct from each other, that there is something biological that separates white people from black people from Asian people, but the truth is that there is nothing biological or scientific or genetic that separates these groups. Race is a **social construct**, meaning that it is constructed, or created, by society, by people, by human beings; in other words, race is an invention. However, while race may be an invention, racism is very real.

When I say that race is not biological, I mean that there is no scientific test I could take where the results would come back and say "white." Of course, if you ask a group of random people (at least in the US) to look at a photo of me and identify my race, they would all likely say "white," or you could ask me what race I check on questionnaires, and I would indicate "white," but as I will get to, that doesn't mean there is any scientific or biological way of defining my race.

As this book will discuss, the initial invention of race depended on two dangerous beliefs. One is the false idea that humans can be subdivided into biologically distinct groups, often based on skin color. The second dangerous and false belief is that these groups are hierarchical, meaning that they can be positioned on a **racial hierarchy** from superior to inferior, with whites at the top, blacks at the bottom, and indigenous people, Asians, and Latinx people occupying various intermediary positions depending on the moment. As this book will explain, humans invented the false ideas that race is biological and hierarchical, and these ideas became powerful justifications for racism, genocide, and slavery.

Racism is one form of oppression, in this case based on race, and oppression is always connected to power, systems, structures, and institutions. An individual bias can reflect racism, but as the Introduction briefly explained, focusing on the individual level does not allow us to understand the larger systems of power. If racism only existed within a few individuals, racism would not be a serious problem, but it is a serious problem, and that's because it is embedded in our institutions and structures of power, whether we are aware of it or not. This book will show how racism, as a system of oppression, was built in colonial America based on false ideas about race being biological and hierarchical, embedded in our nation's founding, and reinforced throughout our history to the present day.

Sociologists Michael Omi and Howard Winant have made a significant contribution to the way we understand race today through their concept of "racial formation":

> Race is a fundamental organizing principle of social stratification. It has influenced the definition of rights and privileges, the distribution of resources, and the ideologies and practices of subordination and oppression. The concept of race as a marker of difference has permeated all forms of social relations. It is a template for the processes of marginalization that continue to shape social structures as well as collective and individual psyches. . . .
> The process of race making, and its reverberations throughout the social order, is what we call *racial formation*. We define racial formation as *the sociohistorical process by which racial identities are created, lived out, transformed, and destroyed.*
> (Omi and Winant 107–108, emphasis in original)

Omi and Winant's term racial formation highlights the never-ending process of racialization.

In order to show the creation of race and the history and persistence of systemic racism, I use the metaphor of the **Racism Machine**. As I began to outline in the Introduction, this metaphor allows me to emphasize that racial categories are an invention by humans, not a natural or biological phenomenon. The Racism Machine is a massive, complex apparatus with wheels, gears, chains, and pulleys that perpetuate racism by connecting systems as varied as education, the media, criminal justice, government, finance, housing, and healthcare. The Machine works so efficiently because it is constantly adjusted and adapted to meet changing times, and this process has occurred for centuries, since colonial America to the present.

The Racism Machine is so powerful and complex because interlocking forces of capitalism and patriarchy operate within it to preserve the status quo and protect the interests of the elite. While Step 2 will define these terms in more depth, I will say here that **capitalism** is an economic system based on private ownership and accumulation of wealth and property. With profit highly valued, those with the most wealth have the most power, and those with the least wealth are marginalized and oppressed. This system is often rationalized with the idea that everyone has the opportunity to become wealthy, a mentality that attempts to justify this system as fair. **Patriarchy** is a method of structuring society that grants power to men, and this power can manifest itself at home in men's roles as husbands or fathers, in the community in men's roles in government, in the workplace in men's roles in management, or many other arenas. Patriarchy depends on sexism, a belief in clearly defined gender roles for men and women and for boys and girls, where men and boys have more power than women and girls. This power manifests itself in relation to behavior and expectations: how to dress, act, and speak; what to study in school; what types of jobs to get and how high a position in that job to hold; how much money to make; and more. In addition to patriarchy depending on sexism, patriarchy also depends on heterosexism, oppression on the basis of sexual orientation. In other words, patriarchy depends on **heteronormativity**, a belief that heterosexuality is the norm and that LGBTQ people are outside of the norm.

We cannot focus solely on one type of oppression in hopes of addressing all types of oppression, meaning that we cannot focus just on economic equality and hope that racism, sexism, and heterosexism get resolved in the process. We need to explicitly address how racism, patriarchy, and capitalism reinforce each other, which is why the concept of intersectionality is so important, as the Introduction began to address. We need to understand how race, gender, sexual orientation, gender identity, class, and other methods by which people are oppressed intersect with each other. For example, transwomen of color are one of the most vulnerable populations in the US; they face a horrifying rate of attack and murder. If we are not intersectional, then trans women of color can be ignored.

If most people recognized and acknowledged the existence of the Racism Machine, then there would be no need for this book. The problem is that we are often taught to ignore this machine. We are taught it doesn't exist, or if we catch a glimpse of it, we are told it's something else. Or we focus on the distractions it creates to divert our attention from systemic racism. We often deny our country's history of racism because we are rarely taught about the Racism Machine. If we don't recognize it, then we can't confront it and dismantle it. As writer James Baldwin tells us, "Not everything that is faced can be changed; but nothing can be changed until it is faced" (38).

So why exactly don't we recognize the Racism Machine?

- Some people might say that racism doesn't exist any more, that it's over, and that now everyone has equal opportunity. In other words, this belief assumes that if people aren't successful, it's their own fault. It's not a surprise that people would believe that today, given how pervasive these messages are and how many different forms the messages come in. The election of President Obama in 2008 was frequently used as evidence that our society is now **post-racial**, as if racism existed in the past but we've moved beyond it, which Step 4 addresses. In this belief, there might be recognition that black and Latinx people don't have the household wealth of white people or are not represented in upper management, higher education, Hollywood, or politics at the same level as white people. However, while people might recognize this disparity, they rationalize it with what could be called a cultural explanation, a view that black and Latinx people just don't care enough about education or about being successful, that they don't work hard enough. This belief blames black and Latinx individuals and their communities for their status.

- Another belief acknowledges that racism exists today, but it focuses on a few individual culprits, a few bad apples who commit hate crimes, a few bad apples in police departments, a few bad apples in an otherwise nonracist community. The solution within this view is to focus on prosecuting individual racists for their crimes. This view would focus on hate groups like the KKK as the cause of white supremacy today.

- Yet another belief focuses on the idea that racism exists, but it exists primarily against white people, a belief described as **reverse racism**. This belief criticizes affirmative action with the view that unqualified people of color are taking spots in schools or at jobs that "belong" to white people. This belief also relates to anti-immigrant rhetoric, sometimes called **nativism**, a belief in the US that foreigners who don't fit in are taking over a country that "belongs" to white people. This belief is grounded in white people's fear of becoming the minority, something that will be addressed in Step 4, especially in relation to the media's response to the census.

While there are other reasons why people may not recognize the Racism Machine, these three reasons seem to be some of the most common. They boil down to a belief that racism no longer exists and that people just need to work hard so they can achieve the American Dream, a belief that a few individual racists are the problem today, and a belief that racism today targets white people. People may support one or more of these beliefs.

Recognizing the Racism Machine means recognizing the faults, some quite egregious, in these beliefs. One of the main limitations of these beliefs is that they tend to focus on individuals and ignore systems. To clarify, we can't ignore individuals, but our tendency is to focus solely on individuals, and that means we're missing a big part of the picture. Systems have a powerful impact in a variety of ways; they can block access to resources (education, housing, jobs, etc.) for people of color and facilitate access for white people. The beliefs described here assume that everyone has equal access to resources and blame individuals when they're not successful, a mentality our individualistic society helps fuel. The emphasis on the individual also appears in the misguided belief that today, racism only appears in the form of hate groups like the KKK. While these groups certainly exist and can commit heinous crimes, this book will show how the Racism Machine involves systems and structures throughout our society.

As outlined, another misguided belief is that if people do think there are racist systems, they think white people are oppressed, which reflects a serious misunderstanding of how systems and oppression operate. Likewise, this false belief relates directly to the false belief that people of color can be racist. As described in this section and in the Introduction, individuals of any race can have prejudice about anything. However, this prejudice becomes oppression, or racism in particular, only when it is directly connected to a system of power. People of color are not the beneficiaries of power in an oppressive system based on race, just like women are not the beneficiaries of power in an oppressive system based on gender, and LGBTQ people are not the beneficiaries of power in an oppressive system based on sexual orientation. While it's true that marginalized people can develop **internalized oppression**, something, in the context of race, that novelist Toni Morrison calls "racial self-loathing" (210), it is not true that those who are marginalized by an oppression can also carry out that oppression. More specifically, people of color are not racist because people of color are oppressed by racism.

One of the main goals of this book is to help readers understand the powerful role that systems and structures have had and continue to have in perpetuating **white supremacy**. As this manual will describe, the forces of racism, patriarchy, and capitalism operate throughout our society to position whiteness at the top of the racial hierarchy and protect its position. White supremacy can operate without our awareness, something we can start to understand if we add another layer of metaphor to the Racism Machine. Let's consider how the Racism Machine produces toxic pollution that those of us living in the US inhale. (Many other countries have their own version of the Racism Machine, which can look similar to or different from ours, but that is not the focus of this book.)

Many of us are not aware that we are inhaling this pollution, so we are unaware of how it has affected us. In her classic text on race and racism, *"Why Are All the Black Kids Sitting Together in the Cafeteria?" and Other Conversations about Race*, psychologist Beverly Daniel Tatum uses the metaphor of "smog" to represent "the cultural images and messages that affirm the assumed superiority of Whites and the assumed inferiority of people of color" (6). She describes the smog: "Sometimes it is so thick it is visible, other times it is less apparent, but always, day in and day out, we are breathing it in" (6). Furthermore, she asks, "if we live in a smoggy place, how can we avoid breathing the air?" (6). I find her metaphor of "smog" to connect very clearly to my metaphor of the Racism Machine, and rather than focus on smog, which is created by many different types of machines (factories, cars, etc.) as well as natural fog, I will narrow down this metaphor to "pollution" and consider it a product of the Racism Machine.

Just like Tatum's smog, we breathe the pollution of the Racism Machine every day, and it varies in its visibility. We can't avoid it, and it's toxic. Even though racism benefits some people and hurts or even kills other people, the pollution of the Racism Machine is toxic to everyone and to our society. This metaphor of the pollution of the Racism Machine can help connect the macro-level to the micro-level, or the systems to the individuals interacting with those systems. Most white people would likely say they are not racist, but they are often not aware of the pollution they have breathed in, of how they have been socialized by the media, family, education, and other systems into taking racism for granted as the norm. They are not necessarily aware of how this pollution affects the decisions they make about where to live, who to vote for, who to hire, and how to perceive and treat people of color. This pollution can have a profound effect on how white people do their work and the decisions they make at work, even if they are not aware of it, whether they are a police officer, a teacher, a journalist, a social worker, a judge, a politician, a lawyer, or an entertainment executive. They can perpetuate the Racism Machine every day without even knowing it. Likewise, white people are often unaware of the unearned advantages they receive and take for granted as the norm, otherwise known as **white privilege**. Furthermore, white supremacy continues to function because the Racism Machine has so many powerful mechanisms to block white people from developing a greater awareness about race and racism, as this book will address.

As an educator both inside the classroom and in the community, I have found that one of the biggest obstacles that blocks our view of the Racism Machine is the false belief that racial categories are not invented, that they are not socially constructed, that they are real, genuine, and natural. This way of thinking manifests itself in the false belief that some racial groups don't care about education or don't work hard. In other words, there is a foundational way of thinking here that views races as inherently different from each other. Another way of understanding that belief is to recognize it as the belief that race is biological. Even though this idea will appear outdated to some readers, I have found, and many scholars now report, that the belief that race is biological is the basis on which contemporary popular notions of race rest. Furthermore, this belief is getting more common, not less.

I've chosen to devote attention to the false belief that race is biological because I believe it is one of the most important foundational beliefs in the history of racism in this country and in contemporary manifestations of racism. I also believe this false belief is one of the biggest obstacles that prevents us from recognizing and examining the Racism Machine. If we don't examine the Racism Machine, then we can't fully understand how race is socially constructed, how patriarchy and capitalism intersect with racism, how racism is embedded in systems and structures, and how the Machine affects individuals.

Even when people don't explicitly reference race being biological and focus instead on race as cultural, there is still a biological foundation that's implied, as I'll demonstrate. Why would people so consistently believe that race is biological? Perhaps the more reasonable question is: why wouldn't they? After all, we're bombarded with messages from the criminal justice system, the media, the healthcare industry, and other systems that reinforce the myth that race is biological. For example, black people are much more likely to be perceived as and treated like criminals than white people. The American Civil Liberties Union (ACLU) reports that black adults are arrested at a much higher rate than white adults for drug possession despite comparable rates of drug use ("Report: The War on Marijuana in Black and White"). The Office for Civil Rights in the US Department of Education reports that in preschool and K–12, black children are much more likely to be suspended from school than white children despite comparable behavior ("2013–2014 Civil Rights Data Collection: A First Look"; Klein; "Racial Profiling in Preschool").

We can see this belief in black criminality at work in the grand jury testimony of white police officer Darren Wilson. In describing his shooting of unarmed black teenager Michael Brown in Ferguson, Missouri, on August 9, 2014, Wilson stated, "'And when I grabbed him, the only way I can describe it is I felt like a 5-year-old holding onto Hulk Hogan. . . . [Michael Brown] had the most intense aggressive face. The only way I can describe it, it looks like a demon, that's how angry he looked'" (qtd. in Calamur). If Officer Darren Wilson thought the unarmed black teenager Michael Brown looked like a "demon" with overwhelming strength, then Wilson perceived Brown as inherently different from himself. Notably, this quote was not an offhand remark but Wilson's testimony to a grand jury. Furthermore, this grand jury did not indict him in the shooting of Michael Brown. The belief that black people are inherently, biologically criminal has operated in this country for more than a century, as this book will discuss.

To further illustrate the way we are surrounded by messages that race is biological, let's consider two seemingly innocuous examples. For example, the website for BiDil, a medication for heart failure, states, "BiDil is the first heart failure (HF) treatment specifically for African Americans" ("About BiDil"). In 2005, the US Food and Drug Administration (FDA) approved the heart medication BiDil expressly for African Americans, and the drug's website still features black patients. Why would the FDA and the pharmaceutical industry alike promote the idea that African Americans need to receive special heart medication made just for them? Doesn't this imply that there is something biologically unique about African Americans so that they would benefit from this medicine in a way that white people or Asian people would not? Most people will likely not take the time to read *Race in a Bottle: The Story of BiDil and Racialized Medicine in a Post-Genomic Age*, an insightful analysis by legal scholar Jonathan Kahn, of how BiDil reinforces the falsehood of biological race. Most people who see an ad for the drug will likely instead accept it without question, and their assumptions about race as biological will likely be reinforced.

Furthermore, another seemingly innocuous trend today that ends up reinforcing assumptions about race being biological is the popularity of DNA testing for ancestry and genealogy. Many companies now offer these services, and while I don't want to minimize the value of identifying and connecting with previously unknown relatives, one consequence of this work is that it can affirm existing myths about race. While these companies tend not to use the word "race," it's easy for consumers to make this short leap when they see the advertising. For example, the website for Ancestry, a company that provides access to genealogical records and family trees as well as DNA testing, states: "Unlock the family story in your DNA. Your DNA can reveal your ethnic mix and ancestors you never knew you had—places and people deep in your past where records can't always take you. Try AncestryDNA, and get a new view into what makes you uniquely you" ("Ancestry"). If "your DNA can reveal your ethnic mix," then wouldn't the average consumer's likely preexisting belief in race as biological be reinforced with this language?

Evolutionary biologist Joseph Graves published an article in the *Teaching Tolerance* magazine to try and correct these misguided assumptions. The article's title, "Race ≠ DNA," foregrounds the key issue here, and the subtitle "If Race is a Social Construct, What's Up with DNA Ancestry Testing?" asks a critical question more people need to ask and discuss. The overly simplified DNA results that people receive can make some think that there is a gene for being white, but that's simply not true. The test examines a tiny amount of one's DNA to compare it to a database of DNA markers from people around the world who were determined to have lived in one specific region for several generations. As Matt Miller wrote in *Slate*, "So when a DNA test comes back saying you are 28 percent Finnish, all it's really saying is that of the DNA analyzed (most companies don't analyze all of your DNA), 28 percent of it was most similar to that of a completely Finnish person" (Miller). These tests look at a few markers that seem to be unique to people who have lived in a very specific region for generations, but even that can be hard to prove. Also, what people don't realize is that these markers are an extremely tiny fraction of our DNA. The idea that, as Ancestry's website states, these results can help you identify "what makes you uniquely you" can be quite misleading and instead can contribute to our nation's ongoing obsession with racial categorization.

I'm not claiming that the individuals or companies behind these quotes are consciously saying that race is biological, but I am saying that this is the message they convey regardless of intended meaning, an example of **intent versus impact**. While I wouldn't want to ignore intention completely, we must acknowledge the power of impact, something that is often swept aside when we hear people focus on their intention with comments like, "But that wasn't my intent," or "I didn't mean it that way." The examples I just described reveal how impact matters, and they each repeat the same message, day after day, that race is biological. This message is all the more powerful because different types of systems repeat it, whether it's the healthcare industry, the media, or the criminal justice system. These messages all reinforce, in various ways, a belief that there is some essential, inherent, natural core identity that relates to race; in other words, they take for granted the idea that race is biological.

Demystifying the myth that race is biological involves several steps because this falsehood is such a powerful belief system that has evolved over centuries. The remainder of Step 1 will take you through that process by focusing on the following:

- simple strategies for chipping away at the myth of biological race
- an introduction to the concept of ideology (a belief system) as a way of understanding the powerful impact of this myth
- historical examples that illustrate the pervasiveness of the myth of biological race
- a brief analysis of how this false belief operates today

This approach will allow you to develop a basic understanding of the dangerous falsehood that race is biological in order to discredit it. Then, once you fully understand the way that race has actually been socially constructed, or invented by people, then that will lead to questions addressed in Step 2 of this manual: If race was invented, then who invented it? When? Why? How? Keep those questions in the back of your mind for now.

Some might argue that most people don't believe in biological races anymore, but it's becoming clearer that there has been a resurgence of this belief, even by people who don't consciously realize they are supporting this belief. Even if one were to argue that today everyone has evolved past this way of thinking, we can't deny that for the vast majority of the existence of the US, the ideology of race as biological was explicitly acknowledged as the only way of understanding race. It would be impossible to deny the ideology's profound impact on our systems and institutions during the span of two centuries. However, as scholars in many disciplines have determined, we have not evolved past this way of thinking as much as we would like to think we have. For example, communication scholar Peter A. Chow-White writes, "Many scholars and activists assumed that the decoupling of race and biology and the enclosure of racial identity in a social constructivist paradigm was a *fait accompli* at the close of the twentieth century" (Chow-White 94). In other words, by 2000 there was so much evidence that race was not biological, it seemed like the myth was on the verge of disappearing, once and for all. However, as Chow-White and other scholars who study race have observed, the myth that race is biological "has not only been raised once again, but given new currency" (Chow-White 94). The fact that this false belief became more popular and widespread from 2000 to the present, notably the years that overlap with the Obama presidency, is not a coincidence and emerges as part of the backlash against his presidency and against the civil rights movement more generally, as Step 4 will discuss. The false belief that race is biological allows racism to continue, so if we want to address racism, we must examine the history and persistence of the idea that race is biological.

Some people might say that believing in biological races by itself is not a dangerous thing because it only becomes dangerous if you believe some races are biologically better than others. I take the position that one cannot pick and choose which parts of a dangerous belief system to keep and which to get rid of. The belief that biological races exist is inseparable from the belief that some races are biologically inferior, which reflects our national obsession with categorization and ranking. I argue here that in order to dismantle racism, we must dismantle the belief system that biological races exist, which includes the belief that some are inferior.

How Is Race *Not* Biological?

Scholars who study race and racism have spent decades refuting the notion that race is biological, and these scholars come from a wide range of disciplines, including anthropology, biology, history, law, and sociology. Let's consider the language of a few recent titles to illustrate their consistent focus on debunking the falsehood that race is biological:

- *Fatal Invention: How Science, Politics, and Big Business Re-Create Race in the Twenty-First Century* by legal scholar Dorothy Roberts
- *The Myth of Race: The Troubling Persistence of an Unscientific Idea* by anthropologist Robert Wald Sussman
- *The Race Myth: Why We Pretend Race Exists in America* by evolutionary biologist Joseph Graves
- *Race: The Power of an Illusion*, a PBS documentary that interviews scholars from various disciplines

In looking at the language of these titles, do you see a pattern? Roberts gives us the word "invention," Sussman refers to a "myth" and an "unscientific idea," Graves also uses the word "myth" and adds "pretend," and the PBS documentary uses the word "illusion" and links it to "power." These titles and the research they share consistently reinforce the fact that race is an idea that humans invented and that a significant amount of power has been attached to this idea.

Over the past one or two decades, we should have seen the disappearance of the idea that race is biological, but instead, we have witnessed the opposite, a resurgence of the idea that race is biological, showing the power of this idea. Scholars point to the pharmaceutical industry, the growing popularity of ancestry DNA testing, and the criminal justice system as social forces that, consciously or not, reinforce the falsehood that race is biological. I'm less concerned here with going into detail about exactly how these social forces have fueled a resurgence in the belief that race is biological, especially since several scholars have successfully mapped that out (see Recommended Resources). Instead, I'm more interested in providing clear, concrete strategies for debunking the myth and then considering why such discrediting matters so much. The impressive work that scholars have collectively carried out needs to reach the general public so that we can chip away at the false ideas blocking our view of the Racism Machine. We cannot allow this scholarship to remain what sociologist Ann Morning calls "lost in transmission" (6).

Let's consider some specific strategies for explaining to the general public what it means to say that race is not biological but rather a social construct. These are the kinds of key points I've found helpful in my classroom and in the community:

- Human DNA is 99.5% to 99.9% identical (Kahn, "Forensic DNA" 117; Yudell 25). Genetic differences between humans are miniscule compared to our similarities. Furthermore, when looking at the .1 to .5% where we do differ, most of that difference (specifically 85%) does not correlate with race or even where our ancestors lived ("The Difference Between Us"). Such variation is spread around the globe. The tiny part (15% of the .1 to .5%) that does correlate to where our ancestors lived still doesn't relate to racial categories.
- Skin color, which we often use in the US to assign a racial category, is an extremely recent adaptation in terms of human evolution. The most significant human evolution all occurred in Africa (meaning that's where we developed language, intelligence, and abstract thought). After some humans started migrating on various paths, those who went north benefited from genetic mutations that selected for lighter skin so they could absorb more sunlight. Skin color is only skin deep; it doesn't correlate with any deeper, more significant genetic information ("The Difference Between Us"; Goodman et al.).
- There is more genetic variation between two randomly selected members of the same race than there is between one randomly selected member of one race and one randomly selected person of another race ("The Difference Between Us").
- There is no way to scientifically separate people into racial categories and say that everyone in one racial group shares a certain biological feature that nobody in another racial group has ("The Difference Between Us").

These brief examples represent a very small selection of the volumes of scholarship available that unequivocally discredit the myth of race as biological. Unfortunately, this considerable research has not adequately reached the public in order to shift their understanding or even the understanding of scholars who don't specialize in race and racism.

So, if racial categories have no biological or scientific meaning, then what is race? Why does the idea that race is biological persist? As scholars have said for decades, race is a social construct. If you think about that phrase, consider what it means for something to be "constructed." It means it is built, created, or invented. And if it's a "social" construct, then society, meaning people and institutions, are the ones creating it. In other words, people made up the idea that race is biological. And that idea gained momentum, so much momentum that it surrounds us, despite the overwhelming amount of evidence we have to dispute it. As legal scholar Dorothy Roberts writes,

> Like citizenship, race is a political system that governs people by sorting them into social groupings based on invented biological demarcations. Race is not only interpreted according to invented rules, but, more important, race *itself* is an invented political grouping. Race is not a biological category that is politically charged. It is a political category that has been disguised as a biological one.
>
> (Roberts 4)

Roberts's repetition of the word "invented" is very important here. She describes two layers of invention when it comes to race, the invented rules associated with defining each race and then the invented overall concept of race in the first place. The entire system is an invention, a creation, but as Roberts writes, the system is "disguised" to appear scientifically sound and legitimate.

In order to understand how the invention of the idea that race is biological can be so powerful, I find it helpful to consider the work of French philosopher Louis Althusser (1918–1990). He studied issues of power and control, specifically ways in which people are controlled; one type of control he called "repressive" and the other he called "ideological" (Althusser 95–100). In the "repressive" form, the control is physical, so you might be locked inside a cage or physically restrained in some way. Perhaps that's the easier type of control to understand, because you can see it, and it's more obvious. The other type of control is what he called "ideological," and it's less visible. Here, your own thinking controls you. You're taught to take something for granted, to fear something, so it becomes automatic. Therefore, an **ideology** is a belief system taken for granted as a given, as the truth, without question. It doesn't occur to us to question it because there doesn't seem to be any other way it could be. I think it's helpful to identify the belief that race is biological as an ideology because it has been used for centuries to control people. As historian Carter G. Woodson wrote almost a century ago, "When you control a man's thinking you do not have to worry about his actions" (Woodson). An ideology can become especially powerful if people hear the same ideological message from different sources, like the media, school, and family, so it starts to appear normal or normalized. Understanding how an ideology operates helps explain how white people can become socialized into taking systemic racism for granted as the norm.

One of the most important points I want to convey here is that the ideology that race is biological has permeated American history and culture for centuries. As anthropologist Robert Wald Sussman writes: "over the past 500 years, we have been taught by an informal, mutually reinforcing consortium of intellectuals, politicians, statesmen, business and economic leaders, and their books that human racial biology is real and that certain races are biologically better than others" (Sussman 2). For the ideology of biological races to develop such a stronghold in this country, it had to get support from all of our institutions, as Sussman makes clear. Leaders throughout our systems literally and metaphorically bought into this ideology, reaping financial, business, cultural, and political success because of it. These institutions, at least in the US, were developed along with or after the ideology that race is biological, so it's hard to imagine how they could not have been immune to this ideology, especially if the leaders of these institutions supported this ideology so explicitly. Furthermore, the people who interacted with these institutions as readers, clients, patients, students, and more would take this ideology for granted, even unknowingly.

Furthermore, another significant point is the horrifying damage that the ideology of biological races has caused throughout its existence in this country (and elsewhere, too, but my focus in this book is on the US). The ideology of biological races is the foundational rationale for how slavery could be sustained in a democracy. If slaves were not considered fully human, the ideology goes, then slavery could exist in a democracy without it being hypocritical. In other words, the ideology's message is that slavery is just the natural state for those not fully human, so it's not the government choosing slavery. The ideology that race is biological not only means that races are biologically distinct but also and even more importantly that races are hierarchical, meaning that they are ranked on a hierarchy with superior and inferior positions. If, as the ideology's message claims, whites were identified as biologically superior, then it was nature that gave them freedom and citizenship, not the government; the government just followed nature. Likewise, there are also ideologies related to gender (men are superior to women) and class (the rich are superior to the poor). In each case, using Althusser's thinking, the ideology serves as a justification for those in power to remain in power via patriarchy in the former and capitalism in the latter.

One of the reasons I use ideology as a way of thinking about the myth of biological races is because it allows us to understand that once we recognize something as an ideology then we can take a step back, take off our blinders, and question how we've been indoctrinated into that ideology. In other words, we can question why the FDA would approve a drug "specifically for African Americans" when African Americans are not a biologically distinct group of people. Then we might consider how the powerful and profit-driven pharmaceutical industry might have played a role in that decision. We can also question why the company Ancestry would advertise its services with language that implies there are biological races, and we can question why its marketing department would find that strategy effective in terms of its appeal. Finally, thinking about biological race as an ideology can help us question the language that Officer Darren Wilson used when describing to a grand jury the unarmed black teenager he shot. Furthermore, the ideological nature of this language can help us see that this shooting was not an isolated event but a symptom of a much larger association that many people have between blackness and inherent criminality, an example of the dangerous belief in biological races that has devastating consequences.

Recognizing that the idea of biological races is an ideology can help us work on actively resisting that indoctrination. We can instead see the ideology for what it is and consider the dynamics of power, control, and fear. This first chapter focuses on helping readers understand the false ideology of biological races because that is the first obstacle in a path toward racial justice. If we chip away at that obstacle and recognize that race is a social construct, we then have two important tools available: hope and responsibility. We have hope because if we realize that race is an invention, something humans made up, then that means racism is not inevitable. If we built it, we can dismantle it. Furthermore, once we realize that we can dismantle racism, we have the responsibility to do that work. Race was not invented by anyone alive today, nor their parents, nor even their grandparents. We all inherited this invention, and once we realize it's an invention that we inherited, we have a responsibility to understand this invention, including the systems it impacts, and take it apart. That is the purpose of this book. However, before we can talk about action, we need to understand this invention of race and racism. First, we need to understand how our country has embedded the ideology of biological races throughout our history and culture; that's the only way we can understand how pervasive this ideology is today and chip away at it.

How Did the Ideology of Race as Biological Emerge?

Let's consider a few key moments in the historical creation of the ideology of race as biological and its path to the present. We begin in the 1700s, in Europe, in the Age of Enlightenment, a period that emphasized reason and science. This was also a time when the burgeoning field of science encouraged its experts to identify, label, and categorize. This emphasis on identification was especially noteworthy in the new field of natural history, which focused on identifying not only animals and plants but also humans. Public health scholar Michael Yudell provides an introduction to one of the first scientists in this field:

> While the term race existed before the eighteenth century, mostly to describe domesticated animals, it was introduced into the sciences by the French naturalist Louis LeClerc, Comte de Buffon, in 1749. . . . To Buffon, the natural state of humanity was derived from the European, a people he believed "produced the most handsome and beautiful men" and represented the "genuine color of mankind."

(Yudell 15–16)

Even from the beginning, we can see that the language used to identify humans within the field of natural history was not what we would consider objective science, even though Buffon (1707–1788) presumably took this language for granted as reasonable and objective. This language allows us to see the process of ideology formation at work. From the beginning, the field of natural history, as it applied to humans, included subjective judgments about the biological nature of human races. With such an approach embedded in the field, we can see how this ideology had an impact on the field of science and the public at large as the ideology of biological races took shape, grew, and became taken for granted. Soon after, Swedish naturalist Carolus Linnaeus (1707–1778) took that work even further.

Linnaeus's work on taxonomy (a classification system for plants and animals) became profoundly influential; within this system, he also developed four categories of humans, based on geography. It's important to consider the type of language Linnaeus used to describe each group. Consider these excerpts from his revised edition of *Systema Naturae*, published in 1758, and think about what subjective words you notice as they are applied to the developing idea of biological races:

- "American: red . . . obstinate, merry, and free; paints himself with red lines; regulated by customs" (qtd. in Goodman et al. 20)
- "European: white, sanguine, muscular, gentle, acute, and inventive . . . governed by laws" (qtd. in Goodman et al. 20)
- "Asian: sallow, melancholy, stiff, severe, haughty, avaricious . . . governed by opinion" (qtd. in Goodman et al. 20)
- "African: black, phlegmatic, relaxed, crafty, indolent, negligent . . . governed by caprice" (qtd. in Goodman et al. 20)

Legal and bioethics scholar Pilar N. Ossorio explains that Linnaeus's language is not objective science, though he may have thought it was. Instead, she writes, "He commingled sociocultural traits and biological ones as though all had the same cause. . . . Linnaeus was constructing a social hierarchy in which whites (the group to which he belonged) were at the pinnacle and blacks were at the bottom" (Ossorio 175). As the "science" of race developed, its proponents focused more and more on developing a subjective hierarchy as if it were objective. Then, as readers and the public became more and more interested in it, they accepted it as objective, as a given, thereby establishing its power as an ideology. As science became more and more prominent, especially through the Enlightenment, ideas presented as objective fact (that were neither objective nor fact) were taken seriously, despite a lack of evidence.

The work of one scientist laid the groundwork for another scientist, and so on. German scientist Johann Blumenbach (1752–1840) extended the work of Linnaeus, especially as it related to the idea of human biological races. While Linnaeus identified four human races and only implicitly arranged them in a hierarchy from superior to inferior, Blumenbach identified five human races (adding the race "Malay"), and he created an overt, explicit hierarchy of human biological races, with white at the top, which he called "**Caucasian**." Blumenbach's overt emphasis on a hierarchical ranking of human races from superior to inferior cannot be underestimated; it was exactly the type of development that solidified the power of the growing ideology of biological human races. As paleontologist Stephen Jay Gould writes, "The shift from a geographic to a hierarchical ordering of human diversity must stand as one of the most fateful transitions in the history of Western science—for what, short of railroads and nuclear bombs, has had more practical impact, in this case almost entirely negative, upon our collective lives?" (Gould, "The Geometer of Race"). Blumenbach's description of human races as a biological hierarchy, with some races worthier than others, was presented and recognized as objective science, which reveals the power of ideology.

This history should make us pause over today's continued use of the word Caucasian to describe white people in the US. As this history makes clear, Blumenbach invented this word as part of his scientific explanation of white biological superiority and black biological inferiority. The word Caucasian gives a scientific tone to a completely unscientific concept. I suspect most people who use this word today are unfamiliar with this history, but sharing that history is one goal of this book so that people can reconsider and take action (see Step 5 action #4). In my teaching experience and work in the community, white people and people of color sometimes use the word Caucasian because they think it is the more appropriate, respectful term. Until I spent years researching these issues, I thought so, too.

Furthermore, it is unlikely that many people in the US who identify as Caucasian actually have ancestors from the Caucasus region that borders Europe and Asia, which is the origin of Blumenbach's term. This region includes present-day countries of Russia, Armenia, Turkey, Iran, and Azerbaijan. People in the US who have emigrated from this region might not even be perceived as white in the US today. The two brothers who perpetrated the Boston Marathon bombing in 2013 had lived in that very region and were not exactly represented by the US media as lily white, especially with their Muslim identity. It's not surprising that the word Caucasian is so popular today; after all, it still appears on a wide range of official documents, including government, employment, and education documents. Why wouldn't the American public take this term seriously? I consider it a symptom of a larger problem that we begin to see when we become aware of the history of the false ideology that race is biological.

As the ideology of biological human races developed in the 1700s in Europe and European thinkers were attempting to create scientific definitions of racial categories and place these categories on a hierarchy, the same type of work was also going on in the very new country of the United States. Since the US is the focus of this manual, understanding the profound impact that the ideology that race is biological has had on American history and culture is very important. I begin with Thomas Jefferson (1743–1826) for several reasons. One reason, as Michael Yudell writes, is that "Jefferson himself was the author of some of America's earliest ideas about race and science" (Yudell 14). Two, his role as a Founding Father is critical. It's not a coincidence or even a contradiction that he developed some of the foundational aspects of the ideology that race is biological and that he developed our country's foundational governing principles and documents. We need to understand that these two histories are very much intertwined. While some might accuse me of bashing a Founding Father, I think it's important to know our full history, because only then can we understand the ideology we've been taught all these years. We need to understand how Jefferson's writing about race, his role as a slave owner, and his rape of his slave Sally Hemmings (1773–1835) were actually not inconsistent with his work on the Declaration of Independence. To Jefferson and his contemporaries, "life, liberty, and the pursuit of happiness" only applied to the people they saw as the superior biological race and only to the men of this race. We can see how examining the Racism Machine reveals the intersecting forces of racism, patriarchy, and capitalism.

Jefferson clearly believed that whites and blacks had inherent, biological differences, and his book *Notes on the State of Virginia* (published in 1788) not only describes the natural history of his state (its land and wildlife) but also applies the same approach to describing the differences between races. Jefferson wrote, "I advance it therefore as a suspicion only, that the blacks, whether originally a distinct race, or made distinct by time and circumstances, are inferior to the whites in the endowments both of body and mind" (153). He repeatedly emphasizes the inherent differences when he refers to "the real distinctions which nature has made" (147) or states that "the difference is fixed in nature" (147). The repetition of "nature" is important because that speaks to an intrinsic, biological difference he sees between whites and blacks. He not only emphasizes their biological differences, but he also clearly positions whites at the top of this racial hierarchy. This overt racial hierarchy is an explicit example of white supremacy.

Jefferson catalogs racial differences related to the body, stating that in comparison with whites, blacks have a "very strong and disagreeable odour" (148), are "more tolerant of heat, and less so of cold" (148), "seem to require less sleep" (148), and are "more ardent after their female" (148). He also focuses on mental differences, writing about blacks: "In imagination they are dull, tasteless, and anomalous" (149) and "Their griefs are transient" (148). Again, Jefferson's language focuses on inherent differences, as he keeps saying, rooted in "nature." These descriptions consistently represent blacks as less than human, as animal-like; such descriptions also serve as rationales for slavery. If blacks were seen as more like animals and not fully human, then their slave status was seen as more natural, whether it was because they "require less sleep" and therefore can be forced to work long hours or because they are "more tolerant of the heat" and can therefore stay out in the hot sun working all day. If they are "more ardent after their female," then they are hypersexual, again like animals. Slave owners frequently raped their female slaves, and this ideology that identifies slaves as subhuman and hypersexual animals served as a rationale to justify rape. In other words, rape was not seen as rape because the female slaves were not seen as fully human. Furthermore, this objectification extends to any children who resulted from this rape because these children would, by law, become additional property for the slave owner. Finally, if, as Jefferson says, their "griefs are transient," then they wouldn't be too upset about losing their family members at slave auctions. All of these ideas reinforce the false ideology that race is biological that was used to justify slavery.

Jefferson is clear that he believes not only that whites and blacks are biologically different but also that whites are unequivocally positioned above blacks on a racial hierarchy. When writing about indigenous people, however, Jefferson, at least in *Notes on the State of Virginia*, focuses more on how they have the potential to be equal to whites but that they need whites to help them get there. His language about indigenous people focuses on the potential he sees in them but that they are noticeably behind whites on the path toward civilization. For example, he states, "they will crayon out an animal, a plant, or a country, so as to prove the existence of a germ in their minds which only wants cultivation. They astonish you with strokes of the most sublime oratory; such as prove their reason and sentiment strong, their imagination glowing and elevated" (149). They have potential ("a germ in their minds") but without European guidance ("cultivation"), it will not grow. As I will explain more in Step 3, Jefferson's attitude toward indigenous people became much more negative later as the American desire for their land grew. Jefferson clearly does not see the same potential in black people because he continues in this passage to state: "But never yet could I find that a black had uttered a thought above the level of plain narration; never see even an elementary trait of painting or sculpture" (149–150). To Jefferson, black people are not fully human and, unlike indigenous people, do not have the potential to be.

While one might think it impossible for the same person to publish these ideas and to write the Declaration of Independence, perhaps it is not so impossible as we might think. As Michael Yudell states, "The contradiction between the Declaration and *Notes* may be understood, however, by Jefferson's view of humanity itself. If blacks were of a separate creation and set apart from the definition of 'all men,' then the equality set out in the Declaration did not apply to all" (15). Rather than ignore this history, I believe the only way we can move closer to racial justice is to acknowledge this history, which includes both the popularity of the belief in biological races and specifically Jefferson's belief in this dangerous ideology.

Recognizing this history is part of chipping away at the false ideology I've been describing. Acknowledging this history is also very much connected to the current **#BlackLivesMatter** movement. Beginning on Twitter as a response to the acquittal of the killer of black teenager Trayvon Martin in 2013, this phrase galvanized activists across the country protesting police shootings of unarmed black men and women. As Alicia Garza, one of the movement's cofounders, later wrote, "It was a response to the anti-Black racism that permeates our society" (Garza). The phrase "black lives matter" clearly speaks to the way in which black people in the US today are not seen as fully human. After all, no one would need to even say "black lives matter" today if black people were perceived as equal human beings. Racial inequality exists today because of its long history, and this history of how black people have been valued less than white people is painful but important to acknowledge, especially for those who question why the phrase "black lives matter" needs to be spoken today (see Step 5 action #1B). Recognizing the history of this racial hierarchy and its persistent impact on the present is part of the process of chipping away at the false ideology that race is biological. The response "#AllLivesMatter" is a sometimes naïve, sometimes hostile response to "#BlackLivesMatter" that denies the history of racism and its persistence that prompted the call for this movement in the first place.

In the 1800s, as philosophers, biologists, and other scientists in both Europe and the US became more and more invested in the ideology that race is biological, a debate emerged about whether different races were different species. Polygenesis was the belief in different origins for different races, and monogenesis was the belief in one origin for different races. Much was written in support of each side of this debate, which is noteworthy for a few reasons. One, regardless of the position in this debate, both sides took for granted that races differ biologically and can be positioned on a hierarchy from superior to inferior. The fact that prominent philosophers and scientists were not even questioning that ideology but rather moving beyond it as if it were already proven is important. It shows how much momentum this ideology had developed.

Second, two scientists who worked in the US in the 1800s were especially significant in providing so-called evidence for the polygenesis side of the debate, and their work became very influential. Louis Agassiz (1807–1873), a Harvard professor of biology, wrote that blacks were "'a degraded and degenerate race'" and that "'it is impossible for me to repress the feeling that they are not the same blood as us'" (qtd. in Roberts 32). He strongly believed that whites and blacks had separate ancestors and focused on "'the relative rank among these races, the relative value of the characters peculiar to each, in a scientific point of view'" (qtd. in Roberts 32). Note the power of words like "rank" and "value" in connection to "scientific." Agassiz was not a fringe scientist; he was one of the most respected biologists of the nineteenth century, helping create the National Academy of Sciences and serving as a "regent of the Smithsonian Institution" (Roberts 32). In March 2017, Harvard University sponsored a conference described in a *New York Times* article titled "Confronting Academia's Ties to Slavery" that explicitly critiqued Harvard's own role in supporting Agassiz and the false ideology that race is biological (Schuessler).

Samuel Morton (1799–1851), another very prominent scientist who led the Academy of Natural Sciences, collected so-called evidence to support polygenesis. For Morton, this evidence came in the form of skulls, and he collected more than a thousand, measuring them to determine brain size, which he wrongly associated with intelligence. His publications supported the established racial hierarchy with whites at the top and blacks at the bottom, not only as different races but also as different species. In 1981, Stephen Jay Gould published *The Mismeasure of Man*, which thoroughly revealed the flaws of Morton's methodology and explained the danger of Morton's racial ideology.

As I've tried to explain, whether an ideology becomes effective depends on how much people take it for granted, and the ideology that race is biological, without a doubt, became extremely effective because mainstream scientists and the general public took it for granted. Samuel Morton became famous for his publications, perceived by many as objective science, where he used data of human skull measurements to propagate the false claim of white superior intelligence. When he died in 1851, the *New York Tribune* honored him with the statement that "'probably no scientific man in America enjoyed a higher reputation among scholars throughout the world than Dr. Morton'" (qtd. in Roberts 34). Note that this is "world" scientific opinion, not just American scientific opinion. Even though his polygenesis side of the debate dwindled in favor of the monogenesis side, keep in mind that both sides didn't question the fundamental ideology of human biological races with whites ranked as superior. Such thinking set the stage for the impending eugenics movement, both in the US and in Europe, and this was a movement that not only embraced and reinforced the ideology of biological races but also put it into practice, to an extreme.

How Did the Eugenics Movement Carry Out the Ideology of Race as Biological?

While the theory of polygenesis faded as the work of Charles Darwin (1809–1882) became popular, scientists and other thinkers in both the US and Europe still held fast to the idea that human races were biologically distinct and hierarchical, even if they did share a common ancestor. Francis Galton (1822–1911), an Englishman who studied math and science, became interested in connecting the burgeoning work in heredity (by scientists like Darwin) with the new field of statistics (Black 14). Galton published *Hereditary Genius*, which, as the name suggests, argued that genius is hereditary by focusing on a few families with many brilliant thinkers and artists. In 1883, Galton coined the term eugenics to mean well-born (Black 16). **Eugenics** grew into an American and European movement that focused on protecting what its proponents identified as white racial purity. Galton sought "'the study of all agencies under social control which can improve or impair the racial quality of future generations'" (qtd. in Black 18). For example, he believed marriages should be regulated in order to encourage "well-born" couples to reproduce (Black 18). This concept of encouraging supposedly biologically superior people to reproduce became known as positive eugenics. In the US, there were, among other activities, "Fitter Families Contests" held at state fairs around the country that would give prizes to families considered to be eugenically "fit."

Then, as you might suspect, there also developed what became known as negative eugenics: preventing the supposedly biologically inferior people from reproducing. I raise this here because the US was at the forefront of this approach. Black writes, "In America, eugenics would become more than an abstract philosophy; it would become an obsession for policymakers" (Black 19). The eugenics movement became very powerful in the early 1900s in the US, with financial support from names still familiar today: "Eugenics was mainstream, and it was financed by the nation's wealthiest entrepreneurs, including the Carnegie, Harriman, and Kellogg dynasties" (Roberts 38). The word mainstream is critical because this work was not fringe science; it was widely popular and well regarded. In the early 1900s, the eugenicists were "some of the nation's most respected and educated figures" (Black 31). Mainstream American science and culture collectively supported not only the belief that human races could be ranked biologically from superior to inferior but also the belief that something should actually be done to encourage the "superior" white race to reproduce and prevent "inferior" races from growing. As Step 3 will discuss, this was a period of extreme fear of racialized others, whether they were freed blacks, quickly labeled "criminal," or immigrants.

Charles Davenport (1866–1944) was a Harvard zoology professor and president of the American Society of Zoologists who became one of the primary leaders of the eugenics movement in the US, founding the Eugenics Record Office (ERO) in 1910 at Cold Spring Harbor Laboratory in Long Island, New York. Consider two quotes from Davenport and think about the language he uses to reinforce the ideology of biological races, an ideology that was becoming more powerful every year:

- "'Can we build a wall high enough around this country so as to keep out these cheaper races, or will it be a feeble dam . . . leaving it to our descendants to abandon the country to the blacks, browns and yellows'" (qtd. in Black 37).
- "'We have in this country the grave problem of the negro, a race whose mental development is, on the average, far below the average of the Caucasian'" (qtd. in Black 38).

These statements were part of a mainstream movement that believed wholeheartedly in the ideology of biological races, especially the positioning of races on a hierarchy with whites at the top. I include the first quote because we heard this demand to "build a wall" again in 2016 by Republican presidential candidate Donald Trump and in 2017 by President Trump. Davenport's statement made in 1903 cannot be seen as a mere relic of history but rather as a symbol of the persistent ideology that race is biological that still impacts our society today.

In the US, the principles of the eugenics movement were not merely abstract ideas people talked about; the ideology that some humans were biologically superior to other humans was put into practice, implemented through a series of influential and far-reaching and dangerous laws, policies, and court decisions. There were essentially three different ways in which negative eugenics was carried out within the US:

- preventing someone deemed "fit" from marrying someone deemed "unfit";
- sterilizing people deemed "unfit" so as to prevent the "unfit" population from reproducing;
- preventing those deemed "unfit" from immigrating into the US.

Furthermore, throughout the early 1900s, many state legislatures, Congress, and the Supreme Court supported all of these practices, which reinforced and legitimized the ideology that races are biologically distinct and hierarchical.

In 1924, the Virginia legislature passed the Racial Integrity Act, which prohibited interracial marriage. Prominent American eugenicist Madison Grant (1865–1937), author of *The Passing of the Great Race*, identified interracial marriage as a "'social and racial crime of the first magnitude'" (qtd. in Roberts 41). The "crime" was that the blood of one supposedly inferior race would infect the blood of one supposedly superior race. I'd like to point out again that these thinkers were not fringe writers, extremists we imagine to occupy the margins of society. Instead, Grant's work was so popular that it was a bestseller with multiple editions, praised by President Theodore Roosevelt and by the *Saturday Evening Post* as something "'every American should read'" (qtd. in Roberts 42).

In further strengthening the ideology of biological races, at the same time as Virginia banned interracial marriage, Virginia also passed a law that allowed for involuntary sterilization of people confined to state institutions who were labeled "feeble-minded" (Roberts 40). This 1924 law went all the way to the Supreme Court, which, in 1927, decided in *Buck v. Bell* that the Virginia legislature did have the right to involuntarily sterilize the supposed "feeble-minded." In this case, the person labeled "feeble-minded" and thus targeted for involuntary sterilization was a young woman named Carrie Buck who was confined to the Virginia Colony for Epileptics and Feebleminded because she became pregnant when raped by a member of her foster family (Roberts 40). Rather than address her rape, the Supreme Court identified Carrie as promiscuous and supported the testimony of Eugenics Record Office Superintendent Harry Laughlin (1880–1943), who identified Carrie as a member of the "shiftless, ignorant, and worthless class of anti-social whites of the South" (qtd. in Roberts 40). While one might think her whiteness would give her immunity from such treatment, her low socioeconomic status tainted that whiteness and made her vulnerable to being involuntarily sterilized.

Supreme Court Justice Oliver Wendell Holmes (1841–1935) supported involuntary sterilization by stating, "'It is better for all the world if, instead of waiting to execute degenerate offspring for crime, or let them starve for their imbecility, society can prevent those who are manifestly unfit from continuing their kind'" (qtd. in Roberts 41). The label feeble-minded provided what sounded like a scientific and medical diagnosis for what was really an opportunity to involuntarily sterilize anyone deemed outside the desired ideal. Involuntary sterilization of those seen as biologically unfit to reproduce continued throughout the 1900s in the US. With the ideology that race is biological and hierarchical, Puerto Rican and Native American women were especially targeted (Black 400). It was not until recently that states (Virginia, for example, in 2002) began to formally apologize for involuntary sterilization and to create funds to compensate victims. While we'll never know exactly how many people have been involuntarily sterilized, the *New York Times* reported in 2011 that "more than 60,000 people nationwide had been sterilized by state order" (Severson).

In addition to involuntary sterilization and bans on interracial marriage, American eugenicists also looked to immigration laws as a way to shift the American population to become a supposed biologically superior white population, and these eugenicists were influential and powerful.

In 1924, Congress passed the Immigration Act, otherwise known as the National Origins Act, which set quotas for immigration that prioritized people from northwestern Europe (like England, for example). Eugenicist Harry Laughlin helped support this legislation, especially his research that found "'the recent immigrants (largely from southern and eastern Europe), as a whole, present a higher percentage of inborn socially inadequate qualities than do older stocks'" (qtd. in Roberts 41). Here, "inborn" reinforces that race is biological, and "socially inadequate" essentially means not white enough, which applied to Jews, Italians, and other southern and eastern Europeans.

Just a few years earlier, in 1921, then soon-to-be Vice President of the US Calvin Coolidge (1872–1933) published an article in the popular magazine *Good Housekeeping* titled "Whose Country Is This?" Here, Coolidge makes the case for the immigration restriction legislation he signed as president in 1924. He writes, "Biological laws tell us that certain divergent people will not mix or blend. The Nordics [Northern Europeans] propagate themselves successfully. With other races, the outcome shows deterioration on both sides" (Coolidge 14). Again, "biological laws" mean that race is biological. And if the "Nordics propagate themselves successfully," then they are the superior race, the superior biological race. Congress was able to support this eugenic mission with the 1924 Immigration Act by making it very difficult, if not impossible, for anyone living outside northern Europe to immigrate to the US. The timing of this law blocked the immigration of many Jewish refugees from Europe.

If the American eugenics movement is starting to sound like something under Hitler's Nazi Germany, that is no coincidence. It should come as no surprise that the American eugenics movement had a profound influence on Hitler and Nazi ideology. For example, Hitler wrote, "'The Germanic inhabitant of the American continent, who has remained racially pure and unmixed, rose to be master of the continent; he will remain the master as long as he does not fall a victim to defilement of the blood'" (qtd. in Black 275). Again, this emphasis on "blood" reinforces the ideology that race is biological. In 1935, the Nazis granted American eugenicist Harry Laughlin an honorary degree for his work "as a champion of the eugenic sterilization," and Laughlin, thrilled by this honor, called it "'evidence of a common understanding of German and

American scientists of the nature of eugenics as research in and the practical application of those fundamental biological and social principles'" (qtd. in Black 312). Meanwhile, the Nazis had taken American eugenics theory and policy to an extreme with a goal of complete annihilation of anyone deemed "unfit," and American eugenicists were not only supportive but also envious. Leading American eugenicist Lothrop Stoddard (1883–1950) visited Nazi Germany in 1940, long after the Nazis' goal was clear; Stoddard "celebrated Hitler and Nazi eugenics," and Hitler admired him so much that he invited him to a private meeting (Black 317–318). Likewise, when Hitler read *The Passing of the Great Race*, referenced earlier, Hitler contacted the American author, Madison Grant, calling the book his "Bible" (qtd. in Goodman et al. 33).

As American scientists had to come to terms with the role of eugenics in the atrocities of the Holocaust, there finally developed a significant school of thought that focused on race as socially constructed, not biological, refuting the very core of American and German eugenics. In 1950, the *New York Times* published a front-page headline, "No Scientific Basis for Race Bias Found by World Panel of Experts" based on the "Statement on Race" by the United Nations Educational, Scientific, and Cultural Organization (UNESCO) that explained that race "'is not so much a biological phenomenon as a social myth'" (qtd. in Roberts 43). Even though the world had just witnessed the horrifying results of taking the belief in biological races to an extreme, with the genocide of millions of people, there was still substantial criticism of approaching race as a social construct.

What Now?

Maybe at first, some of this early history seems innocuous. So what if biologists in the 1700s applied natural history to humans and identified humans as different biological races? So what if they thought some humans were superior to others? Hopefully, though, seeing not only the early stage of this history in the 1700s but also the momentum this ideology developed, culminating in the horrors of the eugenics movement and the Holocaust, gives you a new perspective. You should now be able to understand how dangerous and terrifying this ideology has been. Once you recognize that the ideology of biological race is not only false but also dangerous, you can hopefully understand that we need to chip away at this ideology. This act of chipping away at the false ideology of biological race forces us to question how and why we've been indoctrinated to believe this myth, and the key concepts and historical examples presented in this chapter should have provided you with some strategies for questioning this ideology (see Step 5 action #1A).

I will conclude this section with a recent and powerful example of the persistence today of the false belief in biological races. This example should reinforce why we must chip away at this ideology once and for all. In April 2016, the *Washington Post* reported on recent scholarship that revealed the racial beliefs of white University of Virginia medical students and residents, including their belief in "inaccurate and at times 'fantastical' differences about the two races—for example, that blacks have less sensitive nerve endings than whites or that black people's blood coagulates more quickly" (Somashekhar). Furthermore, not only is it disturbing that white medical students at a prestigious medical school would believe in the false ideology that race is biological but also that this belief would impact their future decisions enough to cause a devastating impact on their future patients. The research showed that "those who held false beliefs often rated black patients' pain as lower than that of white patients and made less appropriate recommendations about how they should be treated" (Somashekhar).

This study shows the persistence of the ideology that race is biological and its dangerous consequences. In looking at the types of statements researchers shared with participants about blacks and whites being biologically different, these statements are not that unlike the types of statements that Jefferson made, especially researchers' statements like "Blacks' skin is thicker than whites," "Blacks have a more sensitive sense of smell than whites," and "Black couples are significantly more fertile than white couples" (Somashekhar). These beliefs, shared by at least some medical students today, and by Jefferson and presumably most of his readers, focus not only on blacks and whites being biologically different but also on blacks being closer to animals, with assumptions about their "thicker" skin, "more sensitive smell," and greater fertility. Of course none of the statements in the study were true, but that didn't stop both medical students and laypeople who participated in this study from thinking otherwise.

This study is just one of many contemporary examples that reveal how important it is for us to recognize the ideology of race as biological for what it is, something we have been taught over and over again, for centuries, to distract us from examining the Racism Machine. Instead of being distracted by the ideology the machine is producing, we need to resist the lure of such ideologies, chip away at them, look over their rubble, and focus our attention on the Racism Machine, its wheels and gears, its pulleys and chains, to see exactly how systems are perpetuating racism. These systems include the media, healthcare, criminal justice, finance, education, and politics. This careful examination can allow us to understand what other ideologies are connected to the ideology of race as biological and how they work together to indoctrinate us to support racism. For example, we need to explore the ideology of the American Dream, the popular belief in **meritocracy** whereby our society rewards merit, or hard work, which leads to success. If we really lived in a meritocracy, then why would our parents' income be such a significant predictor of our success? Why would child abuse and domestic violence be predictors of incarceration? Why would race be a predictor of wealth and exposure to pollution? In other words, if the American Dream were available to all, then these predictors wouldn't exist.

As Dorothy Roberts writes, "The diabolical genius of making this political system seem biological is that the very unequal conditions it produces become an excuse for racial injustice" (24). We can ignore injustice, ascribe unequal outcomes to biological differences, and just say that's the way nature intended it. That's a very convenient way of thinking, one that does not hold anyone accountable. My hope is that the approach of this book will resist that way of thinking and urge you instead to take responsibility with this newfound awareness of our history. If you recognize the idea of biological races as an ideology and chip away at it, you can then turn your attention to the inner workings of the Racism Machine and see how it has been built and how to take it apart, as the rest of this manual will address. That approach will allow you to choose how you can participate in dismantling the Racism Machine.

Now that you can see the Racism Machine, we'll move on to Step 2, which will allow you to explore the construction of the Racism Machine and consider: Who built it? When? Why? How?

Reflection Questions

1. Did you already know that race is a social construct? If so, when and where did you learn it? If not, how would you describe how you're processing this information?
2. Where do you notice the persistence of the false ideology that race is biological? (Consider examples from your daily interactions with other people, the media, your educational experience, or other situations.)
3. What do you think can be done to make people more aware at a younger age that race is a social construct?
4. Take another look at one or more of the historical quotes in this chapter by one of the scientists or eugenicists who reinforced the ideology that race is biological. Look carefully at each word, and consider how the language in the quote reinforces the power of the false belief in biological races.
5. If you were to explain to a friend or family member the idea that race is not biological but rather a social construct, what would you say? Would you even consider having that conversation? Why or why not?
6. What reflection question would you create to respond to Step 1, and why?

Recommended Resources

Films

Africa's Great Civilizations. PBS, 2017.

The African Americans: Many Rivers to Cross. Inkwell Films, Kunhardt McGee Productions and THIRTEEN Productions, LLC, 2013.

"The Difference Between Us." *Race: The Power of an Illusion*, California Newsreel, 2003.

No Más Bebés. Directed by Renee Tajima-Peña, ITVS, 2015.

Online Videos

"The Surprisingly Racist History of 'Caucasian'." *Decoded*, created by Franchesca Ramsey, MTV, 2016, www.youtube.com/watch?v=GKB8hXYod2w&t=20s.

Websites

"Cold Spring Harbor Laboratory's Image Archive on the American Eugenics Movement." www.eugenicsarchive.org/eugenics/.

Race: Are We So Different? American Anthropological Association, 2016, www.understandingrace.org/.

Race: The Power of an Illusion. California Newsreel, www.pbs.org/race.

Articles

Flam, Faye. "Science's Biggest Blunder." *Bloomberg*, 6 October 2016, www.bloomberg.com/view/articles/2016-10-03/science-s-biggest-blunder.

Graves, Joseph L. "Race ≠ DNA: If Race Is a Social Construct, What's Up With DNA Ancestry Testing?" *Teaching Tolerance*. Southern Poverty Law Center, Summer 2015, www.tolerance.org/sites/default/files/general/Race%20does%20not%20equal%20DNA%20-%20TT50.pdf.

Hoffman, Kelly M., et al. "Racial Bias in Pain Assessment and Treatment Recommendations, and False Beliefs About Biological Differences Between Blacks and Whites." *Proceedings of the National Academy of Sciences (PNAS)*, vol. 113, no. 16, 19 April 2016, pp. 4296–4301, m.pnas.org/content/113/16/4296.full.pdf.

Howard, Jacqueline. "What Scientists Mean When They Say 'Race' Is Not Genetic." *Huffington Post*, 9 February 2016, www.huffingtonpost.com/entry/race-is-not-biological_us_56b8db83e4b04f9b57da89ed.

Ko, Lisa. "Unwanted Sterilization and Eugenics Programs in the United States." *Independent Lens*, 29 January 2016, www.pbs.org/independentlens/blog/unwanted-sterilization-and-eugenics-programs-in-the-united-states/.

Books

Black, Edwin. *War Against the Weak: Eugenics and America's Campaign to Create a Master Race*. Four Walls Eight Windows, 2003.

Cohen, Adam. *Imbeciles: The Supreme Court, American Eugenics, and the Sterilization of Carrie Buck*. Penguin, 2016.

Duster, Troy. *Backdoor to Eugenics*. 2nd ed., Routledge, 2003.

Goodman, Alan H., et al. *Race: Are We So Different?* Wiley-Blackwell, 2012.

Graves, Joseph L., Jr. *The Emperor's New Clothes: Biological Theories of Race at the Millennium*. Rutgers University Press, 2002.

———. *The Race Myth: Why We Pretend Race Exists in America*. Dutton, 2004.

Kahn, Jonathan. *Race in a Bottle: The Story of BiDil and Racialized Medicine in a Post-Genomic Age*. Columbia University Press, 2013.

Kendi, Ibram X. *Stamped from the Beginning: The Definitive History of Racist Ideas in America*. Nation Books, 2016.

Krimsky, Sheldon and Kathleen Sloan, editors. *Race and the Genetic Revolution: Science, Myth, and Culture*. Columbia University Press, 2011.

Omi, Michael and Howard Winant. *Racial Formation in the United States*. 3rd ed., Routledge, 2015.

Painter, Nell Irvin. *The History of White People*. W.W. Norton & Company, 2010.

Roberts, Dorothy. *Fatal Invention: How Science, Politics, and Big Business Re-Create Race in the Twenty-First Century*. The New Press, 2011.

Selden, Steven. *Inheriting Shame: The Story of Eugenics and Racism in America*. Teachers College Press, 1999.

Sussman, Robert Wald. *The Myth of Race: The Troubling Persistence of an Unscientific Idea*. Harvard University Press, 2014.

Tattersall, Ian and Rob DeSalle. *Race? Debunking a Scientific Myth*. Texas A&M University Press, 2011.

Tatum, Beverly Daniel. *"Why Are All the Black Kids Sitting Together in the Cafeteria?" and Other Conversations About Race*. Basic Books, 2003.

Wailoo, Keith, Alondra Nelson and Catherine Lee, editors. *Genetics and the Unsettled Past: The Collision of DNA, Race, and History*. Rutgers University Press, 2012.

Works Cited

"About BiDil." *BiDil*, Arbor Pharmaceuticals, LLC, www.bidil.com/about-bidil. Accessed 17 May 2017.

Althusser, Louis. "Ideology and Ideological State Apparatuses: Notes Towards an Investigation." *Lenin and Philosophy and Other Essays*. Monthly Review Press, 2001, pp. 85–126.

"Ancestry." *Ancestry*, 2017, www.ancestry.com. Accessed 17 May 2017.

Baldwin, James. "As Much Truth as One Can Bear." *New York Times Book Review*, 14 January 1962, p. 1+, nyti.ms/2rRBFC7.

Black, Edwin. *War Against the Weak: Eugenics and America's Campaign to Create a Master Race*. Four Walls Eight Windows, 2003.

Calamur, Krishnadev. "Ferguson Documents: Officer Darren Wilson's Testimony." *The Two-Way*, NPR, 25 November 2014, www.npr.org/sections/the two-way/2014/11/25/366519644/ferguson-docs-officer-darren-wilsons-testimony.

Chow-White, Peter A. "The Informationalization of Race: Communication, Databases, and the Digital Coding of the Genome." *Genetics and the Unsettled Past: The Collision of DNA, Race, and History*, edited by Keith Wailoo, Alondra Nelson and Catherine Lee. Rutgers University Press, 2012, pp. 81–103.

Coolidge, Calvin. "Whose Country Is This?" *Good Housekeeping*, February 1921, pp. 13+.

"The Difference Between Us." *Race: The Power of an Illusion*. California Newsreel, 2003.

Garza, Alicia. "A Herstory of the #BlackLivesMatter Movement." *Feminist Wire*, 7 October 2014, thefeministwire.com/2014/10/blacklivesmatter-2/.

Goodman, Alan H., et al. *Race: Are We So Different?* Wiley-Blackwell, 2012.

Gould, Stephen Jay. "The Geometer of Race." *Discover*. Kalmbach Publishing Co., November 1994, discovermagazine.com/1994/nov/thegeometerofrac441.

———. *The Mismeasure of Man*. W.W. Norton & Company, 1996.

Graves, Joseph L. *The Race Myth: Why We Pretend Race Exists in America*. Dutton, 2004.

———. "Race ≠ DNA: If Race Is a Social Construct, What's Up With DNA Ancestry Testing?" *Teaching Tolerance*, Southern Poverty Law Center, Summer 2015, www.tolerance.org/sites/default/files/general/Race%20does%20not%20equal%20DNA%20-%20TT50.pdf.

Jefferson, Thomas. *Notes on the State of Virginia*. Electronic Ed. The University of North Carolina Library, 2004, docsouth.unc.edu/southlit/jefferson/jefferson.html. Accessed 17 May 2017.

Kahn, Jonathan. "Forensic DNA and the Inertial Power of Race in American Legal Practice." *Genetics and the Unsettled Past: The Collision of DNA, Race, and History*, edited by Keith Wailoo, Alondra Nelson and Catherine Lee. Rutgers University Press, 2012, pp. 114–142.

———. *Race in a Bottle: The Story of BiDil and Racialized Medicine in a Post-Genomic Age*. Columbia University Press, 2013.

Klein, Rebecca. "Black Students in the U.S. Get Criminalized While White Students Get Treatment." *Huffington Post*, 28 July 2015, www.huffingtonpost.com/entry/racial-disparities-american-schools_us_55b67572e4b0074ba5a576c1?67pvte29=&utm_hp_ref=black-voices.

Miller, Matt. "A DNA Test Won't Explain Elizabeth Warren's Ancestry." *Slate*, 29 June 2016, www.slate.com/articles/technology/future_tense/2016/06/dna_testing_cannot_determine_ancestry_including_elizabeth_warren_s.html.

Morning, Ann. *The Nature of Race: How Scientists Think and Teach About Human Difference*. University of California Press, 2011.

Morrison, Toni. Afterword. *The Bluest Eye*. Plume, 1993.

Ossorio, Pilar N. "Myth and Mystification: The Science of Race and IQ." *Race and the Genetic Revolution: Science, Myth, and Culture*, edited by Sheldon Krimsky and Kathleen Sloan. Columbia University Press, 2011, pp. 173–194.

"Racial Profiling in Preschool." *New York Times*, 8 October 2016, nyti.ms/2jDOxHX.

"Report: The War on Marijuana in Black and White." ACLU, June 2013, www.aclu.org/report/report-war-marijuana-black-and-white?redirect=criminal-law-reform/war-marijuana-black-and-white. Accessed 17 May 2017.

Roberts, Dorothy. *Fatal Invention: How Science, Politics, and Big Business Re-Create Race in the Twenty-First Century*. The New Press, 2011.

Schuessler, Jennifer. "Confronting Academia's Ties to Slavery." *New York Times*, 5 March 2017, nyti.ms/2ltQXuU.

Severson, Kim. "Thousands Sterilized, a State Weighs Restitution." *New York Times*, 9 December 2011, www.nytimes.com/2011/12/10/us/redress-weighed-for-forced-sterilizations-in-north-carolina.html?pagewanted=all&_r=0.

Somashekhar, Sandhya. "The Disturbing Reason Some African American Patients May Be Undertreated for Pain." *Washington Post*, 4 April 2016, www.washingtonpost.com/news/to-your-health/wp/2016/04/04/do-blacks-feel-less-pain-than-whites-their-doctors-may-think-so/?utm_term=.d734eeb4be39.

Sussman, Robert Wald. *The Myth of Race: The Troubling Persistence of an Unscientific Idea*. Harvard University Press, 2014.

Tatum, Beverly Daniel. *"Why Are All the Black Kids Sitting Together in the Cafeteria?" and Other Conversations About Race*. Basic Books, 2003.

"2013–2014 Civil Rights Data Collection: A First Look." U.S. Department of Education Office for Civil Rights, 2016, www2.ed.gov/about/offices/list/ocr/docs/2013-14-first-look.pdf.

Woodson, Carter Godwin. *The Mis-Education of the Negro*. Seven Treasures Publications, 2010.

Yudell, Michael. "A Short History of the Race Concept." *Race and the Genetic Revolution: Science, Myth, and Culture*, edited by Sheldon Krimsky and Kathleen Sloan. Columbia University Press, 2011, pp. 13–30.

STEP 2

SEE THE RACISM MACHINE

Why was the Racism Machine built? When? Where? How? By whom?

Step 1 began by identifying one of the most significant obstacles blocking our recognition of racism, and that obstacle is the false ideology that race is biological. As Step 1 explained, many people don't identify this as an ideology because they just take it for granted as the truth. That's how ideologies work; they are taken for granted as the truth rather than identified as beliefs one is taught. The ideology that race is biological traps people into a way of thinking that perpetuates racism, whether they know it or not. Step 1 showed how this ideology can be very dangerous in the way it manifested itself in slavery, genocide, the eugenics movement, and the Holocaust. However, this ideology can also be dangerous today in a quieter, more subtle and insidious way. Believing that race is biological perpetuates stereotypes based on race, and it serves as a justification for various visible examples of racial inequality today. The false ideology that race is biological supports these deceptive beliefs and allows them to go unquestioned:

- The police shoot a disproportionately high number of black and Latinx people, but many believe that's because black and Latinx people are naturally criminal.
- Black and Latinx children have lower standardized testing scores, but many believe that's because they're less intelligent.

In other words, believing that race is biological becomes a convenient way to support the status quo. The false ideology that race is biological serves to divert people from recognizing the persistence of racism.

As Step 1 explained, this ideology has purposefully misled people in the US into believing that races are distinctly biological and can be positioned on a hierarchy from superior to inferior, with whites at the top, blacks at the bottom, and indigenous peoples, Asians, and Latinx people occupying various intermediary positions depending on the needs of the moment. While many believe this ideology has faded, Step 1 shared evidence that since the year 2000, the belief that races are biological has shown a resurgence. Because this ideology has been such a major obstacle preventing many people from seeing the Racism Machine since the creation of this country, Step 1 attempted to discredit this ideology by showing how it's untrue and dangerous. Hopefully, Step 1 chipped away enough at that ideology so that you can at least begin to see past it, to see over its rubble to the Racism Machine, with its complex and intricate interlocking wheels, cogs, gears, chains, and pulleys.

Now that you can begin to see the Racism Machine, hopefully you're starting to wonder: What is it? Where did it come from? Who built it? When? Why? How?

Feeling confused and maybe overwhelmed by these questions is actually a good spot for you to be in right now. Here, Step 2 will provide some introductory answers to these questions so you can, in Step 3, get even closer to the Racism Machine and begin to understand how it has strengthened from the founding of this nation to the 1960s. Then Step 4 will consider how the Racism Machine became recalibrated from the 1960s to today, even though it's common for people to say we are in a "post-racial" period, as if the Racism Machine has already been dismantled. Finally, Step 5 will focus on tools for disassembly, so you can start to take apart the Racism Machine, piece by piece.

Since you can begin to see the Racism Machine, you may have a lot of questions. I know I still do, and I've been researching these issues for more than twenty years. As I noticed in working on Step 1, there's a significant gap between what scholars take for granted and what the public (including my students) understands. Scholars sometimes get so focused on how they differ in their views from other scholars regarding details and nuances that they can sometimes lose sight of their common ground and the need to impart their shared knowledge of the larger picture to the general public. While scholars do disagree about exactly how race and racism originated, which is a thought-provoking debate, I am less concerned here with taking sides and exploring the detailed nuances of that debate and much more concerned with the bigger picture.

Even though I will soon turn to the construction of the Racism Machine in colonial America, I first want to look at the global picture to help readers understand that the parts used in building this machine already existed. Yes, the specifically American construction of this machine was unique, and that will be my focus, but the colonial elite didn't build it from thin air. The raw materials had already been developing for more than a century prior to the English settlement of James-town, Virginia, in 1607, the first permanent English settlement in what is now the US.

I've heard plenty of students say: Hasn't slavery always been around? Hasn't racism always existed? Isn't that just the way it is? The textbook I use, *Race: Are We So Different?*, is very helpful in providing a fundamental explanation that responds to these types of questions. The authors distinguish between racism and **ethnocentricity**:

> To be sure, past peoples were *ethnocentric*. They frequently believed themselves culturally superior to others and sometimes exhibited the nasty habit of painting others as uncultured and brutish or savage, even to the point of justifying enslavement and killing on this basis. Yet . . . ethnocentric and later racial logics differed significantly. . . . Prior to the inception of race, people were much less likely to link cultural practices instinctively and irrevocably to physical differences.
>
> (Goodman et al. 11)

In other words, if people believed themselves superior, it was not because of some unchangeable physical trait; they were being ethnocentric because they thought their "language, religion, food, adornment, or other behaviors" were superior, and the significant issue here is that these traits can be changed (Goodman et al. 11). An ethnocentric way of thinking leads to the belief that one's group is superior due to its traits, but other people could learn and adapt to these traits as well. Slavery, in the form of taking prisoners of war for example, certainly dates back to ancient civilizations and is related to these ethnocentric beliefs. However, the system of racialized slavery that emerged in the American colonies was something new. Here, this system depended on a belief that traits that defined a group were unchangeable, inherent, and natural, the false ideology that race is biological, which Step 1 explained.

The creators of the documentary *Race: The Power of an Illusion* developed a handout, "Ten Things Everyone Should Know About Race," which can be a helpful supplement to classroom or community discussions (see Step 5 action #1A). While this list may not include the nuance of longer works about complex historical and sociological concepts, it's a useful place to begin. For my purposes in this section, it offers clarification about the relationship between slavery and race:

> Slavery predates race. Throughout much of human history, societies have enslaved others, often as a result of conquest or war, even debt, but not because of physical characteristics or a belief in natural inferiority. Due to a unique set of historical circumstances, ours was the first slave system where all the slaves shared similar physical characteristics.
>
> ("Ten Things Everyone Should Know About Race")

I raise the distinction between ethnocentricity, slavery, and racism here because it's important to emphasize that the creation of a racialized system of slavery that developed in colonial America was not inevitable. If students think slavery and racism always existed, they consider them just automatic aspects of human existence. I don't believe the facts support this conclusion, and it's certainly not a helpful strategy for change. The racialized system of slavery that developed and the interconnected systems of racism were choices, active choices that were made; the system was built for a purpose, and that was to protect the interests of a small elite. Looking briefly at the global picture will help us understand what that means, and if readers want to know more about these issues at a global level, there are plenty of sources that analyze it in depth.

What Was the Global Context for the Construction of the American Racism Machine?

Often in the US, we're taught to think about people like Christopher Columbus as "explorers," which carries with it a sense of curiosity and innocence. That's a dangerous perception. When Spain and Portugal began voyaging by sea in the 1400s, it was not generally for the sake of knowledge. They explored for the sake of conquering and gaining wealth and resources in order to expand their empire. Columbus Day is still proudly celebrated in many schools, towns, and cities in the US, and what get ignored are the motivations and actions of his voyage. Columbus's own record from his very first encounter with indigenous people in Hispaniola (today, the island with the countries of the Dominican Republic and Haiti) just reinforces his motivation. Since he was not aware the Americas existed, he thought he was near India. He wrote, "'As soon as I arrived in the Indies, on the first Island which I found, I took some of the natives by force in order that they might learn and might give me information of whatever there is in these parts'" (qtd. in Zinn 2). Columbus's own report is very explicit about his hostile approach to the indigenous people, and it's important to understand that his violence was not a response to hostility from indigenous people.

Regardless of the welcoming behavior of the indigenous peoples, as historian Howard Zinn explains, Columbus had his goals established from the beginning. Zinn writes, "The information that Columbus wanted most was: Where is the gold? He had persuaded the king and queen of Spain to finance an expedition to the lands, the wealth, he expected, would be on the other side of the Atlantic—the Indies and Asia, gold and spices" (2). Columbus's zealous quest for gold was more important than treating the indigenous people as human beings; instead, he took indigenous people as captives back to Spain to be sold and forced others into slave labor to search for gold (Zinn 4).

Therefore, Columbus's first encounter reflected his mission to acquire gold at any cost. There never was a period of innocent discovery, a quest for knowledge. Historian Roxanne Dunbar-Ortiz explains how "Gold fever drove colonizing ventures" (43). She writes,

> Thus was born an ideology: the belief in the inherent value of gold despite its relative uselessness in reality. Investors, monarchies, and parliamentarians devised methods to control the process of wealth accumulation and the power that came with it, but the ideology behind gold fever mobilized settlers to cross the Atlantic to an unknown fate.
>
> (Dunbar-Ortiz 43–44)

This emphasis on "wealth accumulation" goes hand in hand with the burgeoning capitalism developing in Europe.

If we look to England in particular, we can see the gradual emergence of capitalism, a system that values private ownership, private property, profit, and acquisition. For example, in England in the 1500s, what was once common (or communal) land used by peasants to farm and raise cows and sheep became private property owned by the small, wealthy elite minority, who evicted the peasants (Dunbar-Ortiz 34–35). The growing value of private property was one of the reasons English colonizers in what is now the US didn't acknowledge the land rights of the indigenous peoples, who didn't use the English system of private property and instead focused more on communal land and resources. The rulers of England were desperately trying to move away from a communal approach to land so that they could take a much greater command of power, so it's no surprise that the last thing they wanted to do was to acknowledge the value of such a system. Instead, they saw communal land as no one's land, available to be claimed and taken for their own.

Starting in the 1400s, Spain and Portugal dominated in the early phase of sea voyages through **imperialism** and **colonialism**. These related terms reveal systems of power and control whereby one nation exerts control over other nations through a variety of means. Imperialism is a broader, more abstract concept of exerting that control, and colonialism is more specific in establishing a government in another nation to take control over its peoples. Spain and Portugal identified resources and claimed land deemed valuable in order to increase the wealth of the elite in their respective nations. In 1455, a papal bull (issued by the Pope) declared a "Doctrine of Discovery," which set the stage for European colonization of land outside of Europe, starting with Portuguese colonization of West Africa (Dunbar-Ortiz 199). In 1493, another papal bull included Spain, and then the Treaty of Tordesillas in 1494 divided the non-Christian world in half between these two imperial powers, with Portugal claiming Africa and Brazil and Spain claiming the Caribbean and the Americas (Dunbar-Ortiz 199). Spain and Portugal sought land and resources, and they used indigenous slave labor to search and mine for resources, especially gold. As the indigenous population died from murder, disease, and deadly slave labor conditions, the Spanish and Portuguese imported African slaves to extract resources that could be shipped back to Europe.

How does this global context help us understand the construction of the Racism Machine in the English colonies in what is now the US? We first need to consider how England became a competitor in colonization. England attempted to compete in the slave trade before they had colonies, but that wasn't very lucrative. Because they didn't have colonies, they didn't have the same need for cheap labor as Spain and Portugal (Hazlewood 309). However, England's first attempt to compete with Spain and Portugal in the slave trade is still important to understand because it establishes a foundation that they returned to. In 1562, under Queen Elizabeth I, John Hawkyns (1532-1595) is considered "the first Englishman to trade in slaves, and the first to benefit from the triangular trade, whereby goods were carried to Africa, slaves to America, and precious commodities to England at a massive profit" (Hazlewood 312). However, with Spain and Portugal dominating and without England having its own colonies, England didn't launch itself into the slave trade immediately.

Within a few decades, England established its first permanent colony in what is now the US in Jamestown, Virginia, in 1607. Not too long after, in 1619, colonist John Rolfe wrote that in Jamestown, Virginia, "'About the last of August came a Dutch man of war that sold us twenty negroes'" (qtd in. Hazlewood 307). (A "man of war" is a ship.) Many historians and other scholars have spent a lot of time considering this one sentence. Who were these "twenty negroes"? Were they slaves? How were they perceived by English colonists? If they began as slaves, did they remain slaves? Before we look more carefully at Jamestown, let's take one more step back at the global picture to consider how people in England perceived Africans. After all, since the English colonists in Jamestown in 1619 were likely raised in England, English perceptions of Africans would have a serious influence on how English colonists in Jamestown perceived these "twenty negroes."

By the late 1500s, the black population in England was increasing; some were servants while others had higher status (Hazlewood 319). Slavery, theoretically, did not exist in England. Queen Elizabeth I responded to England's increasing economic problems by scapegoating the growing black population, and so in 1596 and in 1601, she decreed that black people should be sent to Africa, but neither call for banishment worked. For those of us living in the US, it can be easy to ignore fundamental aspects of European, African, and Asian geography. We need to recognize that by this period, there would already have been centuries of peoples mixing between the continents of Europe, Africa, and Asia. While obviously venturing to the Americas required technological innovation to cross the Atlantic, the continents of Africa, Europe, and Asia are all in close proximity, something that those of us in the US may not fully recognize. Europe and Africa are less than ten miles apart by water when considering the close proximity of Spain (in southwestern Europe) and Morocco (in northwestern Africa) at the Straight of Gibraltar. Africa and Asia are connected by land, and so are Asia and Europe. Scholars and many others in the US take this geography for granted, but many students and the general public in the US don't necessarily have this geography in mind, so it's important to acknowledge the movement and mixing of peoples among Africa, Asia, and Europe goes back thousands of years.

Furthermore, literature and artwork from two thousand years ago reflect communication, trading, and warfare among various groups of people in Asia, Africa, and Europe, long before the English colonized Virginia. Power shifted within and between groups in these continents for centuries. Many students assume Europe always dominated the world, and they don't know that there were wealthy and powerful African civilizations known for important inventions. Students also don't realize that there were people of all skin colors from many parts of Europe, Asia, and Africa taken as slaves at some point over the course of centuries, depending on who was in power. This is all to say that while, by the time of European colonization, slaves tended to be African, that was not always the case.

Sociologist Eduardo Bonilla-Silva provides a helpful overview about the era of European colonization:

> When race emerged in human history, it formed a social structure (a racialized social system) that awarded systemic privileges to Europeans (the peoples who became "white") over non-Europeans (the peoples who became "nonwhite"). Racialized social systems, or white supremacy for short, became global and affected all societies where Europeans extended their reach. I therefore conceive a society's racial structure as *the totality of the social relations and practices that reinforce white privilege.* Accordingly, the task of analysts interested in studying racial structures is to uncover the particular social, economic, political, social control, and ideological mechanisms responsible for the reproduction of racial privilege in a society.
>
> (Bonilla-Silva 8–9)

The purpose of this manual is to provide an introduction to some of the very "mechanisms" that Bonilla-Silva describes here.

Sometimes referred to as the "origins debate," scholars explore the "issue of which came first, racism or slavery" (Sweet 143). In other words, why did African slavery become "the primary form of exploited labor in the Americas" (Sweet 143)? Were Africans used as slaves because they were already seen as inferior, or were they seen as inferior because they were used as slaves? This debate is a much larger issue than this book is addressing, so I'm not going to take sides, but it's important to acknowledge the debate exists. For example, historian Benjamin Isaac, author of *The Invention of Racism in Classical Antiquity,* focuses on the origin of racism in ancient Greece and Rome, especially in the form of "ambivalence and hostility towards foreigners, strangers, and immigrant minorities, rather than internal marginalized groups" (4). While Isaac acknowledges that early racism "did not exist in the modern form of a biological determinism" and did not take the form of "systemic persecution of any ethnic group by another," he does highlight how "some essential elements of later racism have their roots in Greek and Roman thinking" (5). Likewise, in "The Iberian Roots of American Racist Thought," historian James H. Sweet argues that "the racism that came to characterize American slavery was well established in cultural and religious attitudes in Spain and Portugal by the fifteenth century" (Sweet 144). (Note that Spain and Portugal comprise Iberia or the Iberian Peninsula.)

On the other hand, historian David R. Roediger focuses more on the relatively recent development of race and racism. He discusses the work of W.E.B. Du Bois (1868–1963), preeminent historian, sociologist, and civil rights activist who was the first African American to graduate from Harvard University with a PhD (in 1895). Roediger writes,

> "The discovery of personal whiteness among the world's peoples," [Du Bois] wrote, "is a very modern thing." "The ancient world would have laughed at such a distinction," he continued, further noting that in the Middle Ages skin color would have provoked nothing more than "mild curiosity." Despite a good deal of scholarship that has tried to read modern notions of race back into such curiosity, Du Bois was, characteristically, right. . . . Though influenced by the ways that anti-Semitism, anti-Islamic crusading and the conquest of Ireland created "others" against whom a "Christian Europe" and its various empires could begin to fashion themselves, personal whiteness would have to await the slave trade and the settler-colonial conquest of indigenous peoples in the Americas.
>
> (Roediger 1)

Roediger emphasizes how while perceptions of "others" go back to ancient times, significant meaning connected to skin color did not emerge until European colonization of the Americas and the transatlantic slave trade.

For our purposes here, I think it's helpful to focus on a few broader points. By the time of European colonization, there was clearly antiblack sentiment. However, it was still evolving. Not all Africans in Europe or their colonies were necessarily slaves or even servants. If racism and racialized slavery were already inevitable by the time the English established their colony at Jamestown, then it wouldn't have taken almost a century for them to build the Racism Machine. They actively made choices in building the Racism Machine, albeit with parts and materials that already existed, but they still built a uniquely American Racism Machine, and that's what I want to turn to now.

Jamestown, Virginia, *before* the Racism Machine Was Built

Why focus on Jamestown, Virginia? As the first permanent English colony in what is now the US, Jamestown provides a window into the development of racialized thinking in the burgeoning American colonies. Virginia's documented legal codes provide language whose evolution we can analyze as a way to understand the hardening of attitudes and the very creation of racial categories and a racial hierarchy, not to mention the racial ideology described in Step 1. In other words, we can catch glimpses of the construction of the Racism Machine. While scholars disagree about certain aspects of attitudes in the 1600s toward indentured servitude and slavery in colonial America, there seems to be little doubt that race was ambiguously defined in the early 1600s, at least compared to a stricter definition a century later. In early Jamestown, race was an amorphous concept; the line between slave and servant was murky at best, and "black" and "white" as racial categories were not defined.

There are several factors that need to be highlighted in order to understand why the Racism Machine would have been built in the first place. One is the worsening status of European laborers, who represented the majority of the laboring population in Jamestown during much of the 1600s. Historian Theodore Allen explains this worsening status by describing the transition from tenancy to indentured servitude that occurred during the early 1620s. Jamestown was founded in 1607, and Allen argues that the tenant farmers of the 1610s had more rights and opportunities, whereas that changed in 1616 when former tenants no longer had a guaranteed right to land (61–62). Furthermore, in 1619, "independent capitalists were given . . . legal jurisdiction over the control of their tenants and laborers" (Allen 59). For example, Allen points to a 1622 mandate by the Virginia Company that allowed laborers to be "assigned," in which the laborer loses legal power by being traded or sold to another master. Furthermore, the laborer was not previously responsible for his or her transportation costs, but now, with indentured servitude, the servant had to pay off the transportation costs by working for a designated master for a certain number of years. Allen argues that this shift represented a calculated choice to save labor costs. Indentured servants were bought and sold, "'merchandize for sale,'" as a Colony Secretary called it in 1638 (qtd. in Allen 108). The majority of such workers were European, not African.

This shift from tenancy to indentured servitude brought with it a loss of power for laborers at many levels that, not surprisingly, led to great dissatisfaction among the laborers, enough to prompt many to run away and to rebel. While we may have a mental picture of an indentured servant as someone who freely enters into a contract for a specific number of years, vastly different from the status of a slave, such a picture may be inaccurate. As several scholars point out, the status of indentured servants and the status of slaves during this early period of Jamestown were not all that different (the status of slaves got much worse later, as we will get to). Servants could not always control their period of service; masters would often abuse their power and negate a contract. Or, if there was no written contract, then the servant would often be squeezed for as many years of service as possible. The status of servants got worse and worse as the 1600s progressed. Laborers in England tended to have many more rights than their counterparts in Virginia. Historian Edmund Morgan explains how the Virginia court "supported masters in severities that would not have been allowed in England" (127). In fact, many people in England objected to the notion that English servants were bought and sold in Virginia. One servant complained of being sold "'like a damnd slave'" (qtd. in Morgan 128).

Servants in Virginia were treated abysmally, and those in power in Virginia and in England thought very poorly of them. Historian Betty Wood quotes one description of servants as "'idle, lazy, simple people such as have professed idleness and will rather beg than work'" (qtd. in Wood 15). (We will see this negative attitude about the poor recur in Step 4's discussion of recent cuts to government services.) Furthermore, Wood argues that as the 1600s developed, indentured servants had fewer and fewer chances "to achieve the freedom, the upward social, economic, and political mobility that had lured so many of them across the Atlantic"

(Wood 91). It was difficult to leave servitude due to the power of masters, but even once free of servitude, it was increasingly difficult to obtain land (Morgan 225). Not surprisingly, servants expressed their dissatisfaction in a variety of ways, and that posed a threat to the landowning elite.

There are now impressive online repositories that provide the original language of colonial laws, which give us evidence of these historical trends. In 1823, William Waller Hening published a thirteen-volume compilation of the laws of Virginia called *The Statutes at Large*, and these have been transcribed for a comprehensive website. (Note that the website Hening's Statutes at Large preserves the information of the original volume and page number, which appears to be the easiest way to navigate the site, so that's what I've included with each quote. I've also kept the original spelling.)

Several Virginia laws reveal the growing fear of servant rebellions. For example, one law created in 1663 explicitly states its goal of "better suppressing the unlawful meetings of servants" and instructs masters to make sure their servants do not leave on Sundays without permission (Hening vol. 2, 195).

In addition to the worsening status of European laborers, a second factor that served as a catalyst for the construction of the Racism Machine was the emergence of coalitions between European and African laborers. Given the deteriorating position of European indentured servants in Jamestown, it may not be surprising that there is ample evidence that they had more in common with African laborers they worked with than they had with the landowning elite. While we might look back in time and see these laborers as "white" and "black," that's not how they would have seen themselves or each other; they likely saw themselves simply as laborers. Their focus would not have been the skin color difference between them but rather the difference in power and status between laborers and wealthy landowners. Historian Edmund Morgan writes, "It was common, for example, for servants and slaves to run away together, steal hogs together, get drunk together. It was not uncommon for them to make love together" (Morgan 327). Likewise, historian Lerone Bennett Jr. describes this early population as "a great mass of white and black bondsmen, who occupied roughly the same economic category and were treated with equal contempt by the lords of the plantations and legislatures. Curiously unconcerned about their color, these people worked together and relaxed together" (qtd. in Alexander 23). The Jamestown colonists may have brought some of the raw materials to build the Racism Machine with them to Virginia, but they did not bring the Racism Machine itself with them, nor did they build it when they first got there. The Virginia landowning wealthy elite built it as a response to the evolving conditions in an attempt to stay in power. It was a purposeful act, and it's important for us to recognize what Jamestown was like before this occurred. As I've mentioned before, if we can understand that the construction of the Racism Machine was not inevitable, it can give us hope for dismantling it.

African and European laborers formed powerful coalitions, powerful enough that they served as a threat to the landowning elite. Court decisions of colonial Virginia (some of which are compiled on the website Virtual Jamestown) and laws of colonial Virginia (compiled, as previously mentioned, in *Hening's Statutes at Large*) reveal the attempts to break these coalitions. If the coalitions hadn't been perceived as dangerous, there wouldn't have been a need to respond in such a recurring, formal, and legal way. Let's consider a few of these court decisions and laws.

In 1640, the General Court of Colonial Virginia punished two Europeans and one African for running away together. They decided the following: "*Victor*, a *dutchman*, the other a *Scotchman* called *James Gregory*, shall first serve out their times with their master according to their Indentures, and one whole year apiece after the time of their service is Expired" ("The Practise of Slavery"). In other words, the man from the Netherlands and the man from Scotland were punished with an extra year of servitude added to their original indenture. The Court also determined the following for the third runaway in the group: "a negro named *John Punch* shall serve his said master or his assigns for the time of his natural Life here or elsewhere" ("The Practise of Slavery"). This latter decision is the first known instance of an African mandated to serve as a slave for life in Virginia.

This record reveals several important things. To begin, Europeans and Africans were running away together (and there are recordings of many such instances), which reveals that they found common ground with each other. Their different skin color did not prevent them from forming this coalition. However, those in power, in this case the General Court of Colonial Virginia, found this coalition to be a threat. They gave the same punishment to two Europeans from different European countries (perhaps a decision we can see as a precursor to the invention of the category "white" that they would both soon occupy) and a vastly different and significantly worse punishment to the man we would call "black." We can identify an antiblack sentiment with this decision. We can also identify an attempt to divide and conquer the laborers by treating them differently based on skin color; this divide-and-conquer strategy represents an attempt to disrupt their coalition. Finally, if lifelong servitude is the punishment for the African man, then that means his status was not that of a slave prior to the court decision.

Interestingly, twenty years after this first legal decision to give different punishments to a group of servants running away together based on what we would call race clearly had not deterred more groups from running away together. For example, one law passed in 1661–1662 identified the problem of "run-aways" and strengthened their punishment. Furthermore, there was additional punishment if an "English servant" ran away "in company of any negroes" (Hening vol. 2, 116–117). Coalitions of laborers (coalitions we would today call interracial) were constantly forming and constantly punished, revealing that such punishment was not a strong deterrent.

We can also acknowledge the ambiguity of race in this early period in Virginia by considering the situation of an African man, Anthony Johnson. In 1621, when Anthony Johnson reaches Virginia, we don't know whether his status is as servant or slave. Either way, he works his way to becoming a free man who owns his own land and slaves. He is even able to take a white farmer to Virginia court and win, in 1655 (Goodman et al. 18–19). Not only was this man we would today call black able to earn his own freedom, but he also could own his own slaves, testify in court, and win in court. You'll see how these rights were taken away from free blacks once the Racism Machine was built, but his experience shows that while the people who settled Jamestown did bring the raw materials of the Racism Machine with them, they didn't build the Machine right away. If the Racism Machine had been built immediately, Anthony Johnson never would have been allowed to gain the rights he did.

Another way of understanding how the governing bodies of Virginia did not immediately launch themselves into this racialized system of chattel slavery or build the Racism Machine right away is to consider their laws that referred to Irish servants. For example, the Virginia General Assembly passed a law in 1654–1655 that stated that the Irish servants brought to Virginia without a specified time of indentured servitude must serve six years if they're older than sixteen or until they're twenty-four if they're under sixteen (Hening vol. 1, 411). In other words, Irish servants specifically were targeted for serving more time than they would if they were from another country.

However, that decision only lasted a few years, and the Virginia General Assembly in 1659–1660 passed a new law explaining that the additional time had deterred too many people from Ireland. The law states it was an "inconvenience" and that potential Irish immigrants were "being discouraged" (Hening vol. 1, 538–539). This same law also stated that any servant from a "christian nation" that came without a specified time of servitude couldn't be made to serve more time than servants from England (Hening vol. 1, 538–539). This law again serves as a precursor to what we'll see in a few decades, a blending together of separate European national identities (English, Irish, Scottish, Dutch, etc.) into a single European identity that will become known as "white." Note that the word "white" is not used and will not be used in Virginia legal language until 1691. Identifying people by religion or nation of origin was more common in the earliest years of the colony.

While there were many rebellions of exploited laborers, **Bacon's Rebellion** of 1676 is probably the most well known. Nathaniel Bacon led a coalition of laborers, some free, some not, and some we would call white and some we would call black. By this time, there were already decades of unrest by the laborers who objected to their conditions and their exploitation. As I've tried to make clear, the line between servant and slave was still ambiguous, as was the line between black and white, since these racial categories were not quite yet articulated. The coalition that Bacon led included people denied land by the colonial government, and this coalition resisted. It's crucial to keep in mind that this coalition formed at the expense of the indigenous people, whose land the elite and the laborers were fighting over. The rebellion was successful in that it scared the elite, but their response essentially led the way to the construction of the Racism Machine.

As legal scholar Michelle Alexander, author of *The New Jim Crow*, states, "The events in Jamestown were alarming to the planter elite, who were deeply fearful of the multiracial alliance of bond workers and slaves. Word of Bacon's Rebellion spread far and wide, and several more uprisings of a similar type followed" (24). Laborers significantly outnumbered the wealthy planter class. For a variety of reasons, it became in the interest of the wealthy landowners to separate poor whites and blacks as a method of control and containment. Such separation involved lowering the status of blacks and raising the status of whites, although not enough that they would be in a competition with the wealthy elite.

Gathering the Raw Materials to Build the Racism Machine

Several Virginia colonial laws reveal examples of the gradual lead-up to the construction of the Racism Machine. In 1662, the General Assembly passed a law mandating "Negro womens children to serve according to the condition of the mother" (Hening vol. 2, 170). Before that, English precedent tended to have children follow the status of the father and not the mother. The law goes on to state, "Whereas some doubts have arrisen whether children got by any Englishman upon a negro woman should be slave or ffree, *Be it therefore enacted and declared by this present grand assembly*, that all children borne in this country shalbe held bond or free only according to the condition of the mother" (Hening vol. 2, 170). This law imposes control through intersecting categories of race, gender, and economic status. We can see this even more clearly in the next part of the law, which states, "And that if any christian shall committ ffornication with a negro man or woman, hee or shee soe offending shall pay double the ffines imposed by the former act" (Hening vol. 2, 170). This law is attempting to prevent interracial relationships at the same time that a male landowner with a black female servant or slave could increase his property by raping her, and now that child would inherit the mother's servant or slave status. The owner would likely be above the law and not be held accountable for breaking the law because his economic class is what the law is designed to protect.

Another colonial Virginia law, this one passed in 1680, further creates the materials for the Racism Machine. Titled "An act for preventing Negroes Insurrections," it bans "any negroe or other slave" from carrying weapons, leaving the master's property without permission, and threatening a "christian" (Hening vol. 2, 481–482). Anyone who violates this law and runs away can be legally killed (Hening vol. 2, 481–482). Finally, this law states that it must be published every six months at every court and church in Virginia, reinforcing its perceived urgency (Hening vol. 2, 481–482).

We can see the materials for the Racism Machine continue to be collected in a significant 1691 Virginia law called "An Act for suppressing outlying slaves," which includes language drastically limiting interracial marriage:

> And for prevention of that abominable mixture and spurious issue which hereafter may encrease in this dominion as well by negroes, mulattoes, and Indians intermarrying with English, or other white women, as by their unlawfull accompanying with one another, *Be it enacted by the authoritie aforesaid, and it is hereby enacted,* That for the time to come, whatsoever English or other white man or woman being free shall intermarry with a negroe, mulatto, or Indian man or woman bond or free shall within three months after such marriage be banished and removed from this dominion forever, and that the justices of each respective countie within this dominion make it their perticular care, that this act be put in effectuall execution.
>
> (Hening vol. 3, 86–87)

While it's challenging to read the original style of language from more than three centuries ago, there are certain words we must pay attention to. From the beginning of this excerpt, the language regarding the children of an interracial couple could not be more disparaging, insulting, and offensive. First, the focus is on "prevention" of the existence of such children, which is already negative. Then such children are identified as "abominable," meaning repulsive and monstrous, and "spurious," meaning fake and inauthentic. Interracial couples cannot remain in Virginia for more than three months, so this law actively discourages such couples from being together in the first place, much less marrying and having children. However, what is not obvious from this excerpt without some context is that this law appears to be the very first time the word "white" was used to identify a person in Virginia, at least in the written legal record (Goodman et al. 44). Remember that Jamestown was settled in 1607, and the legislature of colonial Virginia started documenting laws in 1619. If the concept of "white" as a racial category were already determined from the outset, it wouldn't have taken the legislature more than seventy years of writing laws before using the word "white."

Building the Racism Machine

In understanding the construction of the American Racism Machine, I find it helpful to focus on three fundamental wheels central to the functioning of this Machine: the wheels of white, black, and native. While we might take for granted that such categories always existed, that was not the case. They were created during the period of European colonialism, capitalism, and slavery, and they were created with a purpose: to maintain the power and status quo of the elite. Consider the following fundamental traits of each wheel:

- White: built with benefits, attached to freedom, and connected to civilization, humanity, and a newly blended European identity
- Black: built by removing rights and chained to chattel slavery with the sub-human status of "animal"
- Native: built by blending distinct indigenous nations into one group often seen as savage and without national identity, with limited or no rights, especially not to the land

All three wheels homogenized (or blended) people who tended not to be previously grouped together. Different European nations certainly didn't see themselves as equal and homogenous; various nations and groups within nations had been fighting for centuries. In Africa, there were a significant number of ethnic, linguistic, national, and religious differences, so Africans didn't see themselves as homogenous. Likewise, indigenous peoples in the Americas didn't see themselves as the same either; they had national, linguistic, and cultural differences. Certainly, when it suited colonists to exploit tribal rivalries in order to gain control over more land, the colonists did distinguish between tribes. However, those distinctions were in the service of conquering indigenous peoples and taking their land.

In 1705, Virginia passed a series of laws referred to as the "**slave codes**." These laws were pivotal in legalizing racialized slavery. Consider these laws as the blueprint for part of the Racism Machine. Roediger explains that "Liberal and radical scholars alike have emphasized that race is not a natural category; rather, racial slavery was a laboriously constructed system. Even in colonies deeply associated with plantation agriculture, it took time for white supremacy to emerge as a centerpiece of the legal and labor systems" (2). While we tend to think that black people in the American colonies never had any rights, these laws show that black and, in some cases, indigenous people initially had rights that were taken away, one after another. For example, in these laws, "any negro, mulatto or Indian" cannot hold office (Hening vol. 3, 251–252). And "negroes, mulattoes and Indian servants, and others, not being christians, shall be deemed and taken to be persons incapable in law" and cannot serve as witnesses (Hening vol. 3, 298). These laws create a racial hierarchy and build the Racism Machine wheel by wheel.

The most powerful and horrific part of these 1705 slave codes was the law titled "An act declaring the Negro, Mulatto, and Indian slaves within this dominion, to be real estate" (Hening vol. 3, 333–335). As its name makes explicitly clear, identifying slaves as "real estate" overtly categorizes them as **chattel**, or property. They are not human beings with rights; they are objects to be moved around and passed along and exploited as their owners see fit. The law states they can be inherited "according to the manner and custom of land of inheritance" (Hening vol. 3, 333–335). Just like other property, human beings could now be inherited, passed down from one generation to the next. The law that mandated slaves to be "real estate" focused on those already living in Virginia.

Then, to categorize those who enter Virginia in the future, a related 1705 law, "An act concerning Servants and Slaves," states,

> That all servants imported and brought into this country, by sea or land, who were not christians in their native country, (except

Turks and Moors in amity with her majesty, and others that can
make due proof of their being free in England, or any other christian country, before they were shipped, in order to transportation
hither) shall be accounted and be slaves, and such be here bought
and sold notwithstanding a conversion to christianity afterwards.

(Hening vol. 3, 447–448)

In other words, while conversion to Christianity may have prevented
some people from being forced into slavery in the past, that is no longer the case. This law would identify the increasing numbers of Africans
being sent to Virginia from non-Christian sub-Saharan Africa as slaves.

The slave code established a system of racialized chattel slavery,
meaning slaves were property, "real estate," and this system became one
of the most fundamental parts of the Racism Machine. Law after law
reinforced this system, each one an additional gear, wheel, or pulley
to reinforce and strengthen the Racism Machine. While the foundational 1705 slave code helped build the Racism Machine by identifying
"Negro, Mulatto, and Indian slaves . . . to be real estate," thereby drastically lowering the status of laborers of color, it also increased the status
of white laborers, specifically white servants. Here we see the persistence
of the divide-and-conquer strategy: split this large, threatening group of
laborers into two groups by dividing them through different labels and
conquering them by positioning one higher than the other on a hierarchy. Roediger explains, "The decisive turn to African slave labor in the
late seventeenth century thus responded to the need to avoid a repetition
of the interracial uprisings that had so threatened colonial rule in the
time of Bacon" (7).

The 1705 "act concerning Servants and Slaves" further reveals the
divide-and-conquer mentality. Servants and slaves, once an ambiguous
group, were made distinct from each other, divided, and one was elevated while the other was lowered, essentially conquering them both.
Then comes an extremely important line marking the difference between
free and slave, where freedom is attached to the emerging category of
whiteness, and slavery is attached to the emerging category of blackness. The slave codes essentially established a system in which European
indentured servants (a shrinking group) would maintain their status as

servants only for a specific time period, and after that, they would be free. This applied to European servants who did not arrive in Virginia with a specific period of indenture; the law required that they be freed by the age of twenty-four (Hening vol. 3, 447). Moreover, this law also mandated that European servants had to have masters who were white and that people of color could only own servants or slaves "of their own complexion" (Hening vol. 3, 449–450).

Furthermore, when the period of servitude was completed for European servants, this law provided legal protection to ensure that they either receive wages or goods and food:

> That there shall be paid and allowed to every imported servant, not having yearly wages, at the time of service ended, by the master or owner of such servants, viz: To every male servant, ten bushels of indian corn, thirty shillings in money, or the value thereof, in goods, and one well fixed musket or fuzee [types of guns], of the value of twenty shillings, at least: and to every woman servant, fifteen bushels of indian corn, and forty shillings in money, or the value thereof, in goods: Which, upon refusal, shall be ordered, with costs, upon petition to the county court, in manner as is herein before directed, for servants complaints to be heard.
>
> (Hening vol. 3, 451)

Once the line between white and black was drawn, the line between servant and slave was also clarified. Before, the status of servants and slaves was ambiguous, and there was not a clear distinction. However, with this law, not only did the status of the slave become lowered and much more controlled, but the status of the servant was elevated, albeit not significantly, but raised nonetheless. For example, this law also stated that

> all masters and owners of servants, shall find and provide for their servants, wholesome and competent diet, clothing, and lodging, by the discretion of the county court; and shall not, at any time, give immoderate correction; neither shall, at any time, whip a christian white servant naked, without an order from a justice of the peace.
>
> (Hening vol. 3, 448)

In other words, white servants were supposed to be treated distinctly better than slaves. Furthermore, while European servants outnumbered Africans in the American colonies for much of the 1600s, "By 1709 Africans in slavery for life overwhelmingly outnumbered Europeans held for a term in Virginia, South Carolina, and Maryland" (Roediger 5).

In order to understand the significance of these laws, it's important to keep in mind that **whiteness** was an invention. It was created to have something to give to the European servants whose rebellions needed to be suppressed. Michelle Alexander refers to this strategy as a "racial bribe," in which white laborers were given a bribe, whiteness, in order to turn against black slaves (25). She writes,

> Deliberately and strategically, the planter class extended special privileges to poor whites in an effort to drive a wedge between them and black slaves. White settlers were allowed greater access to Native American lands, white servants were allowed to police slaves through slave patrols and militias, and barriers were created so that free labor would not be placed in competition with slave labor. These measures effectively eliminated the risk of future alliances between black slaves and poor whites. . . . Their own plight had not improved much, but at least they were not slaves.
>
> (Alexander 25)

In other words, European workers could become white in order to move up one rung on the hierarchy. Though the landowning wealthy elite were still way above them, they could at least feel closer to them and perhaps hope to aspire to be them, at the same time as they now had a group to look down on. They were no longer at the very bottom, which served as a very powerful divide-and-conquer strategy.

Roediger explains the invention of whiteness as follows:

> The notion that one could own a skin color—what the legal scholar Cheryl Harris calls "whiteness of property" and the historian George Lipsitz calls the "possessive investment in whiteness"— came into being alongside the reality that only peoples who

were, increasingly, stigmatized by their color could be owned and sold as slaves. It matured alongside the equally brutal notion that land on which the suddenly "nonwhite" peoples lived would be better managed by "white" people.

(Roediger 2)

In other words, white supremacy was built into the invention of whiteness. The racial category of whiteness was created in order to sit at the top of the racial hierarchy. Forces of capitalism and patriarchy interlocked with white supremacy in order to define status and property in the context of whiteness. One's relationship with freedom directly related to one's relationship with whiteness. While the term white privilege tends to be applied to more recent situations, we can clearly see the creation of this fundamental set of unearned advantages that whiteness allowed: freedom and access to land.

One of the most important pieces of information that can help us acknowledge that the construction of the Racism Machine was not inevitable, that racialized slavery didn't just happen on its own but was rather a deliberate choice, is the reaction of governing officials in England to the decisions of the colonial officials in Virginia. Historian Theodore W. Allen refers to a statement by the Attorney-General in England, Richard West, who raised a concern about a law Virginia passed in 1723. The Virginia law barred any "'free negro, mulatto, or indian'" from voting in any election (qtd. in Allen 241). West questions why skin color alone would be a determining factor in allowing someone to vote or not, as long as the person was free and possessed property and was not a criminal. He writes, "I cannot see why one freeman should be used worse than another, merely upon account of his complexion'" (qtd. in Allen 241). He explicitly questions why a divide-and-conquer approach is being used against free whites and blacks.

West goes on to say that

when several negroes have merited their freedom, and obtained it, and by their industry, have acquired that proportion of property . . . it cannot be just, by a general law . . . to strip all free persons, of a black complexion . . . from those rights, which are so justly valuable to every freeman.

(qtd. in Allen 241)

It's also quite noteworthy to consider the official response from Virginia, and this was made by Governor William Gooch, who explained that they passed the law barring free blacks from voting "'to fix a perpetual Brand upon Free Negroes & Mulattos'" (qtd. in Allen 242). Allen's analysis of this response reinforces my approach here, that the Racism Machine was built through deliberate choice and decisions. In referring to Governor Gooch's response, Allen explains that the Virginia law barring free blacks from voting "was a deliberate act by the plantation bourgeoisie; it proceeded from a conscious decision in the process of establishing a system of racial oppression, even though it meant repealing an electoral principle that had existed in Virginia for more than a century" (Allen 242). To the landowning wealthy elite of Virginia, the most important thing was to preserve their power, wealth, and status, even if it meant building the Racism Machine.

This chapter has attempted to explain what motivated the colonial elite to construct the Racism Machine, reinforcing the key concept that the construction of this Machine was not inevitable. Yes, there were preexisting raw materials used to build it, but it took many decades after the settling of Jamestown before the elite wealthy landowners made deliberate choices to build the Racism Machine in order to protect their interests.

Next, we'll move on to Step 3 and see how the Racism Machine was strengthened in the creation of the newly formed United States and how the Racism Machine was fortified in the almost two centuries after that formation, taking us to the civil rights movement of the 1960s.

Reflection Questions

1. Were you aware of the history presented in Step 2? If not, what surprised you the most, and why?
2. Do you think that this history is regularly taught? Why or why not?
3. Do you think our society would be more racially just if more people were aware of this history? If so, how might that occur?
4. What reflection question would you create to respond to Step 2, and why?

Recommended Resources

Films

Africa's Great Civilizations. PBS, 2017.

The African Americans: Many Rivers to Cross. Inkwell Films, Kunhardt McGee Productions and THIRTEEN Productions, LLC, 2013.

Websites

Race: Are We So Different? American Anthropological Association, 2016, www.understandingrace.org/.

Race: The Power of an Illusion. California Newsreel, www.pbs.org/race.

Articles

Harris, Cheryl I. "Whiteness as Property." *Harvard Law Review*, vol. 106, no. 8, June 1993, pp. 1707–1791. JSTOR, www.jstor.org/stable/1341787.

Books

Berlin, Ira. *Many Thousands Gone: The First Two Centuries of Slavery in North America.* Harvard University Press, 1998.

Bonilla-Silva, Eduardo. *Racism Without Racists: Color-Blind Racism and the Persistence of Racial Inequality in America.* 4th ed., Rowman & Littlefield Publishers, 2014.

Du Bois, W.E.B. *The Souls of Black Folk.* Vintage Books, 1990.

Dunbar-Ortiz, Roxanne. *An Indigenous Peoples' History of the United States.* Beacon Press, 2014.

Farrow, Anne, et al. *Complicity: How the North Promoted, Prolonged, and Profited From Slavery.* Ballantine Books, 2005.

Goodman, Alan H., et al. *Race: Are We So Different?* Wiley-Blackwell, 2012.

Johnson, Charles, et al. *Africans in America: America's Journey Through Slavery.* Harcourt Brace & Company, 1998.

Kendi, Ibram X. *Stamped from the Beginning: The Definitive History of Racist Ideas in America.* Nation Books, 2016.

Kolchin, Peter. *American Slavery: 1619–1877.* Hill and Wang, 1993.

Morgan, Edmund S. *American Slavery, American Freedom: The Ordeal of Colonial Virginia.* W.W. Norton & Company, 1975.

Painter, Nell Irvin. *The History of White People.* W.W. Norton & Company, 2010.

Reilly, Kevin, Stephen Kaufman and Angela Bodino, editors. *Racism: A Global Reader.* M.E. Sharpe, 2003.

Roediger, David R. *How Race Survived U.S. History: From Settlement and Slavery to the Obama Phenomenon.* Verso, 2008.

Warren, Wendy. *New England Bound: Slavery and Colonization in Early America.* Liveright Publishing Corporation, 2016.

Zinn, Howard. *A People's History of the United States: 1492–Present.* Perennial Classics, 2003.

Works Cited

Alexander, Michelle. *The New Jim Crow: Mass Incarceration in the Age of Colorblindness.* The New Press, 2012.

Allen, Theodore W. *The Invention of the White Race: The Origin of Racial Oppression in Anglo-America.* Verso, 1997.

Bonilla-Silva, Eduardo. *Racism Without Racists: Color-Blind Racism and the Persistence of Racial Inequality in America.* 4th ed., Rowman & Littlefield Publishers, 2014.

Dunbar-Ortiz, Roxanne. *An Indigenous Peoples' History of the United States.* Beacon Press, 2014.

Goodman, Alan H., et al. *Race: Are We So Different?* Wiley-Blackwell, 2012.

Hazlewood, Nick. *The Queen's Slave Trader: John Hawkyns, Elizabeth I, and the Trafficking in Human Souls.* William Morrow, 2004.

Hening, William Waller. "Hening's Statutes at Large." 19 July 2009, www.vagenweb.org/hening/index.htm. Accessed 17 May 2017.

Isaac, Benjamin. *The Invention of Racism in Classical Antiquity.* Princeton University Press, 2004.

Morgan, Edmund S. *American Slavery, American Freedom: The Ordeal of Colonial Virginia.* W.W. Norton & Company, 1975.

"The Practise of Slavery: Selected Virginia Records Relating to Slavery." *Virtual Jamestown*, Crandall Shifflett, 1998, www.virtualjamestown.org/practise.html. Accessed 17 May 2017.

Roediger, David R. *How Race Survived U.S. History: From Settlement and Slavery to the Obama Phenomenon.* Verso, 2008.

Sweet, James H. "The Iberian Roots of American Racist Thought." *The William and Mary Quarterly*, vol. 64, no. 1, January 1997, pp. 143–166. *JSTOR*, www.jstor.org/stable/2953315.

"Ten Things Everyone Should Know About Race." *Race: The Power of an Illusion*, California Newsreel, 2003, newsreel.org/guides/race/10things.htm.

Wood, Betty. *The Origins of American Slavery: Freedom and Bondage in the English Colonies.* Hill and Wang, 1997.

Zinn, Howard. *A People's History of the United States: 1492–Present.* Perennial Classics, 2003.

STEP 3

EXAMINE THE RACISM MACHINE'S POWERFUL MECHANISMS

How did the founding of the US strengthen the Racism Machine?
How did the Racism Machine become even stronger during the nation's first two centuries, leading up to the civil rights movement of the 1960s?

Step 1 urged you to recognize the false ideology of biological race as an obstacle that prevents people from seeing the Racism Machine. Furthermore, Step 1 attempted to chip away at this ideology by revealing it as false and dangerous and by explaining race as a social construct. Then Step 2 started to address the questions you would likely have upon seeing the Racism Machine: What is this? Who invented it? Why? When? How? Step 2 provided some introductory answers to these questions by exploring the invention of race as a means of power and control, of divide and conquer. Step 2 took you through the initial construction of the Racism Machine in colonial America. However, just because the Racism Machine was built in colonial America doesn't explain how it persisted for centuries, to the present day.

Step 3 will highlight how the Racism Machine not only persisted but also was essentially reinforced and fortified through the creation of the new nation, the United States of America. Once Step 3 shows how the Racism Machine became embedded in the nation's founding, it will explain how restricting citizenship to white people and identifying everyone by race through the census became additional mechanisms that reinforced the Racism Machine. Then, with that fortification in place, the elite could drastically expand the landholdings of the United States, thereby increasing the nation's wealth and the role of capitalism in the country's future at the same time as removing the land's indigenous inhabitants and replacing them with white citizens. Lawmakers and many others constantly patrolled the borders of whiteness in order to protect the interests of the elite. Patriarchy also exerted considerable power by identifying white women as needing protection from black men, an ideology that became an increasingly more powerful mechanism of the Racism Machine. Step 4 will then pick up and reveal how, despite popular thinking, the Racism Machine was not dismantled by the civil rights movement of the 1960s but merely recalibrated in order to perpetuate racism in less overt, more subtle ways, taking us to the present.

By the time the American colonists started to organize sustained rebellions against British colonial power in the 1770s, the Racism Machine had already been operating for decades. Keep in mind it was built before the Founding Fathers were even born. However, today in the US, when we celebrate the Revolutionary period, especially in July 4th festivities, it's common to ignore the significant role that slavery and genocide had in the creation of the American colonies leading up to the American Revolution and to ignore their powerful role in the founding of the new nation. We focus on oppression in the context of Britain oppressing the American colonies, but we ignore and deny the oppression of indigenous peoples and slaves. We celebrate the freedom of the American colonies from British rule but ignore the denial of freedom to indigenous peoples and slaves. In other words, we disregard the existence of the Racism Machine in colonial America, how much the colonies depended on it, and how it was strengthened rather than dismantled as the American colonies became the United States of America.

As the Introduction to this manual explained, one of the fields that I have personally found extremely helpful in my understanding of the legal history of systemic racism is critical race theory (CRT), and one of its foundational texts will, I hope, be especially helpful in clarifying exactly how the Racism Machine was strengthened rather than dismantled as our country's founding documents were drafted. CRT scholar and one of its founders Derrick Bell developed a more innovative and creative approach to understanding systemic racism than what traditional legal scholarship provides. He blends legal analysis, history, and science fiction to encourage readers to think in new ways about the history of American racism and the role of the law. In 1987, Bell published *And We Are Not Saved: The Elusive Quest for Racial Justice*, in which he creates a supernatural female lawyer character named Geneva Crenshaw who can transcend time and space. The book's story "Chronicle of the Constitutional Contradiction" imagines what would happen if the Founding Fathers had had an opportunity to consider whether to allow slavery in the Constitution with the knowledge from the future that allowing slavery will lead to more than two hundred years of suffering and injustice.

Keeping Slavery in the New Constitution

In Bell's story, Geneva goes back in time to the Constitutional Convention of 1787, explains to the delegates the impact of their decision to include slavery in the Constitution, and tries to persuade them to reconsider. Bell's creative approach reveals the sheer power and influence of the Racism Machine at the time. His story includes actual statements made by the delegates at the Convention or later as well as statements made by recent historians who analyze this period (but in Bell's story, these statements come from the delegates). This approach provides a much more three-dimensional and creative way of understanding what Bell calls "the permanence of racism" than we would gain through a more traditional method. I will highlight four key themes that emerge in his story that illustrate how the nation's founders strengthened the Racism Machine.

1. All Thirteen American Colonies Depended on Slavery, Not Just the Southern Colonies

First, as a reminder, Step 2 explained that imperialism fueled European colonization of the Americas in order to gather resources that would increase the wealth of the European elite. Like Spain and Portugal, Britain continued this colonialism, and its first permanent American colony of Virginia eventually developed into a very profitable tobacco plantation economy. Similarly, in American colonies farther south, like South Carolina and Georgia, plantation economies were powerful and dependent on race-based slave labor. Therefore, it should be no surprise that the Racism Machine was a powerful force in the American colonies in the years leading up to the Revolution and also in the creation of the new nation. However, what gets less attention, especially in the North today, is that all thirteen colonies, including northern colonies, were dependent on slavery, some directly and some indirectly.

Bell's story does an excellent job of making it clear that all thirteen colonies depended on slavery. When the delegates at the Constitutional Convention calm down after their initial shock of Geneva's arrival, she explains to them the devastation their decision will have on the future. When they defend their decision, one of their rationales for their decision to maintain slavery focuses on how all of the colonies depend on it, not just the Southern colonies, as those of us raised in the North often assume. For example, one delegate states, "'the economic benefits of slavery do not accrue only to the South'" (qtd. in Bell 30). Northern colonies have their own slaves, the delegate continues, Northern markets benefit directly from goods produced by Southern slave plantations, and "'the New England shipping industry and merchants participate in the slave trade'" (qtd. in Bell 31).

Furthermore, Bell helps readers see that this dependence on slavery throughout the colonies also funded the Revolution. While today, we like to think of the Revolution as a symbol of independence, not as something that came at the expense of those enslaved, Bell forces us to question that myth. Bell creatively highlights this point by putting the analysis of a key historian of slavery, Edmund Morgan, into the mouth of a delegate, who says, "'Slavery has provided the wealth that made independence possible. The profits from slavery funded the Revolution. . . . the goods for which the United States demanded freedom were purchased in very large measure by slave labor'" (qtd. in Bell 34). Bell reveals this multifaceted economic dependence on slavery to show the Racism Machine as a source of economic power.

2. All American Colonies Supported the Protection of Property, a Cornerstone of Capitalism

While the colonies varied in their relationship with slavery, they did share a belief in capitalism and specifically a belief in property, the cornerstone of capitalism. Disagreement focused more on governing that property than on questioning the right to property. In Bell's story, one delegate quotes another actual delegate of the period, General Charles Cotesworth Pinckney of South Carolina, as follows: "'property in slaves should not be exposed to danger under a Govt. instituted for the protection of property'" (qtd. in Bell 29). The word "property," which appears twice in this quote, is extremely important. A key principle of capitalism is the value of private property and its protection.

As Step 2 describes, at the time of European colonialism in the Americas, indigenous peoples did not use a model of private property for land. Because European nations perceived private land ownership as the only appropriate relationship with the land (even though they had shifted from a more communal approach not that long before), European colonizers did not recognize indigenous rights to the land and instead identified the land as theirs for the taking. Step 2 also describes the creation of race as a means of dividing and conquering European and African laborers and the corresponding creation of a racial hierarchy that positioned newly created categories of white at the top as superior and black at the bottom as inferior. The creation of the Racism Machine normalized an ideology that treated Africans as property, indigenous people as expendable, and indigenous land as available. Furthermore, we need to recognize that slave owners owned not only their slaves but also the children of their female slaves. We can see the interlocking forces of patriarchy and capitalism within the Racism Machine here when the slave owners' right to protection of property included not only their rights to their slaves as property but also their rights to their future slaves, which sometimes would be the result of male slave owners raping their female slaves.

When Geneva speaks to the Constitutional delegates, she criticizes "'your slogans of liberty and individual rights'" that protect "'your property rights and those of your class'" (Bell 31). She helps us recognize that the Constitutional delegates were the elite who believed their liberty depended on slavery, on the dehumanization of Africans and indigenous peoples. We know from plenty of historical sources that about half of the delegates owned slaves. Even those who did not personally own slaves were still part of a financial elite who depended directly or indirectly on slave labor. This dependence began decades before, but the Founding

Fathers maintained that dependence as they built the new nation. To be sure, there were certainly some ardent opponents of slavery at the Constitutional Convention, but they were not in the majority.

The delegates' emphasis on property is crucial, and it relates back to Step 2's recognition of the role that property (and the desire for more property) played in European colonization. Even though the American colonists are separating themselves from Europe, the Americans retain a strong belief in the value of property, the cornerstone of capitalism, and they seek to protect private property, even if that property is another human being whose humanity is denied.

The invention of race served a purpose in the late 1600s, in the late 1700s when trying to build a nation, and, as this manual will later show, even today. If the invention of race was supporting the interests of the propertied elite, and they were the primary voices writing the new nation's documents, why would they deviate from a plan that supported their interests? Even if they weren't slave owners themselves and even if they had a record of identifying slavery as a problem or even a sin, they still benefited from it, and they wanted to protect the right to property.

3. Preserving Slavery Was an Acceptable Sacrifice to Those Who Supposedly Disagreed With It

Revolutionary leaders, now at the stage of forming a nation at the Constitutional Convention, believed strongly that slavery could both fund the new nation and unite the disparate colonies in that nation. The racial ideology that Step 1 explains is also extremely important here. As Bell's story makes clear, the Convention delegates, including those who didn't like the idea of slavery in an abstract way, were still willing to support it as an acceptable sacrifice. The delegates found slavery an acceptable sacrifice because of the powerful belief in white supremacy, which included a biological racial hierarchy with whites at the top and blacks at the bottom. Many believed that black people were supposed to be slaves, that it was their natural state. Even those who didn't believe that still believed it was acceptable to build a nation on the backs of black people. In Bell's story, one delegate reinforces the fundamental relationship between the new nation and slavery, stating, "'slavery has been the backbone of our economy, the source of much of our wealth. It was condoned in the colonies and recognized in the Articles of Confederation. The majority of the delegates to this convention own slaves and must have that right protected if they and their states are to be included in the new government'" (qtd. in Bell 37).

When Geneva tries to persuade the delegates to reconsider their position of maintaining the institution of slavery in the Constitution, two of the most famous delegates, George Washington and James Madison, respond. Though, historically, their quotes do not come directly from the Convention records, they do appear in later writings of these two men.

- George Washington states, "'in the aggregate it is the best constitution, that can be obtained at this epoch, and that this, or a dissolution, awaits our choice, and is the only alternative'" (qtd. in Bell 32).
- James Madison states, "'I thought it safe to the liberties of the people, and the best that could be obtained from the jarring interests of States'" (qtd. in Bell 33).

Both Washington and Madison use the word "best" when describing the Constitution they have developed, the one that sanctions the continuation of slavery. Washington's quote emphasizes his perspective that they have no choice if they want a Constitution; it is either this sacrifice or no Constitution and no new nation. Madison's quote references the Constitution as "'safe to the liberties of the people,'" and that just reminds us which "people" are being taken into consideration here. His phrase "the people" clearly does not include the slaves themselves or indigenous peoples, and that reinforces the power of the false ideology that race is biological, described in Step 1. This ideology is extremely powerful at this time and provided the rationale the delegates needed to move forward with a Constitution that celebrated freedom on the backs of black and indigenous peoples. (See Step 5 action #5 for a *Hamilton*-related educational assignment.)

4. Slavery Strengthened White Solidarity across Classes

Finally, the fourth main reason that the Racism Machine was strengthened, which Bell's story helps illustrate, is the way in which the persistence of slavery allowed the elite to control white workers. As Step 2 explains, when whiteness was developed as a legal invention almost one hundred years earlier, it came with the privilege of freedom, of not being a slave. The "better than a slave" status that poor whites gained was the elite's attempt to prevent poor whites from continuing to fight against the wealthy, to instead align themselves with elite wealthy whites and to turn against the burgeoning coalition with laborers of color, who were soon becoming slaves. Geneva helps us see that all of the colonies were complicit in this system, whether it was by explicitly using slavery as a means of labor in their colony or implicitly by using this new racial ideology to control white workers.

One delegate explains to Geneva the benefit of slavery because that allowed the elite to move away from the indentured servitude of Europeans, which produced "'a growing, poverty-stricken class'" (qtd. in Bell 39). This delegate goes on to say,

> "A free society divided between large landholders and small was much less riven by antagonisms than one divided between landholders and landless, masterless men. With the freedmen's expectations, sobriety, and status restored, he was no longer a man to be feared. That fact, together with the presence of a growing mass of alien slaves, tended to draw the white settlers closer together and to reduce the importance of class difference between yeoman farmer and large plantation owner."
>
> (qtd. in Bell 40)

As Step 2 explained, the Racism Machine was built in colonial America in order to support the interests of the wealthy elite landowners. The divide-and-conquer approach that first facilitated the construction of the Racism Machine continued to fuel the Racism Machine's work in the new nation. Whiteness paid white workers what W.E.B. Du Bois later called a "public and psychological wage" because it provided them an alliance with wealthy whites and feelings of superiority over blacks, even if it did not pay a significant financial wage (700). This alliance benefited the wealthy elite much more than poor whites, who received just enough financial benefit to appease them but not so much that they could actually compete with wealthy whites. The Racism Machine maintained power and control. Capitalism could continue, and profit was greatest through the unpaid labor of slavery and the minimal pay of white workers. The ideology of white supremacy within the Racism Machine kept all of this in place, and that only became stronger and more reinforced through the creation of the new nation.

The Racism Machine in the New Nation

The Racism Machine that was gradually built in the late 1600s and early 1700s became fortified through the process of defining and building the new nation decades later. The divide-and-conquer approach that was used in response to Bacon's Rebellion in 1676 became strengthened. The Racism Machine mediated class conflict between whites and curbed rebellion by poor whites. Elite whites built a system in which they extracted massive profits from slave labor and from the land and resources of indigenous peoples. The Racism Machine operated successfully before the Revolution, and it became even more powerful after the Revolution. The Constitution sanctioned the Racism Machine, the very document we look to today as a symbol of freedom and liberty. For example, Geneva points out to the delegates the existence of "'ten different provisions you have placed in the Constitution for the purpose of protecting property in slaves'" (Bell 34). These provisions include a clause that fugitive slaves must be returned to their owners, the Three-Fifths Compromise (which will be discussed shortly), and measures to stop slave rebellions (Mintz). Bell's story reveals the history we tend to ignore, the history that gets little attention when we celebrate President's Day or the Fourth of July.

The divide-and-conquer strategy used in the late 1600s to create a racial hierarchy that established racialized chattel slavery that in turn protected the wealth of the elite was not only maintained in the creation of the United States but also reinforced in the centuries that followed through patriarchy and capitalism. Even though the dominant narrative focuses on celebrating liberty and independence, such freedom was only guaranteed to a select few, given in small doses to some, and denied to others. Over time, the key players changed, but the system remained, and that was due in part to the power of the Racism Machine. It was adapted and re-adapted to suit the needs of the moment, and this maintenance always involved a vigilant patrolling of whiteness and the protection of property, especially the property of the most propertied class, the wealthy elite.

There were several arenas in which this occurred. Step 1 already explained how science was used to perpetuate the false ideology of race, a racial hierarchy that positioned whites at the top, blacks at the bottom, and everyone else in between at various positions depending on the moment. Science was manipulated to normalize this racial hierarchy and present it as undisputable scientific fact.

The Racism Machine was fortified at the nation's founding with mechanisms that normalized the racial hierarchy and established methods to protect and patrol the borders of whiteness. These mechanisms included a definition of citizenship and the creation of the census in 1790, which this next section will explain in more detail. Then, once methods for counting and classifying people were developed, thereby ensuring the protection of the racial ideology explained in Step 1, the country could expand its landholdings in order to increase the wealth of the elite. Once that process was underway in the early 1800s, the divide-and-conquer practices continued through slavery and the oppressive mechanisms that followed the Civil War, including convict leasing (a system that extracted forced labor from people identified as criminal), sharecropping (a system in which those who worked the land didn't own it and were perpetually in debt to the landowners), and Jim Crow segregation (legal racial segregation of transportation and public facilities and institutions). The second half of this chapter focuses on the premise that now that the new nation was established and the Racism Machine had been strengthened, there were several important mechanisms that perpetuated the Racism Machine for almost two centuries, leading up to the civil rights movement of the 1960s.

Persistence of Slavery

One of the most powerful mechanisms of the Racism Machine's fortification in the newly formed US was the persistence of slavery. A few critical points help illustrate the perpetuation of slavery:

- Congress passed the Act Prohibiting Importation of Slaves, which meant that starting in 1808, it was technically illegal to import slaves into the US (even though it did continue). While one might think this law would allow the gradual demise of slavery, that was not the case. The domestic slave trade within the US became very powerful, and the slave population grew as female slaves were treated like animals and used for breeding at an increasing rate. African American history and literature scholar and documentary film host Henry Louis Gates, Jr. explains that families were consistently broken up as "Slave auctions became large and wrenching daily events" in the Upper South, in states like Virginia and Maryland (Gates and Yacovone 79). This domestic slave trade sent more slaves to the Deep South (states like Mississippi, Alabama, and Georgia) than had been shipped from Africa to this region during the Middle Passage of the transatlantic slave trade (Gates and Yacovone 79). The domestic slave trade "became the Second Middle Passage, in many ways just as destructive as the first," and created "a warehouse of exportable human capital" (Gates and Yacovone 79). In 1790, there were about 650,000 slaves in six states, and in 1850, there were about 3.2 million slaves in fifteen states (Gates and Yacovone 77).

- One of the literal mechanisms that strengthened the Racism Machine was the invention of the **cotton gin**, which drastically increased the efficiency of processing cotton and thereby the profitability of cotton. The cotton gin's widespread use starting in the early 1800s created a much greater demand for slave labor. While the land in the northern states may not have been able to sustain agricultural plantations, leaving the plantation economy for the land further south, northern states very much participated in this economy through the widespread development in the northeast of textile mills that manufactured the newly abundant supply of cotton. The cotton gin "would make cotton history's first affordable luxury commodity, speed the growth of the white middle class, and bond the United States to the economics of slavery" (Gates and Yacovone 76). Cotton became "a staple crop that would meet the very specific demands of a large and global industrial machine— the same thing that sugar had done in the Caribbean and Latin America" (Gates and Yacovone 77). Furthermore, the "new planter class" it created "had access to new markets and new sources of capital (much of it, ironically, in the North)" (Gates and Yacovone 77). Gates helps us see how cotton greatly expanded the power and strength of the Racism Machine and its interlocking forces of capitalism and patriarchy throughout the North and South: "The more money the planters made from cotton, the more cotton they wanted to grow. The more cotton the planters wanted to grow, the more slaves they needed to grow the cotton. The world's desire for cotton—and the Southern planters' and Northern industrialists' desire for profits—seemed insatiable" (Gates).

- While Northern states that had abolished slavery were often seen as the endpoint for escaped slaves, the Fugitive Slave Act of 1850 made that much more difficult. While there had been various laws against helping fugitive slaves, including in the Constitution itself, the enforcement of these laws was limited. However, this new law of 1850 increased the power of those searching for escaped slaves and limited the recourse for those accused of being fugitive slaves. This law empowered slave catchers to compel local officials and residents in the North to assist in the capture of escaped slaves, who were returned to their slave owners in the South. Furthermore, any black person identified in the North as a runaway could be sent South, even if the person had never been a slave or lived in the South.

Citizenship as a Mechanism of Strengthening the Racism Machine

The Constitution, written in 1787 and then ratified, took effect in 1789. Then the Naturalization Act of 1790 established **citizenship** for "free white persons" (Goodman et al. 48). While white men did not automatically have access to voting rights in many states, that did shift during the 1800s, as many states relaxed their requirement that free white men own property in order to vote. At the same time, while free black women and men and white women were sometimes initially allowed by states the right to vote (especially if they had property), states restricted their rights more and more throughout the 1800s. This is yet another example of patriarchy operating within the Racism Machine.

The definition of citizenship was challenged throughout American history. Various individuals petitioned in many different ways to be included in the definition of "white" in order to become citizens. As legal scholar and critical race theorist Ian Haney López explains in his insightful book *White by Law: The Legal Construction of Race*:

> In its first words on the subject of citizenship, Congress in 1790 restricted naturalization to "white persons." Though the requirements for naturalization changed frequently thereafter, this racial prerequisite to citizenship endured for over a century and a half, remaining in force until 1952. From the earliest years of this country until just a generation ago, being a "white person" was a condition for acquiring citizenship.
>
> (López 1)

Let's examine a few moments over time to understand the relationship between citizenship and whiteness:

- The *Dred Scott* Supreme Court decision of 1857 stated that black people were not citizens and had no rights and that their status was that of property.
- In 1878, in California, a federal district court determined that a Chinese man named Ah Yup could not become a citizen through naturalization because he wasn't white. The court used the type of pseudoscience described in Step 1, with explicit reference to Blumenbach's racial hierarchy (López, *White by Law* 5–6). Chinese workers had been encouraged to immigrate by companies working on the transcontinental railroad. However, the companies wanted to exploit the workers' labor but not recognize their contribution. Furthermore, white workers resented this growing population. There were riots and the "driving out" in California. This anti-Chinese sentiment culminated in the **Chinese Exclusion Act** of 1882, which, as its name suggests, excluded Chinese immigrants from entering the US and also made sure that any Chinese residents could not become citizens. White fear of Asian immigrants was called "**Yellow Peril**."
- Starting in 1879, indigenous children were taken from their homes and placed in **boarding schools** with the goal of severing

the children's connections to their indigenous heritage. Richard Henry Pratt, the founder of the first school in Carlisle, Pennsylvania, said, "'Transfer the savage-born infant to the surroundings of civilization, and he will grow to possess a civilized language and habit'" (qtd. in Goodman et al. 49). Pratt also justified these schools with the statement, "'Kill the Indian in him, and save the man'" (qtd. in Bear). These schools were founded on the ideology that associated whiteness with civilization. These schools were also nothing short of abusive in their treatment of indigenous children, who were forced to have their long hair cut or even shaved, to bathe in kerosene, and to follow strict gender roles; the children could not wear their own clothes or speak their own language (Bear).

- In 1922, the Supreme Court ruled that a Japanese man named Takao Ozawa was not eligible for citizenship because he wasn't white. Likewise, in 1923, the Supreme Court ruled that a man from India named Bhagat Singh Thind was also not allowed to become a citizen because he wasn't white (Goodman et al. 52–53).

So far, we've focused on explicit, legal decisions about citizenship. However, the issue is not only whether one can become a citizen but also how people are accorded second-class citizen status despite holding citizenship. To be clear, the Civil Rights Act of 1866 did grant citizenship to black people born in the US, and the Fourteenth Amendment to the Constitution reinforced this vital change when it was passed in 1868. However, even though this significant change in citizenship could have had the potential to radically improve the lives of black people, including former slaves and their descendants, the rights of citizenship were sometimes in name only, a pattern we'll also see with voting rights.

- The *Plessy v. Ferguson* decision of the Supreme Court in 1896 made sure that after the Civil War, black people would maintain a second-class status through a "**separate but equal**" policy. Separate was never equal. Children in black-only schools were given old, outdated textbooks and had to make do with inferior, sometimes dilapidated facilities.

- **Jim Crow segregation** also maintained a second-class status for black people through the segregation of many types of facilities, not just schools. Whether it was separate water fountains labeled "white" and "colored" or segregated restaurants, movie theaters, public pools, beaches, or other locations, there may have been a separate and inferior entrance or none at all. Separate but equal was never equal because the very act of separation is based on the belief that humans can be divided biologically and placed on a hierarchy, the racial ideology explained in Step 1. W.E.B. Du Bois explains segregation in the context of the "public and psychological wage" paid to white workers:

  > They were given public deference and titles of courtesy because they were white. They were admitted freely with all classes of white people to public functions, public parks, and the best schools. The police were drawn from their ranks, and the courts, dependent on their votes, treated them with such leniency as to encourage lawlessness. Their vote selected public officials, and while this had small effect upon the economic situation, it had great effect upon their personal treatment and the deference shown them. . . . On the other hand, in the same way, the Negro was subject to public insult; was afraid of mobs; was liable to the jibes of children and the unreasoning fears of white women; and was compelled almost continuously to submit to various badges of inferiority.
  >
  > (Du Bois 700–701)

- After the Civil War, **lynching** became a weapon of fear and terrorism in order to maintain this second-class status. Racial violence emerged as a powerful force, and lynching became a tangible symbol of white fear that went unchecked and often worked in league with local officials and the police, as well as the KKK. Lynchings were often public spectacles, with families and children attending, and photographs of lynchings were sold as postcards (see Allen, et al.). Ida B. Wells-Barnett (1862–1931) was a black feminist, journalist, and antilynching activist who wrote and spoke about how lynching served as an act of terror. In "Lynch Law in America," published in 1900, she wrote:

Our country's national crime is *lynching*. It is not the creature of an hour, the sudden outburst of uncontrolled fury, or the unspeakable brutality of an insane mob. It represents the cool, calculating deliberation of intelligent people who openly avow that there is an "unwritten law" that justifies them in putting human beings to death without complaint under oath, without trial by jury, without opportunity to make defense, and without right of appeal.

(Wells-Barnett 70)

- Recently, the Equal Justice Initiative "documented 4075 racial terror lynchings in twelve Southern states between the end of Reconstruction in 1877 and 1950, which is at least 800 more lynchings in these states than previously reported." This report, *Lynching in America: Confronting the Legacy of Racial Terror*, reinforces not only the horror of lynching but also its legacy:

Lynching profoundly impacted race relations in this country and shaped the geographic, political, social, and economic conditions of African Americans in ways that are still evident today. . . . Most critically, lynching reinforced a legacy of racial inequality that has never been adequately addressed in America. The administration of criminal justice in particular is tangled with the history of lynching in profound and important ways that continue to contaminate the integrity and fairness of the justice system.

(Equal Justice Initiative)

- During the US participation in World War II (1941–1945), President Roosevelt sanctioned the detention of thousands of American citizens of Japanese descent for the sole reason of their Japanese ancestry. They were automatically seen as a threat even though there was no evidence of wrongdoing before, during, or after the war. **Japanese internment** camps were established starting in 1942 throughout the western half of the US. Many have pointed out the hypocrisy that at the same time the US fought to end Nazi concentration camps in Europe, we were building our own ones here.

The Census as a Mechanism of Strengthening the Racism Machine

In 1790, when "free white persons" were deemed citizens, the census also began, and this is important for several reasons. The census has been conducted every ten years since 1790, and every decade, there is some type of change to the racial categories in the census or the language describing them. When I work with students and community members alike, I use the census as a tangible example to reinforce the idea that race is a social construct. After all, if race were biological, then would the government need to keep redefining racial categories every ten years for more than two centuries? Furthermore, the census also serves as a window into the way American society at any given particular moment perceives race, so I will focus on a few of these moments here.

From its origin to the present, the census has determined the official count of residents, which in turn determines Congressional district size and representation. Keep in mind, though, that being counted in the census is very different from having the right to vote. For much of our history, more people were counted in the census but excluded from voting, thereby giving more power to the white men who already had power. For example, white women and free people of color were counted in the census but often excluded from voting for much of our history. Furthermore, one of the biggest points of debate in the Constitutional Convention of 1787 was how to count slaves. The **Three-Fifths Compromise** determined that slave states would be able to count three-fifths of the state's slave population toward representation for that state both in Congress (the House of Representatives) and in the Electoral College (which determines who becomes president). This compromise gave states with more slaves more representation in government. Of course, this greater representation didn't mean that slaves were actually being represented in terms of a political voice or a vote, because they were identified as property. The increase in political voice went to those who had the power to vote in slave states, including slave owners. The more a state was invested in slavery, the greater political representation it would receive, bolstering the power of the institution of slavery and the strength of the Racism Machine. Furthermore, the Three-Fifths Compromise also symbolized an enduring legacy still referred to today that reinforced the way in which black people were seen as not fully human.

Many people don't know that it wasn't until 1960 that you could fill out the census for yourself. Before then, for the majority of the history of the census, a census worker, or census enumerator as they were called, would come to your household and fill out the census on your behalf. The directions provided to these census enumerators reveal powerful insight into what we might consider an obsession with deciding who is white and who isn't. The Naturalization Act of 1790 just stated one needed to be "white" to be a citizen, but what exactly did that mean? Since it was an invented category, it had to be constantly defined and redefined as time went on. The census helped normalize the racial hierarchy described in Step 1 and established methods for categorizing people according to this hierarchy, with the ultimate goal of protecting and patrolling the borders around whiteness. Examining the original language in the directions for the census enumerators (see "Enumeration Forms") will help reveal the mechanism of the census in the Racism Machine.

For example, in 1870, the census categories under "Color" were: "White," "Black," "Chinese," "Mulatto," and "Indian." The directions to the census Enumerators stated,

> It must not be assumed that, where nothing is written in this column, "White" is to be understood. The column is always to be filled. Be particularly careful in reporting the class *Mulatto*. The word is here generic, and includes quadroons, octoroons, and all persons having any perceptible trace of African blood. Important scientific results depend upon the correct determination of this class in schedules 1 and 2.
>
> ("1870 Census: Instructions to Assistant Marshals")

Let's pause and take a look at this language. The opening sentence is grammatically quite confusing and unnecessarily complicated. It essentially means that the census worker should not leave the "color" question blank and assume that whoever processes the form will just take for granted that the person was white. The second sentence helps clarify the first one and emphasizes to the census enumerators that they better fill in that box for "Color." They can't leave it blank. It is their duty to determine the race of the person. That type of message to the census enumerator reveals a desperate insistence about categorizing people by race.

Moreover, by this year, 1870, the racial ideology explained in Step 1 will have already had a powerful impact, and this period will see the rise of the eugenics movement, a movement based on the manipulation of science for the purposes of racism. This was the first census taken after the abolition of slavery in 1865, so we can almost hear the desperation in the directions for census enumerators. They must be "particularly careful" filling out "Mulatto" because "any perceptible trace of African blood" must be identified, as if it is a contaminant, and the borders around whiteness must be protected and patrolled. In other words, now that slavery is abolished, new ways of maintaining that racial hierarchy need to be established. In addition, the 1870 census is the first time there is a category for "Chinese," who are perceived as a new threat. This new category on the census set the stage for Congress to identify this group as a growing threat when it passed the Chinese Exclusion Act in 1882, which essentially banned immigration from China, as referenced earlier.

In looking at one more example of the census, this time from 1930, we can see the number of categories is significantly longer. Note that in 1930, the category was called "Color or Race," and it included the following: "White," "Negro," "Mexican," "Indian," "Chinese," "Japanese," "Filipino," "Hindu," and "Korean." You might reasonably say to yourself, isn't Hindu a religion? Yes, it certainly is, but in 1930, the US Census Bureau used the word Hindu to identify someone from India (while Indian meant what the Census Bureau would later call American Indian). This list is not drastically different than it was in 1920, but the category "Mulatto" is no longer on the list, and the category "Mexican" has been added. The complex set of directions for the census enumerator highlights these changes, and the complete list of directions follows (and just note that the word "return" means to fill out the form):

151. Negroes. A person of mixed white and Negro blood should be returned as a Negro, no matter how small the percentage of Negro blood. Both black and mulatto persons are to be returned as Negroes, without distinction. A person of mixed Indian and Negro blood should be returned a Negro, unless the Indian blood predominates and the status as an Indian is generally accepted in the community.

152. Indians. A person of mixed white and Indian blood should be returned as Indian, except where the percentage of Indian blood is very small, or where he is regarded as a white person by those in the community where he lives. ([See] par. 151 for mixed Indian and Negro.)

153. For a person reported as Indian in column 12, report is to be made in column 19 as to whether "full blood" or "mixed blood," and in column 20 the name of the tribe is to be reported. For Indians, columns 19 and 20 are thus to be used to indicate the degree of Indian blood and the tribe, instead of the birthplace of father and mother.

154. Mexicans. Practically all Mexican laborers are of a racial mixture difficult to classify, though usually well recognized in the localities where they are found. In order to obtain separate figures for this racial group, it has been decided that all persons born in Mexico, or having parents born in Mexico, who are not definitely white, Negro, Indian, Chinese, or Japanese, should be returned as Mexican ("Mex").

155. Other mixed races. Any mixture of white and nonwhite should be reported according to the nonwhite parent. Mixtures of colored races should be reported according to the race of the father, except Negro-Indian (see par. 151).

("1930 Census: Enumerator Instructions")

While early census questionnaires focused on multiple categories to identify supposedly different amounts of "black blood," we see now that that's been consolidated so that it's all or none. Anyone with "Negro blood," "no matter how small the percentage of Negro blood," should be identified as "Negro." This reinforces the **"one-drop rule,"** in which one supposed drop of black blood categorizes a person as black, again a way to patrol and protect the category of whiteness described in Step 2 and the racial hierarchy described in Step 1.

It's also noteworthy that for the category "Indian," how one is identified "in the community" plays a critical role in determining how the census enumerator is supposed to identify someone as Indian. That certainly seems quite different from a supposedly "scientific" way of determining racial identity, so even within this single document, we see contradictions. Likewise, the directions for "Other mixed races" state, "Any mixture of white and nonwhite should be reported according to the nonwhite parent." That again reinforces the ideology of the one-drop rule, that nonwhite "blood" contaminates the racial purity of a white identity, so anyone who is biracial must be identified by the part of their identity that is nonwhite, the part that makes them a racial other.

Furthermore, we also see the creation for the first time of the racial category "Mexican." Then the directions state, "Practically all Mexican laborers are of a racial mixture difficult to classify." This statement seems to reflect confusion about a group that does not neatly fit into the supposed preexisting categories. They are "difficult to classify," as if they are sneaky, but they are clearly a "racial group." The textbook *Race: Are We So Different?* reveals that

> The Census Bureau explained that the category was added because of increased immigration to the United States in the wake of Mexico's revolution of the 1920s. . . . During the economic depression of the 1930s, nearly 400,000 Mexicans and Mexican Americans living in the United States were deported to Mexico. Many Mexicans saw a link between the Mexican racial category on the census and this forced expulsion.
>
> (Goodman et al. 160)

Likewise, Ian Haney López explains that the new census category of "Mexican" "helped legitimize federal and state expulsion campaigns" in the 1930s ("Race on the 2010 Census" 44). However, that category did not remain on the census, and the 1940 census enumerator instructions explain, "Mexicans are to be regarded as white unless definitely of Indian or other nonwhite race" ("1940 Census: Instructions to Enumerators").

Westward Land Acquisition and Seizure as a Mechanism of Strengthening the Racism Machine

With the Racism Machine fortified in the new nation through powerful mechanisms that defined citizenship as white and established the census as a way to measure racial identification, the elite could then expand the land holdings of the new nation in order to protect and grow their wealth. The same forces of capitalism, colonialism, and imperialism that created the original thirteen American colonies under English rule continued unabated in the birth and development of the new nation of the United States. It can be easy to look at a map of the current United States and take for granted the appearance of those fifty states as a natural, unified country. However, if you look at a map with dates when land was acquired by the US, it tells a different story.

Most people are likely familiar with the original thirteen colonies along the east coast. It would make sense that this land was colonized first since it was encountered first by ship from Europe. For a time, that land alone probably felt infinite, and anything further west might have seemed unimaginable. However, even before the Revolution, wealthy landowners controlled a significant portion of the best land for growing crops, so poorer farmers, speculators, and others wanted to push past the western border. The Treaty of Paris ended the American Revolution in 1783 and granted independence to the American colonies, but it also roughly doubled the land holdings of the newly formed US, as Britain ceded its holdings west of the original thirteen colonies, what is now Michigan and Wisconsin south to Mississippi and Alabama. While this land expansion might have seemed like the new country was now complete, we can sense, in retrospect, a feeling of "never enough." And that's a fuel for capitalism, a sense that there can never be enough, never enough land, never enough profit, never enough money.

Despite the Treaty of Paris doubling the land holdings of the new nation, twenty years later, the land holdings of the United States roughly doubled again. While Thomas Jefferson is of course quite famous for writing the Declaration of Independence, often we forget (or perhaps never even learned) that under his presidential administration in 1803, the US doubled in size through what is called the "**Louisiana Purchase.**" This term makes it sound quite official and reasonable, but such a name ignores the fact that some or all of nations of "the Sioux, Cheyenne, Arapaho, Crow, Pawnee, Osage, and Comanche" occupied this land (Dunbar-Ortiz 95). This "purchase" was made "without consulting any affected Indigenous nation" (Dunbar-Ortiz 95). Eventually fifteen states would emerge from some or all of this land. If you look at a present-day map of the US, it essentially encompasses the entire middle third of the US.

As the US acquired more and more land, any romantic notion of the Native American as "noble savage" shifted to one of extermination. Thomas Jefferson, as Step 1 noted, believed that indigenous people were capable of being as fully human as Europeans, but they just needed to be civilized and assimilated for that to happen. That belief was bad enough, but it got even worse. As the desire for territorial expansion grew, there was greater and greater hypocrisy with a view of indigenous peoples as capable of becoming fully human. The only view that supported the goal of territorial expansion was one of seeing indigenous peoples as less than human and expendable. This view built on what the new nation had just established, citizenship for "free white persons" only and a census that started keeping track of residents' racial identities. This citizenship law and the census were powerful mechanisms that contributed to the operation of the Racism Machine and its fundamental purpose of dividing and conquering laborers in order to protect the interests of a wealthy elite. Land expansion supported all of these principles even more powerfully.

We can continue to see this emphasis on land expansion as we move forward in the 1800s with just a few examples:

- Congress passed the **Indian Removal Act** of 1830, and President Andrew Jackson (1767–1845) signed it. Consider the name "Indian Removal." People seen as fully human would not be "removed" from their homeland, so this law just reinforces the subhuman way in which indigenous peoples came to be seen. This forced removal on foot from the area of present-day Georgia to the area of present-day Oklahoma became known as the Trail of Tears.
- Furthermore, this forced removal allowed the massive spread of cotton plantations: "White settlers eager to raise cotton pressured the federal government to acquire the Indian land by any means necessary. The result was a relentless and often violent campaign of Indian removal . . . and settlement of their lands by whites who replaced virgin forests with cotton plantations worked by black slaves" (Gates and Yacovone 77).

- **Manifest Destiny** is a term that describes an ideology, so it's not a law or a policy, but it did prompt plenty of laws and policies. Manifest Destiny essentially focused on the idea that white Americans are the most civilized people, and therefore it was their destiny to take over the land that became the United States. This ideology of white supremacy connects directly to the ideology Step 1 describes, that race is biological and that white people are superior. Manifest Destiny then provided a rationale for conquest of indigenous lands and the genocide of their inhabitants. It also provided a rationale for slavery and for other actions against people of color. Andrew Jackson, among other government leaders, is associated with Manifest Destiny, and the Indian Removal Act certainly supports this ideology. Furthermore, as the growing US took over this land and divided it up into states it admitted into the union, the new state constitutions usually reinforced the same tenets of white supremacy as the original states, including limiting citizenship and rights to white people.

- The Mexican-American War (1846–1848) and resulting acquisition for the US of a massive piece of land was yet another example of this same ideology. As with prior land seizures, this land was also already occupied, this time by Mexicans, indigenous peoples, and mixed peoples. After waging war, the US ultimately acquired almost the rest of the current continental US, including some or all of Texas, New Mexico, Arizona, California, Nevada, Utah, and Colorado. This history appeared recently in a speech made at the Democratic National Convention in July 2016 by actress Eva Longoria. She told the audience, "I'm from a small town in South Texas, and if you know your history, Texas used to be part of Mexico. Now, I'm ninth-generation American. My family never crossed the border, the border crossed us" ("Longoria"). Borders are often taken for granted as natural, as a given, but we should really understand them as socially constructed, the result of power and control.

- Not only was there a hunger for land acquisition within the US, but the US also set its sights beyond US borders. The US asserted its authority over Europe in the Monroe Doctrine of 1823, which prevented European countries from colonizing in the same hemisphere as the US. Then, as a result of the Spanish-American War of 1898, the US acquired Puerto Rico, Guam, and the Philippines. While the Philippines became independent a few decades later, Guam and Puerto Rico are still US territories. Their citizens are US citizens and can serve in the US military, but they cannot vote in US presidential elections (only in the party nominating process).

The Persistence of Slavery After Slavery Ended

At the end of the Civil War, the Thirteenth Amendment (1865) abolished slavery, the Fourteenth Amendment (1868) granted due process and equal protection to black people, and the Fifteenth Amendment (1870) granted black men suffrage (the right to vote). While all of that is true, it only tells part of the story. The rest of the story reveals how the Racism Machine was adjusted to continue to maintain white supremacy. The brief period of "**Radical Reconstruction**" after the Civil War until 1877, when federal troops withdrew from the South, allowed for some major changes in black civil rights. Black male suffrage led to black officials being elected at the federal and local levels. Two black senators were elected during this period (in Mississippi), and until almost a century later, they were the only black senators elected anywhere in the US. More than a dozen black representatives were elected during this period, from several Southern states. Furthermore, many black officials were elected at the state, county, and municipal levels in the south during this time.

However, this period was short-lived. As W.E.B. Du Bois wrote in *Black Reconstruction in America: 1860–1880*, "The slave went free; stood a brief moment in the sun; then moved back again toward slavery" (30). Even though the Thirteenth Amendment did abolish slavery in many situations, it did not abolish slavery for people identified as "criminal." While there was not a significant number of people labeled "criminal" when the law was passed in 1865, that changed quickly, as I'll show in a moment. Likewise, even though the Fourteenth and Fifteenth Amendments appeared to provide significant rights to blacks, many mechanisms were soon implemented to circumvent those rights, including local measures to prevent blacks from voting. Here are a few specific examples of the persistence of slavery:

- The 2016 documentary *13th* explicitly focuses on today's crisis of mass incarceration stemming from the Thirteenth Amendment, which stated the following: "Neither slavery nor involuntary servitude, except as a punishment for crime whereof the party shall have been duly convicted, shall exist within the United States, or any place subject to their jurisdiction" ("13th Amendment to the U.S. Constitution"). Michelle Alexander, author of *The New Jim Crow*, and many other racial justice scholars and activists, explain in the film *13th* that laws were created after the end of the Civil War to label black people criminal in order to force them into a system of **convict leasing**, where labor could be extracted from them, just like during slavery.

- Consider how the title of this recent book by journalist Douglas A. Blackmon describes the persistence of slavery: *Slavery by Another Name: The Re-Enslavement of Black Americans from the Civil War to World War II*. This Pulitzer Prize–winning book, which also was developed into a PBS documentary, explains how slavery shifted into convict leasing. Vagrancy laws were created to be broad enough to criminalize almost anyone, but they targeted black people, who would be rounded up and essentially sold for labor. For example, in Alabama, the county identified black people as vagrants, who would then become convicts through "a standing arrangement between the county and a vast subsidiary of the industrial titan of the North—U.S. Steel Corporation" (Blackmon 1). These laws were part of the era's "**black codes**," restrictive laws targeting newly freed black people, modeled after the slave codes described in Step 2.

- For those not caught up in a system of convict leasing, sharecropping was another mechanism of the Racism Machine. Here, black people were often farming the same land that they or their parents' generations farmed for slave owners. Yes, they were technically free, but this system did not allow them to own their own land, and they were consistently in debt to the landowners, who extracted unfair labor demands. While the promise of "forty acres and a mule" would have provided former slaves their own land, that was quickly abandoned, and sharecropping became very common.

- Released in 1915, *The Birth of a Nation* was the first silent feature-length film in the US and considered a leap in technological innovation. While it may seem out of place to include a film here, we cannot underestimate its powerful role as a mechanism of the Racism Machine. If the content had been innocuous, then it wouldn't have been a problem that the film was viewed throughout the US, from movie theaters across the country to the theater in the White House itself. However, the film was anything but innocuous. We might consider it one of the most dangerous and damaging films ever made. The film celebrated patriarchy and the racial ideology described in Step 1. It took place after the Civil War and sent the clear message that life was much better back in the good old days before the Civil War when black people knew their place as slaves and white women were shielded from black male rapists. The film explicitly depicted the period after the Civil War as a chaotic and dangerous time because black people thought they deserved rights. In the film, black characters (often white actors in blackface) are depicted as subhuman and uncontrollable, and black men are hypersexual animals who threaten the safety and purity of white women. The film's heroes are the KKK, who ride in on horseback to protect white women and white supremacy. The film was a massive success, and it established a foundation for cinematography. Its horrifying content reinforced the Racism Machine in very powerful and long-lasting ways. There are countless examples in popular culture throughout the 1900s (and even more recently) of characters and plot lines that reinforce the dangerous narrative established in this film. *The Birth of a Nation* powerfully fueled the Racism Machine and helped sustain Jim Crow segregation and bans on interracial marriage.

The Racism Machine's Twentieth-Century Mechanisms for Advancing White Supremacy

In the early to mid-1900s, the Racism Machine developed powerful mechanisms for preventing people of color from gaining access to whiteness at the same time as it produced mechanisms for providing white people financial and educational opportunities unavailable to people of color. Following are a few examples:

- Immigration: Starting in the late 1800s, as Step 1 explained, the eugenics movement in the US and Europe granted scientific authority and political power to the ideology that races are biologically distinct and that whites are superior. Step 1 identified a variety of mechanisms in which this ideology was put into practice, including the Holocaust. In focusing on US immigration policy, we can recognize the Immigration Act of 1924 as a powerful mechanism that greatly privileged immigrants from the area of the world the eugenics movement identified as most desirable: Northern Europe (England and nearby countries). The law significantly restricted immigration from the rest of Europe, all of Asia, and most of Africa. This law was not significantly altered until the Immigration and Nationality Act of 1965, which ended those restrictions.

- Social Security: President Roosevelt created Social Security in the 1930s to provide financial support for retired people, as well as other types of financial assistance to vulnerable populations, including the unemployed. One might think that seems unbiased, but what does not always get enough attention is that several groups of people were left out of this benefit, including domestic workers and farm workers, many of whom were black, who were limited in the types of employment available to them. The lack of access to Social Security during this time period is one contributor to today's significant racial wealth gap that Step 4 will address.

- G.I. Bill: Likewise, the G.I. Bill was another benefit created by the government, this time for veterans of World War II who came home from war and could go to school and/or receive a low-interest home mortgage. Again, this sounds like a fair benefit, but as political scientist Ira Katznelson explains, white veterans were able to access its benefits, but black veterans were often not able to, especially when it came to housing and finance. Again, this disproportionately implemented benefit is another contributor to today's significant racial wealth gap. Furthermore, men of color, like white men, fought to defend the US during World War II, a war against Hitler and the Nazis, where the US helped free people trapped in concentration camps across Europe. Men of color and white men alike risked their lives overseas to fight for democracy and freedom, but when they came home, that democracy and freedom were not equally available to them.

- Redlining: Northern cities implemented overt racial segregation throughout the first half of the 1900s. We can see concrete evidence when we look at official housing maps of cities like Chicago and see sections outlined in red (see, for example: *Mapping Inequality: Redlining in New Deal America*, dsl.richmond.edu/panorama/redlining). Redlining is not a metaphor; it's literal. Red lines were drawn around neighborhoods deemed risky and undesirable, usually communities of color. Homebuyers of color were funneled to these areas, and they were charged much higher rates. This practice negatively affected intergenerational wealth for black families and serves as yet another contributor to today's racial wealth gap.

- Suburban segregation: After World War II, the US economy was strong, and a man's income alone could provide a home and an acceptable standard of living for his family—that is, if the man was white. In this new era of suburbanization and home buying, these new homes were often limited only to white people. For example, homes in Levittown, NY, one of the first suburban developments, mandated in the lease that the houses could only be sold to white people. When such official rules were no longer in place, they were upheld in other less overt ways. We can also see patriarchal power at work here, as white women who had worked outside of the home in factories to help the war effort were essentially told to return home and fulfill their patriotic duty. Stricter race-based gender roles emerged in which white, middle-class and upper-class women were pressured to stay at home as wives, mothers, and consumers, while black women were often domestic workers in white homes. Women were often prevented from seeking out higher education, and if they tried, white women often encountered sex-based segregation, and women of color encountered both sex-based and race-based segregation. Furthermore, as suburbs were built outside of cities, highways were also built to provide easy access from the suburb to the city, and many of these highways divided and even demolished urban communities of color. The trend of prioritizing the needs of predominantly white suburban neighborhoods over the needs of urban communities of color that began during the mid-1900s grew considerably during the decades that followed, as Step 4 will highlight.

Step 3 has outlined just a few of the mechanisms through which the Racism Machine reinforced white supremacy from the founding of the US to the civil rights movement of the 1960s. Step 4 will take us to the present by showing how the Racism Machine was not dismantled but merely recalibrated for this new era.

Reflection Questions

1. Is it possible for us to redefine patriotism so that we can own our full history and create a future with freedom for all?
2. What mechanisms of the Racism Machine stand out to you the most, and why?
3. What recurring patterns related to the Racism Machine do you notice over the nearly two centuries considered in Step 3?
4. What reflection question would you create to respond to Step 3, and why?

Recommended Resources

Films

The African Americans: Many Rivers to Cross. Inkwell Films, Kunhardt McGee Productions and THIRTEEN Productions, LLC, 2013.

Ku Klux Klan: A Secret History. The History Channel, 1998, www.youtube.com/watch?v=cayCYpxtIyo.

Slavery by Another Name. TPT National Productions, 2012.

13th. Directed by Ava DuVernay. Kandoo Films, 2016. *Netflix.*

Websites

"Measuring Race and Ethnicity Across the Decades: 1790–2010." United States Census Bureau, 2015, www.census.gov/population/race/data/MREAD_1790_2010.html.

Race: Are We So Different? American Anthropological Association, 2016, www.understandingrace.org/.

Race: The Power of an Illusion. California Newsreel, www.pbs.org/race.

Books

Alexander, Michelle. *The New Jim Crow: Mass Incarceration in the Age of Colorblindness*. The New Press, 2012.

Baptist, Edward E. *The Half Has Never Been Told: Slavery and the Making of American Capitalism*. Basic Books, 2014.

Blackmon, Douglas A. *Slavery by Another Name: The Re-Enslavement of Black Americans From the Civil War to World War II*. Anchor Books, 2008.

Bogle, Donald. *Toms, Coons, Mulattoes, Mammies, and Bucks: An Interpretive History of Blacks in American Films*. 5th ed. Bloomsbury, 2016. [See Chapter 3 for history and analysis of *The Birth of a Nation*.]

Collins, Patricia. *Black Feminist Thought: Knowledge, Consciousness, and the Politics of Empowerment*. Routledge, 1991.

Davis, Angela Y. *Women, Race & Class*. Vintage Books, 1983.

Du Bois, W.E.B. *The Souls of Black Folk*. Vintage Books, 1990.

———. *Black Reconstruction in America: 1860–1880*. The Free Press, 1992.

Dunbar-Ortiz, Roxanne. *An Indigenous Peoples' History of the United States*. Beacon Press, 2014.

Giddings, Paula. *When and Where I Enter: The Impact of Black Women on Race and Sex in America*. William Morrow, 1984.

Goodman, Alan H., et al. *Race: Are We So Different?* Wiley-Blackwell, 2012.

Guy-Sheftall, Beverly. editor. *Words of Fire: An Anthology of African-American Feminist Thought*. The New Press, 1995.

Hartman, Saidiya V. *Scenes of Subjection: Terror, Slavery, and Self-Making in Nineteenth-Century America*. Oxford University Press, 1997.

Houston, Jeanne Wakatsuki and James D. Houston. *Farewell to Manzanar*. Bantam Books, 1995.

Ignatiev, Noel. *How the Irish Became White*. Routledge, 1995.

Isenberg, Nancy. *White Trash: The 400-Year Untold History of Class in America*. Viking, 2016.

Jacobson, Matthew Frye. *Whiteness of a Different Color: European Immigrants and the Alchemy of Race*. Harvard University Press, 1998.

Katznelson, Ira. *When Affirmative Action Was White: An Untold History of Racial Inequality in Twentieth-Century America*. W.W. Norton & Company, 2005.

Lee, Erika. *The Making of Asian America: A History*. Simon & Schuster, 2015.

López, Ian F. Haney. *White by Law: The Legal Construction of Race*. New York University Press, 1996.

Phillips, Patrick. *Blood at the Root: A Racial Cleansing in America*. W.W. Norton & Company, 2016.

Roediger, David R. *The Wages of Whiteness*. Revised ed., Verso, 1999.

———. *How Race Survived U.S. History: From Settlement and Slavery to the Obama Phenomenon*. Verso, 2008.

Rothstein, Richard. *The Color of Law: A Forgotten History of How Our Government Segregated America*. W.W. Norton & Company, 2017.

Ruiz, Vicki L. and Ellen Carol DuBois, editors. *Unequal Sisters: An Inclusive Reader in U.S. Women's History*. 4th ed., Routledge, 2008.

Takaki, Ronald. *Strangers From a Different Shore: A History of Asian Americans*. Updated and Revised ed., Little, Brown and Company, 1998.

Wilkerson, Isabel. *The Warmth of Other Suns: The Epic Story of America's Great Migration*, Random House, 2010.

Wu, Frank. *Yellow: Race in America Beyond Black and White*. Basic Books, 2002.

Zia, Helen. *Asian American Dreams: The Emergency of an American People*. Farrar, Straus and Giroux, 2000.

Zinn, Howard. *A People's History of the United States: 1492–Present*. Perennial Classics, 2003.

Works Cited

Alexander, Michelle. *The New Jim Crow: Mass Incarceration in the Age of Colorblindness*. The New Press, 2012.

Allen, James. et al. *Without Sanctuary: Lynching Photography in America*. Twin Palms Publishers, 2000.

Bear, Charla. "American Indian Boarding Schools Haunt Many." *Morning Edition*, NPR, 12 May 2008, www.npr.org/templates/story/story.php?storyId=16516865.

Bell, Derrick. *And We Are Not Saved: The Elusive Quest for Racial Justice*. Basic Books, 1987.

Blackmon, Douglas A. *Slavery by Another Name: The Re-Enslavement of Black Americans From the Civil War to World War II*. Anchor Books, 2008.

Du Bois, W.E.B. *Black Reconstruction in America: 1860–1880*. The Free Press, 1992.

Dunbar-Ortiz, Roxanne. *An Indigenous Peoples' History of the United States*. Beacon Press, 2014.

"1870 Census: Instructions to Assistant Marshals." *IPUMS USA*, Minnesota Population Center, University of Minnesota, usa.ipums.org/usa/voliii/inst1870.shtml.

"Enumeration Forms." *IPUMS USA*, Minnesota Population Center, University of Minnesota, usa.ipums.org/usa/voliii/tEnumForm.shtml.

Equal Justice Initiative. *Lynching in America: Confronting the Legacy of Racial Terror*. 2nd ed., 2015, eji.org/sites/default/files/lynching-in-america-second-edition-summary.pdf.

Gates, Henry Louis, Jr. "What Was the Second Middle Passage?" *The African Americans: Many Rivers to Cross*, PBS, 2013, www.pbs.org/wnet/african-americans-many-rivers-to-cross/history/what-was-the-2nd-middle-passage/.

Gates, Henry Louis, Jr. and Donald Yacovone. *The African Americans: Many Rivers to Cross*. Smiley Books, 2013.

Goodman, Alan H., et al. *Race: Are We So Different?* Wiley-Blackwell, 2012.

Katznelson, Ira. *When Affirmative Action Was White: An Untold History of Racial Inequality in Twentieth-Century America*. W.W. Norton & Company, 2005.

"Longoria: 'My Father Is Not a Criminal or Rapist.'" *Washington Post*, 25 July 2016, www.washingtonpost.com/video/politics/longoria-my-father-is-not-a-criminal-or-rapist/2016/07/25/8930cc88-52d4-11e6-b652-315ae5d4d4dd_video.html.

López, Ian F. Haney. *White by Law: The Legal Construction of Race*. New York University Press, 1996.

———. "Race on the 2010 Census: Hispanics & the Shrinking White Majority." *Daedalus*, vol. 134, no. 1, Winter 2005, pp. 42–52. *JSTOR*, www.jstor.org/stable/20027959.

Mintz, Steven. "The Constitution and Slavery." *The Gilder Lerhman Institute of American History*, 2017, www.gilderlehrman.org/history-by-era/creating-new-government/resources/constitution-and-slavery.

Nelson, Robert K., et al. *"Mapping Inequality: Redlining in New Deal America."*, dsl. richmond.edu/panorama/redlining.

"1930 Census: Enumerator Instructions." *IPUMS USA*, Minnesota Population Center, University of Minnesota, usa.ipums.org/usa/voliii/inst1930.shtml.

"1940 Census: Instructions to Enumerators." *IPUMS USA*, Minnesota Population Center, University of Minnesota, usa.ipums.org/usa/voliii/inst1940.shtml.

13th. Directed by Ava DuVernay. Kandoo Films, 2016. *Netflix*.

"13th Amendment to the U.S. Constitution." *Primary Documents in American History*, Library of Congress, 2015, www.loc.gov/rr/program/bib/ourdocs/13thamendment. html.

Wells-Barnett, Ida B. "Lynch Law in America." *Words of Fire: An Anthology of African-American Feminist Thought*, edited by Beverly Guy-Sheftall. The New Press, 1995, pp. 70–76.

STEP 4

ANALYZE THE RACISM MACHINE'S RECALIBRATION AFTER THE CIVIL RIGHTS MOVEMENT

Why didn't the civil rights movement permanently dismantle the Racism Machine?

How is the Racism Machine different today than it was before the civil rights movement?

While many believe that the civil rights movement of the 1960s ended systemic racism, it's important that we recognize, five decades later, that the Racism Machine was not dismantled but merely recalibrated. Yes, there were significant changes that cannot be underestimated, including momentous cultural shifts as well as court decisions and legislation of the 1950s and 1960s that outlawed Jim Crow segregation. It became illegal to have schools, restaurants, pools, and other institutions and facilities labeled "whites only." However, taking the "whites only" sign down doesn't automatically lead to institutional change, and that is what we are still struggling with today. As critical race theorist and legal scholar Derrick Bell writes, "We have made progress in everything yet nothing has changed" (22). Here are just a few examples of the persistence of racial inequality five decades after the civil rights movement:

- Racial school segregation has worsened significantly since the 1980s, meaning that the number of schools with almost all white children has increased, and the number of schools with almost all children of color has increased. For example, UCLA reports that in 1988, almost 6% of public schools were more than 90% non-white, while in 2013, that tripled to 18% (Orfield et al.).

- The PEW Research Center reports that in 2013, the median net worth of white households was thirteen times greater than the median net worth of black households and ten times greater than the median net worth of Hispanic households (Kochhar and Fry).

- In 2017, the Centers for Disease Control and Prevention (CDC) reports that while overall infant mortality has decreased over the past decade, there is still a persistent racial gap, and the rate of black infant mortality is double that of white infants (Mathews and Driscoll).

- In 2013, the American Civil Liberties Union (ACLU) reports that despite comparable marijuana use between blacks and whites, "blacks are 3.73 times as likely to be arrested for marijuana possession" ("Report: The War on Marijuana in Black and White").

How can this be? After all, there was the Montgomery Bus Boycott, the March on Washington, the Civil Rights Act of 1964, the Voting Rights Act of 1965, and countless sit-ins and protests. Activists worked so hard, and many even died for the cause of racial justice. How can we possibly still experience the same levels of racial segregation today that existed before those boycotts, protests, and legislation occurred?

Derrick Bell can help us answer this question when he explains the Supreme Court under the leadership of Chief Justice Earl Warren, who served from 1953 to 1969. We may think of this Court as ending racism through decisions like *Brown v. Board of Education*, which ruled in 1954 that racial segregation in schools was unconstitutional. However, Bell writes,

the civil rights decisions of the Warren Court were profoundly conservative and protected the economic and political status quo by responding to the pleas for justice by blacks and other severely disadvantaged groups just enough to siphon off discontent, thereby limiting the chances that the existing social order would pay more than minimal costs for the reforms achieved.

(Bell 61)

This quote tells a different story than the one we usually hear. Bell's description of the court's strategy "to siphon off discontent" reveals an approach that is not focused on real change to "the existing social order" but rather on protecting the status quo by appeasing and thereby silencing advocates for racial justice with superficial rather than deep changes. These superficial changes remove the "whites only" signs but do not get to the core of institutional racism because the institution itself doesn't change. Bell's analysis, what critical race theorists call a counter-narrative, can be challenging to understand. This chapter will highlight some ways of recognizing how the Racism Machine was never ultimately disassembled but rather recalibrated to adjust to a new period, a post–civil rights era.

As discussed in Steps 1 and 2, the Racism Machine was built in order to divide and conquer laborers and protect the status quo of the elite, and a false ideology that race is biological and hierarchical provided a rationale to support this system as well as to justify the taking of indigenous lands for the purpose of colonial profit. Step 3 explained how the Racism Machine was fortified in the building of the new nation and the transition from colonial America to the United States of America. Step 3 also identified several mechanisms for policing the boundaries of whiteness in order to maintain the status quo. After the Civil War, there was powerful legislation that had the potential to begin to dismantle the Racism Machine, but instead the Racism Machine was merely recalibrated to adjust to a post–Civil War period. Sharecropping and convict leasing replaced slavery, and the KKK, lynching, and Jim Crow segregation emerged as powerful forces that maintained the Racism Machine and patrolled the boundaries of whiteness.

We can see a parallel between the recalibration of the Racism Machine after the Civil War in the 1860s and after the civil rights movement of the 1960s. There was such potential for change at both moments, and powerful racial justice legislation was passed at both times. In both cases, though, a dominant, multifaceted conservative backlash made adjustments to the Racism Machine that recalibrated it and prevented it from being permanently disassembled. This conservative backlash to racial justice took many forms, and this chapter will highlight a few of those forms. Opponents of civil rights worked to roll back the progress of the civil rights movement, cut social services, and increase the power of corporations by using divide-and-conquer strategies, powerful racial stereotypes, and the fueling of white fear. This backlash succeeded in widening the gap between the rich and the poor at the same time as it conveniently blamed the poor for their poverty and targeted people of color and immigrants as scapegoats.

Divide and Conquer

Though we don't necessarily hear a lot about them today, the interracial coalitions that formed during the 1950s and 1960s to fight for racial justice were significant. Movements emerged that focused on addressing the needs of specific groups, but they also worked together to form interracial coalitions. For example, the American Indian Movement, the Chicano Movement, the Black Panthers, Students for a Democratic Society (SDS), the Student Nonviolent Coordinating Committee (SNCC), the Southern Christian Leadership Conference (SCLC), and many more organizations didn't necessarily agree on every strategy, but their coalitions were important and powerful (see Step 5 action #2G).

Even more significantly for my purposes here, their coalitions were so powerful they became a threat, just like during Bacon's Rebellion in Virginia, when laborers from Europe and Africa ran away together and formed coalitions together to fight back against oppressive landowners, as Step 2 describes. Coalitions can be a threat to the status quo, to the elite, to the powerful and wealthy, so divide-and-conquer strategies are used to disrupt coalitions, to break them apart, to divide them, and to thereby conquer them (see Step 5 action #2). While the divide-and-conquer response to these coalitions in the late 1600s was to create a racialized hierarchy through the building of the Racism Machine, in the 1960s, the divide-and-conquer response can be seen through the FBI's program called **COINTELPRO**, which stands for the Counter-Intelligence Program. This program conducted surveillance, infiltration, and intimidation on a variety of civil rights groups and group leaders in order to break apart burgeoning, increasingly powerful interracial alliances and to discredit leaders. FBI Director J. Edgar Hoover mandated the agency use COINTELPRO to "expose, disrupt, misdirect, discredit, and otherwise neutralize" several civil rights organizations and leaders (qtd. in Taylor).

In 1971, a group of activists broke into an FBI field office in Media, Pennsylvania, stole hundreds of internal FBI documents that revealed COINTELPRO's illegal surveillance, and shared the documents with the news media. Only recently, in 2014, did some of these activists identify themselves in the book *The Burglary: The Discovery of J. Edgar Hoover's Secret FBI*, written by one of these activists, Betty Medsger. She explains specific tactics to divide and conquer civil rights groups and to discredit the Black Panthers:

> The FBI's approach to investigating the Black Panther Party was in the spirit of the worst of COINTELPRO operations—set up people to destroy one another. Testimony at the Church hearings revealed that the bureau's national effort to destroy the Panthers involved using informants and disinformation to promote gang warfare between Panthers and other black organizations and also to promote intramural violence within branches of the party. These bureau efforts were believed to be responsible for the deaths of at least four Black Panthers who were shot to death.
>
> (Medsger 347)

Likewise, *The COINTELPRO Papers: Documents from the FBI's Secret Wars Against Dissent in the United States*, published in 2002, reproduces copies of many of these FBI internal memos, including "forged letters to activists and their supporters, families, employers, landlords, college administrators and church superiors; FBI-authored articles and editorials which 'cooperative news media' ran as their own; cartoon leaflets that the FBI published in the name of certain radical groups in order to ridicule and antagonize others" (Churchill and Wall xi).

For example, one internal FBI memo states,

> "These suggestions are to create factionalism between not only the national leaders but also local leaders, steps to neutralize all organizational efforts of the BPP [Black Panther Party] as well as create suspicion amongst the leaders as to each others [sic] sources of finances, suspicion concerning their respective spouses and suspicion as to who may be cooperating with law enforcement."
>
> (qtd in. Churchill and Wall 125)

The language of this memo clearly and explicitly reveals the divide-and-conquer tactics intended to disrupt racial justice and preserve and protect the Racism Machine. The Black Panthers were trying to end police brutality and build community resources, like a free breakfast program for children. Another internal FBI memo explicitly states the program's purpose, "'to help neutralize extremist Black Panthers and foster split between them and Student Nonviolent Coordinating Committee (SNCC)'" (qtd. in Churchill and Wall 127). The COINTELPRO program served as one explicit example of a powerful divide-and-conquer strategy aimed at discrediting civil rights leaders and organizations and disrupting interracial coalitions.

Divide and Conquer: The Model Minority Stereotype of Asian Americans

In addition to divide-and-conquer strategies overtly orchestrated by the federal government, other divide-and-conquer strategies developed in more subtle and seemingly innocuous ways, like the emergence of specific stereotypes. I'll begin with the creation of the stereotype of Asian Americans as the **model minority**," a stereotype that is still pervasive today. Surfacing in 1966, this stereotype depicted Asian Americans as hardworking, law abiding, smart, and resourceful, otherwise known as the "model minority." What could possibly be wrong with such a positive image? Actually, quite a lot. This stereotype often gets ignored because it appears so positive, but in fact, it is quite damaging. The supposedly positive nature of this stereotype pits Asian Americans against black and Latinx people, who are more likely to be depicted as lazy, criminal, and less intelligent, establishing a "good minority" and a "bad minority." If we look more carefully at the first appearance of the "model minority" stereotype, we can see this dynamic at work.

The first two popular news articles in which the creation of the model minority image was established were published in 1966. In *Yellow: Race in America Beyond Black and White*, legal scholar Frank H. Wu provides helpful context: "The modern model minority myth was born during the civil rights revolution, shortly after comprehensive federal laws were passed against racial discrimination" (62). Many people believed that the major civil rights legislation of 1964 and 1965 was sufficient, and it was now up to members of racial minority groups to work hard. If they did, they'd be successful. With the creation of the "model minority," there was now a convenient group to point to and essentially say, "If they can do it, so can you."

Journalist Helen Zia reinforces this point in her book *Asian American Dreams: The Emergence of an American People*: "Where Asians had previously been the economic wedge to distract labor unrest, in the 1960s they were refashioned as a political and social hammer against other disadvantaged groups. The 'model minority' was born" (46). Think about the imagery she invokes here. In the late 1800s, Asian immigrant workers were used as a "wedge" when they were positioned as scapegoats to be targeted by the white workers, preserving the status quo of the white elite company owners, as Step 3 describes briefly. In a parallel dynamic, rather than being used as a "wedge," a century later, the representation of Asian Americans as the "good minority" became a "hammer" to beat down and silence black and Latinx people. The Black Panthers, for example, were expanding at the same time the "model minority" emerged, and with this movement's perceived threat to the status quo, the "hammer" of the model minority stereotype became a weapon against blacks to protect the status quo of the white elite.

Furthermore, we need to keep in mind that the Immigration and Nationality Act of 1965 lifted race-based immigration restrictions established in 1924, so in 1966, there would have been recognition that the Asian population in the US would likely be growing. If new Asian immigrants could be funneled into this "model minority" stereotype upon arrival and pitted against black and Latinx people, it would be much less likely that interracial coalitions would form.

We can see this divide-and-conquer dynamic at work if we analyze the first two model minority articles up close. Even though these articles are now more than five decades old, a careful examination of their language will reveal that the tenets of the model minority myth established in these two articles are very much alive and well today. However, we can only see that by looking beneath the surface of the seemingly innocent stereotype of the model minority.

On January 9, 1966, the *New York Times Magazine* published an article titled "Success Story, Japanese Style." Though the phrase "model minority" does not actually appear in the article, the author, sociologist William Petersen, sets the stage for this term by describing Japanese Americans as a "success story." His lengthy article establishes all of the important themes of the model minority:

- Overall success
- Success despite a history of racism
- Success without government aid
- Success in contrast to the failure of other minorities

Let's consider the language he uses that we can connect to each theme. First, he focuses on the basic notion of Japanese American success, both economically and educationally. He argues, "By any criterion of good citizenship that we choose, the Japanese Americans are better than any other group in our society, including native-born whites" (21). This emphasis on Japanese Americans as "good citizens" is at the heart of the success image within the model minority stereotype. It essentially tells the story that if you work hard and play by the rules, the American dream is possible. The success of Japanese Americans then reinforces the viability of the American dream, which is available to anyone who works hard and is a "good citizen." As we'll see, though, once the idea of a "good citizen" is invoked, implicit is the notion of a "bad citizen."

Second, Petersen emphasizes that the success of Japanese Americans comes despite the long history of racism this group experienced in the US. He details various discriminatory laws and policies that explicitly targeted and discriminated against Japanese Americans, culminating in their internment during World War II. Petersen's consistent focus, though, is that despite the racism they experienced, they persevered to become successful. It's clear that the theme of playing by the rules and working within the system (rather than resisting the system) is crucial. Petersen writes, "Denied citizenship, the Japanese were exceptionally law-abiding alien residents" (21). Petersen is praising Japanese Americans for abiding by the law even though the law didn't recognize their humanity. The unspoken contrast is with other minorities, particularly blacks, who are perceived as having resisted the law that discriminated against them. Petersen also states that even though Japanese Americans were "Often unable to marry for many years, they developed a family life both strong and flexible" (21), again an unspoken contrast to other minorities. He also writes, "Denied access to many urban jobs, both white-collar and manual, they undertook menial tasks with such perseverance that they achieved a modest success" (21). Petersen praises Japanese Americans for "persevering" at "menial tasks," essentially doing whatever they were told without complaint.

Third, Petersen focuses on how Japanese American success occurred without government aid. He writes in the early part of the article about this success: "They have established this remarkable record, moreover, by their own almost totally unaided effort" (21). In other words, he is saying that Japanese Americans are the most successful and productive citizens, and they did not need government aid to achieve this success. The message is clear that if they can accomplish so much without aid, then anyone should be able to, undercutting the argument for continuing aid. It's important to keep the context in mind: it's 1966, and legislation banning racial discrimination has been passed, but civil rights protestors and the black power movement were seeking greater government action. Petersen's argument would have contributed to the belief racism existed in the past but the government already did all it could or should to address it. This line of thinking opens the door to many key principles: that government aid is not necessary for a racial minority group to succeed, that such aid is not money well spent since it doesn't seem very effective or relevant, that a history of racism does not prevent a racial minority group from succeeding, and, finally, that if the group wants to succeed, it can, and it's up to them. It is not society's or the government's responsibility, so the message goes; it's the responsibility of the individual and their community.

Finally, with the fourth theme of Petersen's model minority myth, success in contrast to the failure of other minorities, Petersen's description of Japanese Americans as successful is in stark contrast to the description of other minorities (and poor whites) as virtual failures. As discussed earlier, the emphasis on "good citizenship" also means there are "bad citizens," and this theme reveals an important mechanism of the model minority myth. If there is to be a "model" minority, then there must be minorities who are clearly not model. Though he doesn't explicitly say this, he infers that blacks are those "bad citizens." The only hope, Petersen appears to argue, is for blacks to resist a history of racism by doing the things that Japanese Americans are doing: abiding by the law, focusing on education, working hard, respecting authority, and maintaining strong families.

Even though one could argue that Petersen's article included some nuance, some hedging, and a bit of hesitation about the model minority image and its implications regarding systemic racism, at the end of that same year, another mainstream news article was published without this nuance, an article that took the four themes from Petersen's article and proclaimed them loudly and clearly. On December 26, 1966, *U.S. News & World Report* published an anonymous article titled, "Success Story of One Minority Group in U.S." While it doesn't use the phrase "model minority," it does use the word "model," which helped prompt the later use of the phrase "model minority."

The bolded headline below the title of the article starts to spell out the themes of Petersen's article. This headline begins: "At a time when Americans are awash in worry over the plight of racial minorities—One such minority, the nation's 300,000 Chinese-Americans, is winning wealth and respect by dint of its own hard work" (73). The statement "Americans are awash in worry over the plight of racial minorities" implies that Americans are quite burdened by concerns over racism, almost as if it is the fault of the "minorities" for causing such undue hardship to the "Americans." It is the end of 1966, and the civil rights protesters have been speaking out against injustice for years now, and the message is almost "enough is enough," as if there has been enough "worry" about these issues, and it's time to move on. The distinction between "Americans" and "racial minorities" also implies that the two groups are mutually exclusive, as if "racial minorities" are not real "Americans." In addition, the quote implies that if Americans are indeed "awash in worry," then they can't possibly be guilty of racism; otherwise they wouldn't be so worried. It implies the burden should be on the "racial minorities" themselves. Those who are experiencing this "plight" should be responsible for their own situation. Such a dynamic retains a certain level of innocence for these Americans, who are unnecessarily blamed and burdened with worry.

This bolded headline continues with the following: "In any Chinatown from San Francisco to New York, you discover youngsters at grips with their studies. Crime and delinquency are found to be rather minor in scope" (73). In other words, young Chinese Americans are not causing trouble; they are focusing instead on their academics, again presenting an unspoken contrast to other racial minorities.

Finally, this bolded headline concludes with this statement, which highlights the themes already identified: "Still being taught in China-town is the old idea that people should depend on their own efforts—not a welfare check—in order to reach America's 'promised land'" (73). The message is clear: Chinese Americans are successful on their own, by making good choices about hard work, education, the law, and authority. They are not burdening anyone with their worries; they are not taking the government's money (taxpayers' money). Their success is presumably evidence that the system works as it should: racism is a thing of the past and does not need further remedy, and the American Dream can be achieved with hard work. The message is that the class system is fluid enough that if you work hard, regardless of your race, you will succeed.

The message that if Chinese Americans can do it, anyone can do it is enforced even more firmly in the article: "At a time when it is being proposed that hundreds of billions be spent to uplift Negroes and other minorities, the nation's 300,000 Chinese-Americans are moving ahead on their own—with no help from anyone else" (73). The article is clearly critical of spending government money on assisting those who have been discriminated against. After all, the article's message says, Chinese Americans experienced "hardship and discrimination," and they have become successful without this government aid. Why, therefore, should any racial minorities receive such aid? If Chinese Americans didn't need this kind of aid to be successful, then no one else should, and claims for such aid are therefore unfounded. The argument is very convenient because it absolves everyone except the unsuccessful individual from responsibility.

While the depiction of Asian Americans as the "model minority" continued throughout the 1970s, it became far more pervasive in the 1980s, which coincides with President Reagan's emphasis on "trickle-down economics," a theory that businesses and the wealthy should have lower taxes so they can invest more of their wealth, and that growth will "trickle down" to everyone else. This approach has persisted despite evidence that only the wealthy benefit. Not surprisingly, this approach paralleled a significant growth in the gap between the rich and the poor, which in turn prompted competition for resources perceived as scarce but in actuality just accumulating much more at the top than before. This vicious cycle corresponded to the backlash against support services for the poor and others in need, which the model minority stereotype helped fuel, with its messages that racism is a thing of the past, that hard work leads to success, and that the government should no longer provide aid.

Following are a few sample headlines from the 1980s that powerfully reinforce this stereotype:

- "Asian-Americans: A 'Model Minority'" in *Newsweek*, 1982 (Kasindorf et al. 39+)
- "A Formula for Success" in *Newsweek*, 1984 (Williams et al. 77–78)
- "To America with Skills" in *Time*, 1985 (Doerner et al. 42–44)
- "The Triumph of Asian-Americans" in *The New Republic*, 1985 (Bell 24+)
- "America's Super Minority" in *Fortune*, 1986 (Ramirez 148+)
- "Why Asians Succeed Here" in the *New York Times Magazine*, 1986 (Oxnam 72+)

These headlines emphasize over and over again that Asian Americans are the superior minority, the example to put on the pedestal, the "political and social hammer against other disadvantaged groups," as I quoted Helen Zia earlier. Because the stereotype appears positive, it seems innocuous, and many people today who are not Asian don't think about a positive depiction as a problem. However, this stereotype has caused a lot of damage through the coalitions it has disrupted and through the sheer fact that the stereotype is simply untrue.

Despite the decades-long perpetuation of the model minority myth, the mainstream media still ignores the mythical nature of this stereotype. Asian Americans who are economically and academically successful get the media's attention, and the media ignores those who are in poverty or who struggle academically. For years, there have been well-researched books and articles published about the inaccuracy of the model minority stereotype, but, unfortunately, that hasn't made much of a dent in the perpetuation of this stereotype. Frank Wu, who contributed to that research, published an op-ed in the *New York Times* on June 22, 2012, stating, "Despite decades of debunking by social scientists and historians, the model minority myth—Asian-Americans as over-achieving nerds—persists" (Wu, "Why Vincent Chin Matters"). The stereotype of Asian Americans as the model minority takes an extremely diverse group of people and labels them as equally successful, as if they don't vary significantly in socioeconomic class, income, education, work, language, religion, country of origin, refugee status, and access to resources.

The model minority stereotype can make it hard for Asian Americans in school to get help if they're struggling because they are perceived as inherently academically gifted and not in need of help. Asian American college students are more likely than white college students to experience mental health distress but less likely to seek help ("Model Minority Stereotype for Asian Americans"). Asian Americans in poverty are not always targeted for needing resources because Asian Americans are perceived as economically successful. However, Asian American poverty is a serious concern. A recent study by the Center for American Progress showed that the wealth gap among Asian Americans is greater than the wealth gap among whites (Weller and Thompson). For example, "Hmong, Laotian, Cambodian, and Filipino Americans remain overrepresented in lower-wage jobs" (Wingfield). (See Step 5 action #2C.)

The Model Minority Stereotype and the Los Angeles Uprising

The stereotype of Asian Americans as the model minority played an important role in the media's portrayal of the 1991 **Los Angeles uprising**; this portrayal yet again reinforced a divide-and-conquer mentality, thereby preserving the status quo and avoiding a confrontation with the Racism Machine. On March 3, 1991, a witness videotaped Los Angeles police officers beating Rodney King, a black man pulled over by the police. Keep in mind that the early 1990s was a period when many people had video cameras at home, but there were not yet any cell phones or social media or technology for individuals to upload videos instantaneously for the world to see. When a local television station began airing this video, it received unprecedented attention. Four white officers were charged with excessive force.

The following year, on April 29, 1992, the four officers were acquitted, and the acquittal sparked the Los Angeles uprising, what many have called a "riot," and the National Guard were called in. This uprising should have prompted the media and the nation to confront the Racism Machine and examine a racially biased criminal justice system, including police brutality, as well as a persistent withdrawal, or divestment, of resources in urban areas, including Los Angeles. However, this uprising did not become such an opportunity to challenge the Racism Machine and instead did just the opposite; the mainstream media identified it as a "riot" that pitted racial minorities against each other, specifically the "good" Korean shopkeepers victimized by the "criminal" black residents of South Central LA. Even though scholars have done an exceptional job of revealing the faulty assumptions that blame the so-called "black/Korean tension" for the Los Angeles uprising, their work goes mostly unacknowledged by mainstream media. Blaming tension between blacks and Koreans rather than confronting the Racism Machine serves only to perpetuate the status quo through yet another divide-and-conquer strategy that builds on the "good" versus "bad" minority at the heart of the model minority myth.

Consider a few examples of how scholars have analyzed the media's portrayal of "black/Korean tension":

- Legal scholar Angela E. Oh explains, "The media, once again, played a critical role in shaping what the public thought it saw. Rather than deliver the truth, which is that we were experiencing the failure of our institutions and political system, the media exploited the hardship and tensions between two communities engaged in a struggle for survival" (1647). In other words, instead of examining the systemic and structural problems at the heart of the uprising, the media maintained the status quo by focusing instead on the tension between blacks and Koreans, depicting it as inevitable.

- Oh also explains how the media highlighted Korean/black conflict and ignored examples of Korean/black cooperation and coalitions: "The missing stories are still missing" (1651). Her analysis highlights how editors and reporters make choices that have serious consequences about how events are represented and perceived. We usually analyze how the media tells the stories it tells, but we don't often enough consider the stories it doesn't tell.

- Philosopher Robert Gooding-Williams argues that we need to understand the systemic nature of the problems that caused this uprising, including "the deployment of public policy and economic power contributing to the devastation of America's cities; the dissemination of racial ideologies that denigrate people of color; and, not least of all, the perpetuation of a contradiction between the practice and the promise of American democracy" (11).
- Sociologists Kwang Chung Kim and Shin Kim explain that during the twentieth century, there was significant migration of African Americans from the South to cities in the North and West (21). However, they were limited to segregated sections of those cities; furthermore, the cities lost industry and employment opportunities, causing widespread poverty and unemployment for those who remained (21–23). South Central Los Angeles exemplifies this situation, with limited job and educational opportunities, where "the basic needs in the community are not being met by state, county, or city agencies" (Kim and Kim 24).
- Anthropologist Kyeyoung Park argues that "In the 1980s the Reagan administration attempted to reverse the political gains of the racial minority movements of the 1960s" (62). More specifically, Park explains that "Under successive Republican administrations, federal and state governments withdrew funds for community-based organizations, undermining key institutions in the community. As in many other inner-city communities throughout the nation, the state abandoned its 'War on Poverty' in South Central long before poverty was eliminated" (63).

Unlike the mainstream media news stories of the time, this scholarship highlights the way that the Racism Machine created the conditions for the Los Angeles uprising to occur and then provided the mechanism of the existing stereotypes of Asian Americans as the good minority and blacks as the bad minority to explain the uprising, deflecting attention from the inner workings of the Racism Machine. The Los Angeles uprising should have prompted serious improvements to urban resources, including jobs, housing, infrastructure, safety, and more. Instead, it reinforced the stereotype of Asian Americans as the good minority and African Americans as the bad minority, thereby maintaining the Racism Machine. (See Step 5 actions #2C, #3A, #3C, and #3E.)

The Model Minority Stereotype and Affirmative Action

While the issue of affirmative action might seem quite different, it actually has some important parallels with the Los Angeles uprising, especially in the way it perpetuates a divide-and-conquer approach that builds on the model minority myth to maintain the status quo, a connection that legal scholar Sumi Cho explains well (202). **Affirmative action** was one of the legal reforms developed during the 1960s to address racism and sexism, and it's one of the reforms that has received the most sustained and virulent backlashes, a backlash that has helped to recalibrate the Racism Machine and bolster a divide-and-conquer mentality.

Also, it's very important to acknowledge that while white women have seemingly gained the most of any demographic from affirmative action policies of the 1960s and 1970s, they have also become some of affirmative action's biggest opposition. Two recent articles help explain this situation, starting with their titles: "White Women Benefit Most from Affirmative Action—and Are among Its Fiercest Opponents" (Massie) and "Affirmative Action Is Great for White Women. So Why Do They Hate It?" (Angyal). A dynamic seems to have emerged in which white women who benefit from decades-old affirmative action policies may not even be aware that they are benefitting; they may just take it for granted as the norm. Then, in turn, they may look to people of color who are not as successful and think they just need to work harder. Affirmative action often has a very negative stigma now among whites, who sometimes believe that people of color get benefits they don't deserve and that people of color don't work hard enough, a belief described in Step 1. This view reveals a lack of awareness of the Racism Machine, and, in turn, this attitude helps perpetuate the Racism Machine because it fuels the backlash against affirmative action. Furthermore, just like there is a potential coalition among workers of all races due to their labor and socioeconomic status (as we saw briefly in Bacon's Rebellion and in aspects of the civil rights movement), we can also imagine the potential coalition among women of all races, and there have been examples of that periodically in our history. However, whether it's a potential coalition among workers of all races or women of all races, one of the biggest barriers to either coalition can be racism. I can't help but think of the recent presidential election of 2016, when more than 50% of white women voted for Trump, a candidate who explicitly advocated rhetoric and policies that would negatively impact people of color. These are all examples of powerful divide-and-conquer strategies at work (see Step 5 action #2).

The most recent Supreme Court case related to affirmative action that highlighted these issues and received national attention was *Fisher v. University of Texas*. The University of Texas accepts all Texas high school seniors who graduate in the top 10% of their class. White female Texas student Abigail Fisher did not make that cut, but the university then takes into account a wide variety of other criteria, including race, and she was not accepted in that round either. While Fisher believed that being white prevented her from getting accepted, the university claimed she would not have been accepted regardless of her race. The university's ability to take race into consideration as one of many criteria, after they admit the top 10% of all seniors in the state, was upheld by the Supreme Court in a 4–3 vote in June 2016 (Liptak).

Fisher's defense employed a divide-and-conquer strategy of using the stereotype of Asian Americans as a model minority to support its own case. Her legal team's narrative reinforced the backlash against the civil rights movement: in addition to deserving white students losing their spots and being discriminated against, the good minority, Asian Americans, were also being discriminated against in this process. This strategy reinforced the pattern of pitting Asian Americans against black and Latinx people in debates about affirmative action. Fisher's legal team received the support of a few Asian American organizations that filed briefs in support of Fisher. In one such brief, the Asian American Legal Foundation stated that the university "discriminates against Asian Americans" and "grants no preferences to Asian Americans even though they are less well represented in UT Austin classrooms than Hispanics, a racial category granted preference in the admissions process" ("Brief of the Asian American Legal Foundation" 15). However, despite this seeming alliance between Fisher's defense and Asian American organizations, many Asian American legal scholars argue that these divide-and-conquer strategies undermine racial justice for Asian Americans as well as black and Latinx people.

Legal scholar Sumi Cho shows that for decades, Asian Americans have been positioned and repositioned in debates about affirmative action as a strategy to preserve the status quo (202). There's evidence that this divide-and-conquer approach to affirmative action goes back to at least the 1980s, when the University of California's director of admissions explicitly stated in a memo, later leaked, "'The campus will endeavor to curb the decline of Caucasian students. . . . A rising concern will come from Asian students and Asians in general as the number and proportion of Asian students entering at the freshman level decline—however small the decline may be'" (qtd. in Chang 117). There was an explicit attempt to reduce the number of Asian American students. As legal scholar Robert Chang explains, "Divide and conquer at its best or worst, depending on your perspective, Asian Americans are pitted against blacks and Latinas/Latinos as if there are only a certain number of seats reserved for minority students. This is true only if a certain number of seats are reserved for white students" (117). Both the coverage of affirmative action and the coverage of the Los Angeles uprising reveal an important parallel in the way that the stereotype of Asian Americans as the model minority operates to protect the status quo.

Divide and Conquer: The Black Criminal Stereotype and Mass Incarceration

At the same time as the media began celebrating Asian Americans as the "model minority" in the 1960s, the stereotype of blacks as "criminal" reemerged, now within the context of a divide-and-conquer mentality to pit the good minority against the bad minority. This dynamic allowed the status quo to remain and the Racism Machine to be maintained and recalibrated. In *The New Jim Crow*, legal scholar Michelle Alexander does an extraordinary job of explaining how mass incarceration became the new iteration of systemic racism after the civil rights movement of the 1960s. Ava DuVernay's 2016 documentary *13th*, which features Alexander and a range of other scholars and activists, reinforces this same concept, specifically focusing on how the Thirteenth Amendment to the Constitution is celebrated for abolishing slavery while the loophole that allowed slavery to continue for those who became incarcerated often gets overlooked.

The film *13th*, as well as the scholarship on which it is based, clearly reveals how, when slavery was officially over, convict leasing was used to extract labor from black people, as Step 3 explained. When Jim Crow segregation was officially dismantled by the civil rights legislation of the 1960s, there was an opportunity for the Racism Machine to be dismantled. However, that did not happen, and the Racism Machine was modified to serve the interests of the elite, to protect the wealth of a few, and to safeguard white supremacy. The 1960s was unmistakably a time when many marginalized groups were rebelling against their marginalized status, including indigenous people, Latinx people, blacks, Asian Americans, women, immigrants, poor people, LGBTQ people, and people with disabilities. As I've discussed, they were a powerful coalition, and many different but complementary divide-and-conquer tactics damaged these coalitions.

One such divide-and-conquer tactic was the creation of the War on Drugs, what Alexander calls the "new Jim Crow," which was based on several false ideologies. One was that drug use was a growing problem, when it wasn't (Alexander 6). This became a convenient excuse. If drugs were criminalized and people identified as threats to the status quo could be targeted as drug users, then they became criminals. With the Thirteenth Amendment still in effect, they could essentially be reenslaved. This "law and order" approach became very effective. Many years after the fact, John Ehrlichman, who was President Nixon's domestic policy chief in the 1960s, explained this exact strategy. The film *13th* reveals that Ehrlichman said the following:

> The Nixon campaign in 1968, and the Nixon White House after that, had two enemies: the antiwar left and black people. You understand what I'm saying? We knew we couldn't make it illegal to be either against the war or black . . . but by getting the public to associate the hippies with marijuana and blacks with heroin, and then criminalizing both heavily, we could disrupt those communities. . . . We could arrest their leaders, raid their homes, break up their meetings, and vilify them night after night on the evening news. Did we know we were lying about the drugs? Of course we did.
>
> (qtd. in *13th*)

This is the blueprint for a divide-and-conquer strategy. We often don't hear such a thing explicitly mapped out like this, and we often are forced to speculate about the thinking process, but here it is, very clearly planned out.

The film also quotes Lee Atwater, chair of the Republican National Committee and advisor to both Presidents Reagan and George H.W. Bush. Atwater explains that after the civil rights movement, the n-word couldn't explicitly be used as a strategy to demonize blacks. Instead, opponents of civil rights needed to use euphemisms that would have the same effect of maintaining white supremacy. Atwater says,

> So you say stuff like forced-busing, states' rights, and all that stuff. You're getting so abstract now. You're talking about cutting taxes. And all these things you're talking about are totally economic things . . . And a byproduct of them is blacks get hurt worse than whites.
>
> (qtd. in *13th*)

Again, we see evidence of an explicit strategy in a post–civil rights era to demonize and criminalize black people in order to preserve white supremacy and the status quo. The euphemisms or code words that Atwater refers to become examples of what legal scholar Ian Haney López calls **"dog whistle politics"** in his 2014 book of that title. These code words, which avoid explicit racism, serve to recalibrate the Racism Machine, not dismantle it. Furthermore, when these explicit words are not used, it's much more challenging to prosecute discrimination. For example, Alexander explains that the 1987 Supreme Court decision *McClesky v. Kemp* determined "that racial bias in sentencing, even if shown through credible statistical evidence, could not be challenged under the Fourteenth Amendment in the absence of clear evidence of conscious, discriminatory intent" (109). In other words, the Court wanted to focus on intent not impact.

The film *13th* highlights several mechanisms that work together within the Racism Machine to support the **"new Jim Crow."** First, it's important to recognize the sheer number of people swept up in mass incarceration in the past few decades in the US. As the film explains at the outset, the US has 5% of the world's population but 25% of its prisoners (*13th*). To emphasize the "new" part of the "new Jim Crow," compare how the US "had a prison population of 300,000 in 1972. Today, we have a prison population of 2.3 million. The United States now has the highest rate of incarceration in the world" (*13th*). Second, those who are incarcerated are disproportionately black and Latinx people, the "Jim Crow" part of the "new Jim Crow." The Sentencing Project reports on the "Lifetime Likelihood of Imprisonment for U.S. Residents Born in 2001" as follows:

- For white men, this likelihood is 1 in 17 ("Criminal Justice Facts").
- For black men, this likelihood is 1 in 3 ("Criminal Justice Facts").
- For Latino men, this likelihood is 1 in 6 ("Criminal Justice Facts").
- For white women, this likelihood is 1 in 111 ("Criminal Justice Facts").
- For black women, this likelihood is 1 in 18 ("Criminal Justice Facts").
- For Latina women, this likelihood is 1 in 45 ("Criminal Justice Facts").

The ideology that associates blackness with criminality has existed since the emergence of convict leasing after the Civil War, as Step 3 explained. The Racism Machine's recalibration supported the creation of the "new Jim Crow" and perpetuates an ideology that criminalizes black and Latinx people through legislation, the media, and corporate power. The film *13th*, Alexander's *The New Jim Crow*, and African American studies scholar Keeanga-Yamahtta Taylor's *From #BlackLivesMatter to Black Liberation* address the following mechanisms:

- mandatory sentencing that enacted the same penalty for one ounce of crack cocaine as for one hundred ounces of powder cocaine (meaning the penalty for the drug used more in urban communities of color was one hundred times harsher than the penalty for the same drug used more often in suburban white communities) (*13th*)
- "three-strikes" laws that increase life sentences

- the Violent Crime Control and Law Enforcement Act of 1994 (the crime bill), which significantly increased funding to the police and prisons and was signed by President Bill Clinton
- the rise of "law-and-order" rhetoric and a fear by politicians of being "soft on crime"
- the way the 1988 campaign for Republican presidential candidate George H.W. Bush against Democratic presidential candidate Michael Dukakis used the story of Willie Horton to provoke fear (Horton was an incarcerated black man who committed a violent crime while he was on a weekend pass)
- the growing relationship between the rise of private prisons (which make their shareholders a significant profit) and the American Legislative Exchange Council (ALEC, which connects politicians and corporations together so that laws can be passed to support the interests of corporations)
- the significant number of plea bargains rather than trials in which people are pressured to plead guilty
- the rise of over-policing of communities of color through policies like stop-and-frisk and racial profiling
- the militarization of police departments
- the massive amount of fines and fees associated with tickets and arrests from overpolicing of communities of color that can lead to "debtors' prison" (Benns and Strode)
- the use of violence by the police against unarmed people of color

These mechanisms and many more have strengthened the Racism Machine over the past few decades, facilitated by a rationale, sometimes spoken, sometimes unspoken, that black and Latinx people are inherently criminal. This powerful ideology goes back to the original construction of the Racism Machine described in Step 1, the racial hierarchy of white supremacy built into the core of the Racism Machine. The ideology of this hierarchy indoctrinates people into a false belief that white people are inherently, biologically superior and that people of color are not fully human. The #BlackLivesMatter movement speaks directly to this fundamental racial ideology through the powerful hashtag that insists that black people are fully human. The fact that anyone would need to hear this today, that it wouldn't just be taken for granted, clearly establishes how the Racism Machine continues to run effectively, five decades after it was supposedly dismantled by the civil rights movement. Furthermore, the #BlackLivesMatter movement has made visible the mechanisms of the Racism Machine described here that relate to police shootings of unarmed black people and the overpolicing of communities of color. The #BlackLivesMatter movement has also demonstrated the power of interracial coalition building, as in its work with indigenous protestors at Standing Rock ("Black Lives Matter Stands in Solidarity with Water Protectors at Standing Rock"). (See Step 5 actions #1B, #2C, #3A, and #3C.)

The criminalization of black people during the past few decades was also facilitated by the demonization of the black family during the 1960s. In 1965, then-Assistant Secretary of Labor Daniel Patrick Moynihan published *The Negro Family: The Case for National Action*, which became known as the Moynihan Report. Much scholarship on this report and its impact emphasizes how Moynihan pathologized black families, with particular criticism about their "matriarchal" structure and high number of single-mother–headed households. His lengthy report appears to acknowledge the persistence of systemic racism, with statements like "the racist virus in the American blood stream still afflicts us," which could lead one to think that this report could have served as a tool to confront the Racism Machine. Ultimately, though, this report does just the opposite and maintains the Racism Machine through the report's conclusion that "The fundamental problem . . . is that of family structure" (qtd. in Geary). Furthermore, the report recommends "a new kind of national goal: the establishment of a stable Negro family structure" (qtd. in Geary). Rather than focus on how the Racism Machine perpetuates structural racism through systems related to housing, finance, education, the media, criminal justice, and healthcare, this report ultimately blames black people themselves for persistent racial inequality. Blaming "Negro family structure" fed the belief in "personal responsibility" that has become so pervasive in the past few decades. This belief, connected to, as Step 1 explains, a "cultural" explanation for racial inequality, essentially blames the individual and the community for their status, removing responsibility from any structures or systems that created the conditions for this inequality. This belief is yet another way to reinforce the message of the model minority myth: work hard, and you'll be successful because racism is a thing of the past, and any problems you experience are of your own doing and are therefore yours to address. In 2015, the fiftieth anniversary of the original Moynihan Report, the *Atlantic* published an annotated version of the report that helps illustrate these concerns (Geary).

In addition to the criminalization of black people and the black family, another dynamic operated to disenfranchise black communities. In the 1970s, many urban centers across the US experienced **white flight**. White people in predominantly white urban neighborhoods worried about their neighborhoods becoming more racially integrated, even with just a few families of color. White people, provoked by real estate agents, feared a loss of their property value, and they also feared school integration, so many left for predominantly white suburbs. Some urban neighborhoods shifted from predominantly white to predominantly black in just a decade (*Black America since MLK*). As white families moved out of urban neighborhoods, resources often left with them. Some middle-class black families also left these urban centers. These urban centers gradually transformed into areas of concentrated poverty with few resources, limited employment opportunities, limited educational opportunities, limited access to healthy food and healthcare, limited access to adequate utilities (like water and heat), and limited maintenance of the infrastructure (streetlights, roads, etc.). (See Step 5 action #3E.)

Divide and Conquer: From the "Welfare Queen" to the Tea Party

Furthermore, the stereotype of the **"welfare queen"** also fueled this vicious cycle of demonizing black individuals and families and helped modify and maintain the Racism Machine. In *Myth of the Welfare Queen*, David Zucchino writes,

> During the 1976 presidential campaign, Ronald Reagan drew roars of approval at rallies by telling the story of a Chicago welfare mother who cheated the system. "She has eighty names, thirty addresses, twelve Social Security cards and is collecting veterans' benefits on four nonexisting deceased husbands," Reagan told one rally. "And she's collecting Social Security on her cards. She's got Medicaid, getting food stamps, and she is collecting welfare

under each of her names. Her tax-free income alone is over $150,000." Reagan had a name for the woman: Welfare Queen.

(Zucchino 64–65)

A recent *Atlantic* article aptly titled "The 'Welfare Queen' Is a Lie" highlights some additional context for this stereotype:

- President Johnson introduced the "War on Poverty" in 1964, and it "focused on the white, rural poor to maintain broad support" (Black and Sprague).
- "In 1964, only 27 percent of the photos accompanying stories about poverty in three of the country's top weekly news magazines featured black subjects; the following year, it rose to 49 percent. By 1967, 72 percent of photos accompanying stories about poverty featured black Americans" (Black and Sprague).
- "By 1989, 64 percent of Americans felt that 'welfare benefits make poor people dependent and encourage them to stay poor,' shoring up the political support for reform" (Black and Sprague).

This history alone reveals the increased racialization of poverty as a strategy to persuade white people to shift their perception of public assistance from positive to negative, despite the actual demographic data that there were more poor white people than poor black people and more white welfare recipients than black welfare recipients. What was once seen as a necessary safety net became something to enable supposedly "lazy" and "criminal" black people defrauding the system. To be clear, there has never been evidence to support the claim of extensive welfare fraud by recipients. If anything, when welfare fraud occurs, it's not committed by the recipients but rather by officials involved in the system. For example, consider the following:

- "Entitlement programs, from food stamps to Medicare, don't see unusually high cheating rates—and the culprits are usually managers and executives, not 'welfare queens'" (Schnurer).
- "CBPP [Center on Budget and Policy Priorities] analysis finds that more than 90 percent of the benefit dollars that these

programs [Supplemental Nutrition Assistance Program and other federal social programs] spend go to assist people who are elderly, seriously disabled or members of working households—not to able-bodied, working-age Americans who choose not to work" (Stone).

In 1996, President Bill Clinton signed the Personal Responsibility and Work Opportunity Reconciliation Act, otherwise known as welfare reform. More than twenty years later, we can clearly see what it meant to "end welfare as we know it," the phrase Clinton used in his campaign, especially with regard to the impact of replacing AFDC (Aid to Families with Dependent Children) with TANF (Temporary Aid to Needy Families), mandating short lifetime limits for these benefits, adding challenging requirements, and cutting people off without other options (Semuels). As with many of our laws, the language of the law's name itself must be unpacked. The phrase "personal responsibility" is a powerful and popular phrase, and it tends to evoke the fundamental tenet of the American Dream: work hard and you'll be successful. In other words, your success is up to you. This focus on meritocracy tends to ignore systems and structures that provide a path to success for some and obstacles to others, often dependent on one's race, socioeconomic status, religion, gender, sexual orientation, and more. The law's phrase "work opportunity" makes it sound like people who benefitted from the prior system did not want to work or were not working and that this new law would simply provide ample opportunities to work, and everyone who wanted to be economically self-sufficient could be. What gets ignored is that there are often very limited job opportunities for people, dependent on where they live, their health, their access to transportation, and their access to childcare. Furthermore, what also gets ignored is the significant gap between the minimum wage and a particular region's living wage. In other words, one could make minimum wage at a full-time job but still have an income well below the cost of living in a particular area, something especially true in my state of New Jersey.

The "welfare queen" stereotype of the 1980s became powerful enough to contribute to a massive drop in support for social services, part of the backlash against the civil rights movement and the recalibration of the

Racism Machine. When the Tea Party rose to power as soon as President Obama was elected, one of the most prominent Tea Party themes identified in a 2010 *New York Times* poll focused on a "conviction that the policies of the Obama administration are disproportionately directed at helping the poor rather than the middle class or the rich" (Zernike and Thee-Brenan). Furthermore, the poll shows that within the Tea Party, "More than half say the policies of the administration favor the poor" and that "Ninety-two percent believe Mr. Obama is moving the country toward socialism" (Zernike and Thee-Brenan).

During this time, the *New York Times* shared videos called "Voices of the Tea Party" in which twenty members described their reasons why they support the Tea Party. While the themes of limited government and reduced taxes run throughout, these comments in particular highlight the same demonization of the poor as the "welfare queen" stereotype:

- An Apollo Beach, Florida, resident states, "government programs . . . promote dependency and thwart motivation. We of the Tea Party are the backbone of this nation. We pay the taxes. We of the Tea Party are hard-working, self-sufficient people. We do not want to become a nanny-state. . . . We of the Tea Party movement want to stay a capitalistic democracy where all do the work for the few who can't work instead of a few doing the work for the many who won't work." ("Voices of the Tea Party")
- A resident of St. Augustine, Florida, states, "motivation, hard work, and achievement is punished via taxes . . . the majority of people pay no income taxes and expect the minority that do the hard work to pay for all the entitlements that they expect." ("Voices of the Tea Party")

The language here is quite telling, especially with "the many who won't work," with "won't" being key, reinforcing the narrative that the poor are lazy "welfare queens" defrauding the system and uninterested in getting a job. "We" work hard, and "they" do not. Furthermore, both statements focus on how only the "few" are actually working hard. This should give us pause to reflect on how someone gets to the point where they believe the majority of people in the US are not working hard.

Furthermore, as political rhetoric, the media, and other systems shifted the public's image of the poor from white to black, it's not a coincidence that President Obama, as the first black president, was especially associated with doing too much to help poor people. For example, when former Speaker of the House Newt Gingrich ran in the Republican presidential primary in 2012, he repeatedly called President Obama the "food stamp president." Moreover, anytime it seemed President Obama tried to address poverty, he would be accused of inciting "class warfare." For example, in September 2011, when he announced a plan to cut the federal deficit in part by implementing the "Buffet Rule," the *New York Times* reported that the idea "was met with derision Sunday by Republican lawmakers, who said it amounted to 'class warfare'" (Cooper). Likewise, when Paul Ryan spoke to the Republican National Convention in August 2012 to accept the nomination of vice president, he said, "None of us have to settle for the best this administration offers—a dull adventureless journey from one entitlement to the next, a government-planned life, a country where everything is free but us" ("Transcript: Rep. Paul Ryan's Convention Speech"). Ryan equates government-sponsored social service programs with a lack of freedom. Granted, these programs don't work perfectly, and there are serious challenges with some of their rules. However, it's illogical and unfair to say that these programs make people lack freedom rather than the lack of freedom stemming from not having enough food to eat, not having a living wage, and not having access to adequate employment or education or healthcare.

The rhetoric that blames the poor for their poverty reinforces the notion that our class structure is fair, that hard work leads to success, that racism is a thing of the past, and that affirmative action is no longer needed. As discussed earlier, these messages are the same ones the model minority stereotype sends. The backlash against the civil rights movement was so powerful because so many different yet complementary stereotypes fed into it. Many influential voices reinforced the platform of the Tea Party, both before and after the group was established. Consider the following comments:

- Paul Ryan, Congressman, Speaker of the House, and 2012 Republican vice presidential nominee, says in the official Republican response to the 2011 State of the Union, "We are at a moment, where if government's growth is left unchecked and unchallenged, America's best century will be considered our past century. This is a future in which we will transform our social safety net into a hammock, which lulls able-bodied people into lives of complacency and dependency" ("Transcript: GOP Response From Rep. Paul Ryan").

- Mitt Romney, former governor and 2012 Republican presidential nominee writes in a 2011 *USA Today* Op-Ed, "Government dependency can only foster passivity and sloth" (Romney).

- Rick Santorum, former senator and a Republican presidential candidate in 2012 and 2016, refers to "'the narcotic of dependency'" (qtd. in Krugman).

These influential voices repeat the same message of the Tea Party, that people who seek social services are "complacent," "dependent," and "passive," "sloths" living in a "hammock." They don't work, they don't want to work, and they drain our society. Social services harms all involved because it creates "welfare queens" and forces a "narcotic of dependency." These toxic beliefs send the clear message that people need to take personal responsibility for their own success. This allows middle- and upper-class white people to attribute their success to their hard work rather than to a system of privileges and benefits that have supported them, and it allows poor white people and people of color to be told they just need to work hard in order to be successful. In this dynamic, various groups are pitted against each other via class- and race-based divide-and-conquer strategies in order to preserve the status quo and protect the white elite.

It is especially important that we understand the context in which these voices are demonizing the poor. As economist and former Labor Secretary Robert Reich has taught us through his documentary *Inequality for All*, the wealth gap between the rich and the poor has grown dramatically during the past few decades. After World War II and up until the 1980s, the gap was much smaller, where the average male worker in 1978 was making $48,302, compared to the average person in the top 1% making $393,682 ("A Graphical Look at Economic Inequality in Three Parts"). There's definitely a gap, but nothing compared to 2010, where the average worker drops to $33,751 and the average person in the top 1% jumps to $1,101,089 ("A Graphical Look at Economic Inequality in Three Parts"). One of the problems is that average workers' wages hit a plateau around 1970 and even went down some, all due to various factors, including deregulation, union busting, emerging technology, overseas markets, and more ("A Graphical Look at Economic Inequality in Three Parts"). The economic growth that has persisted over the past few decades has gone mostly to the top and has not "trickled down." (See Step 5 action #2B.)

While one might think that this increasing disenfranchisement of the poor would prompt a working-class rebellion, there have been many forces to thwart that possibility. Here are just a few examples:

- Large corporations can afford to hire lobbyists to go to Congress and represent their business interests. Such lobbying has led to deregulation, the process of taking away previous regulations that set rules about what companies could do, whether it was related to pollution or other environmental impacts, finances, taxes, minimum wage, or more.
- In 2010, the Supreme Court voted 5–4 in favor of the organization Citizens United in the case *Citizens United v. Federal Election Commission*. This decision increased the power of corporations by essentially saying that "corporations are people too" when it comes to First Amendment rights to free speech, including campaign donations. Corporations had already been gaining a lot of power before this decision, and this Supreme Court's support for business interests only sustained them even more (see Step 5 action #2B).
- The American Legislative Exchange Council (ALEC) is an extremely powerful organization that, as its website states, focuses on "limited government, free markets and federalism." They provide legislative templates to state and local governments to dismantle government services and increase the power of businesses (see Step 5 action #2B).
- Two of the wealthiest Americans, Charles and David Koch, frequently referred to as the Koch Brothers, are another powerful

force in this backlash against the civil rights movement that seeks to curtail the safety net and increase corporate power. Their massive financial resources have allowed them to serve on boards of major organizations and wield the power of their own Koch Industries. They spend their money to exert considerable influence in politics, and their ideology has a clear antipoor, antienvironmental, prowealthy agenda (see Step 5 action #2B).

President Obama inherited a nation with a massive wealth gap between the rich and the poor. He also inherited a nation in backlash against the civil rights movement and social services. However, those who had fueled that backlash, from politicians to media personalities to powerful corporations, persuaded many people that the gap was the fault of government programs for civil rights and social services, so-called "big government." President Obama could not address racial justice without extreme criticism from politicians and voters alike who thought he was giving an unfair advantage to people of color. Even though Trump's election was a shock to many, perhaps it should not have been such a shock given the context of this backlash. Many voters believed that President Obama had been too progressive and that we needed an immediate shift in a conservative direction. Some of these voters were disenfranchised by the very wealth gap that President Obama inherited but blamed him for it rather than the backlash that supported the rise in corporate power, deregulation, and cuts to unions. Furthermore, the conservative backlash against the civil rights movement fueled questions about the very legitimacy of Obama's presidency, especially with accusations from the "birther movement" that he was not born in the US. It should also be noted that one of the more prominent members of this movement was Donald Trump, who, in 2011, began questioning where President Obama was born (Barbaro).

Backlash Against Voting Rights

Another way we can see both the power of the backlash against the civil rights movement and the related growth of the "black as criminal" stereotype appears in the loss of voting rights originally protected in the 1965 Voting Rights Act. This legislation granted voting rights to all Americans,

regardless of race, and barred any racial discrimination that would prevent someone from voting on the basis of race. Furthermore, voting districts with a history of discrimination couldn't make any changes to their
voting laws without approval. According to the ACLU, this law led to
250,000 black people registering to vote in 1965 alone ("Voting Rights
Act: Major Dates in History"). Such increased access to political participation in turn prompted more people of color not only to vote but also to
run for office at all levels of government. Furthermore, Presidents Nixon,
Ford, and Reagan all signed extensions of the Voting Rights Act in the
1970s and 1980s.

However, despite this initial progress, the protection of voting rights is
now going backward. As part of the backlash against President Obama's
administration, states began to restrict voting, whether by passing voter
ID laws, limiting when people can vote, drawing new voting districts, or
other methods. These actions appear to be race neutral in the sense that
they don't explicitly refer to race, but the impact is very much racialized.
As the number of restrictive laws grew in the early 2010s, the Justice
Department in the Obama administration tried to block such laws, leading to the Supreme Court case of *Shelby County v. Holder*. Under the
Voting Rights Act, districts like Shelby County, Alabama, were supposed
to get federal permission before changing voting laws, but they passed a
restrictive voting law without such permission. Eric Holder, President
Obama's Attorney General, tried to hold the county accountable for
defying the law. However, the Supreme Court ruled that districts with
a history of racial discrimination no longer needed to get permission to
pass new voting laws, prompting even more laws.

Let me be very clear here. Just like the creation of the War on Drugs
depended on the myth that black people were much more likely to use and
sell drugs and just like cuts to welfare and other social services depended
on the myth of the "welfare queen" and of "welfare fraud," these new voter
restrictions depend on the myth that a significant number of people are
voting "illegally." There is absolutely no evidence to support this claim.
Furthermore, these new restrictions on voting have and will continue to
prevent eligible voters from voting.

The Brennan Center for Justice, based at New York University School
of Law, has spent considerable time investigating these issues for years.

They issued a report that "reviewed elections that had been meticulously studied for voter fraud, and found incident rates between 0.0003 percent and 0.0025 percent. Given this tiny incident rate for voter impersonation fraud, it is more likely, the report noted, that an American 'will be struck by lightning than that he will impersonate another voter at the polls'" ("Debunking the Voter Fraud Myth").

Furthermore, the Brennan Center's comprehensive work revealed the following:

- "Studies agree: impersonation fraud by voters very rarely happens" ("Debunking the Voter Fraud Myth").
- "Courts agree: fraud by voters at the polls is nearly non-existent" ("Debunking the Voter Fraud Myth").
- "Government investigations agree: voter fraud is rare" ("Debunking the Voter Fraud Myth").

Journalist Ari Berman, author of the insightful book *Give Us the Ballot: The Modern Struggle for Voting Rights in America*, wrote an article in October 2016 aptly titled "Voter Suppression Is a Much Bigger Problem Than Voter Fraud" (Berman). He raises very serious concerns about "the real danger to American democracy" that these new voter restrictions create (Berman). He explains that by the time of the November 2016 presidential election, there were "new voting restrictions . . . in 14 states . . . mak[ing] it harder for millions of eligible voters to cast a ballot. And voters are lacking crucial protections because this is the first presidential election in 50 years without the full provisions of the Voting Rights Act" (Berman).

In May 2017, President Trump established a Presidential Commission on Election Integrity. ABC News reported that "The announcement is the latest indication that the president intends to pursue action, as promised, on his controversial and so-far unsubstantiated assertion that 'millions' of people illegally cast ballots in the 2016 presidential election" (Faulders and Mallin). The phrase "election integrity" in the commission's title is in direct contrast to the existing work of the two leaders of this commission, Vice President Mike Pence and Kansas Secretary of State Kris Kobach, who have already led efforts in their home states to systemically disenfranchise communities of color through various types of voting restrictions. (See Step 5 action #3F.)

The myth of voter fraud, the myth of the "welfare queen," and the myth that provoked the War on Drugs all reinforce the same pattern of inventing a problem, criminalizing it, and blaming black and Latinx people as the perpetrators. This pattern significantly contributes to the "bad minority" stereotype of black and Latinx people implicit within the model minority stereotype of Asian Americans described earlier.

Divide and Conquer: The Latinx "Illegal" Stereotype

Furthermore, the emergence of the stereotype of Latinx people as "illegal" further bolstered the good minority versus bad minority opposition at the heart of the divide-and-conquer mentality. Using the word "illegal" to describe a person reflects an ideology that identifies Latinx people, the primary targets of this slur, as less than human, as inherently of less worth, and as criminals, even though being in the US without authorization is not a crime.

In their "Issue Brief: Criminalizing Undocumented Immigrants," the American Civil Liberties Union (ACLU), addresses ongoing misperceptions:

- "[U]ndocumented presence alone is not a violation of federal criminal law."
- "Despite the anti-immigrant rhetoric, 'criminal alien' is not a legal term and undocumented immigrants are not 'criminal aliens' under federal law."
- "Thus, many believe that the term 'illegal alien,' which may suggest a criminal violation, is inaccurate or misleading."

The "illegal" stereotype sends the message that people called "illegal" don't belong in the US because they are sneaking across the Mexican border, trying to steal American jobs, and ruining an American way of life. This powerful stereotype not only adds to the good minority-versus-bad minority dichotomy, but it also protects the status quo and recalibrates the Racism Machine, further strengthening it.

In *Living "Illegal": The Human Face of Unauthorized Immigration*, Marquardt et al. describe how four major themes of the "illegal" stereotype emphasize the way undocumented people:

- "flood across the U.S.-Mexico border to take advantage of public benefits and social services, while contributing very little to U.S. society"
- "are a burden on the U.S. economy"
- "are closely associated with criminality, violence, drugs, and gangs"
- "cannot be integrated into U.S. society because they bring values that are contrary to the values of this nation" (Marquardt et al. 5)

The news media has been, in part, responsible for perpetuating this word "illegal." In April 2013, the Associated Press, which establishes a writing style for journalists, changed its guidelines to end the use of the word "illegal" to describe a person. This change occurred after much heated debate and a dramatic rise in mainstream news media's use of the term "illegal immigrants." The higher frequency of the word "illegal" within the media fuels white fear of immigration and of becoming the minority.

The writers of *Living "Illegal"* explain: "The media have tended to magnify the raw passions elicited by the term *illegal*, contributing to an overall climate of mistrust, hostility, and incivility, which as we shall show, stymies constructive public debate, impeding the search for rational, pragmatic, and long-term repairs to the broken immigration system" (Marquardt et al. 10). One researcher in the field of applied experimental psychology conducted an experiment on undergraduate university students and determined that "'illegal aliens' invoked greater prejudice than 'undocumented workers,' indicating that the term 'illegal aliens' is associated with increased perceptions of threat" (Pearson 118). This research just reinforces the fact that words carry baggage, and the choice of wording can have a real impact on a reader or listener.

Politicians also fuel white fear of immigration by highlighting the danger of "illegal immigrants." In 2005, a marketing research firm (Luntz, Maslansky Strategic Research) issued a report for the Republican Party to guide their use of the word "illegal" and to recommend how Republican candidates and policy makers can best use the word "illegal" to stoke fear, elect their candidates, and pass their policies. The report, "Respect for the Law & Economic Fairness: Illegal Immigration Prevention," essentially serves as a manual for Republicans to instill fear into people over the issue of immigration. It recommends language that candidates can use, like: "Those who flaunt the rule of law should be held accountable" and "The best way to show compassion for illegal immigration is to END illegal immigration" (Luntz 1). The report makes the following recommendations: "Always differentiate LEGAL from illegal immigration" and "Always focus on those who are hurt most by illegal immigration—American citizens and immigrants who came here legally and played by the rules" (Luntz 3).

Furthermore, the emphasis here on legal versus illegal immigration makes the situation sound so simple. There's a common myth that people in the US without documentation can just "go back to where they came from" and "get in line" to come here. Many people here without documentation don't have a home they even remember, and there is usually no "line" to simply enter. Many people here without papers entered the US with papers, but those papers expired.

In addition, the overly simplified notion of legal versus illegal immigration ignores the conditions under which people leave their homes and how US foreign policy may have contributed to those conditions. Many people who come to the US feel they have no other choice: "The widespread use of the term *illegal* leaves no room to consider the moral and policy contradictions that are behind the need for people to leave their homes and risk their lives crossing the border without authorization or to overstay visas and live in a precarious status" (Marquardt et al. 9–10).

Journalist Juan Gonzalez wrote *Harvest of Empire*, which was adapted into a documentary. In this film, Gonzalez says,

> There's a reason why there are so many Mexicans, Puerto Ricans, Dominicans, Salvadorans in the United States because, really, the major migrations come precisely from those countries that the United States once dominated and even occupied. They never teach us in school that the huge Latino presence here is a direct

result of our own government's actions in Mexico, the Caribbean, and Central America over many decades, actions that forced millions from that region to leave their home and journey north.

(Harvest of Empire)

A destructive policy like NAFTA just reinforces this point. In 1994, President Clinton signed the North American Free Trade Agreement (NAFTA), which prompted the growth of **maquiladoras**, factories in this Mexican zone near the US border. Companies could build factories and other types of plants in this region without the same kind of taxes and fees they would normally experience in other regions not within such a zone. Companies could benefit from these incentives in addition to the cheap labor, far below the cost of labor in the US. The documentary *Harvest of Empire* includes a news report that states,

"While the trade agreement opened U.S. markets to Mexican corn farmers, they haven't been able to sell any corn in America. Meanwhile, American farmers have flooded Mexico with cheap corn, thanks to generous U.S. government subsidies. As many as 2 million farmworkers have lost their jobs. The vast majority headed north across the U.S. border, looking for better pay."

(Harvest of Empire)

Likewise, in his book, Gonzalez writes,

During the second half of the twentieth century a momentous shift occurred in American economic life. U.S. transnational firms searching for cheap labor and maximum profit shifted much of their manufacturing to Third World countries, especially to Latin America. As part of that shift, the U.S. government led a worldwide campaign to convince developing nations to lower the high tariffs protecting their domestic industries and to adopt "free trade" policies. That campaign . . . has further distorted Latin America's economic development, increased the income gap between rich and poor, and accelerated labor migration to our shores.

(Gonzalez 228)

After all, if companies want to increase their profit, then why be constrained by higher American wages and benefits and American environmental regulations when these companies can set up shop in Mexico, the Caribbean, or South America? However, as Gonzalez makes clear, the only ones who benefit are corporate executives pocketing the higher profit. The rest of the US doesn't benefit, and the countries with free trade zones certainly don't benefit either.

Gonzalez further writes:

> As quickly as industrial plants were shuttered in the Northeast and Midwest, scores of shiny new industrial parks and factory towns . . . sprang up south of the border. . . . Thus, free trade, which was supposed to stabilize the economies of the countries involved, has actually made conditions worse, and the free trade zones, instead of providing Latin Americans with living wage jobs, have probably fueled massive Latin American emigration to the United States.
>
> (Gonzalez 229)

Furthermore, the destructive policies have only continued. In 1996, the Illegal Immigration Reform and Immigrant Responsibility Act significantly increased funding and support for immigration enforcement and control. The same year, also under President Bill Clinton, welfare reform legislation (previously discussed) ended benefits to undocumented immigrants (Rubin and Melnick 265). More recently, in 2010, Arizona passed the "Support Our Law Enforcement and Safe Neighborhoods Act" (SB 1070), controversial legislation identified as anti-immigrant and anti-Latinx. The law's title begs the question: "safe" neighborhood for whom? The Supreme Court ruled in 2012 that some of its provisions were not constitutional, but it upheld what the ACLU calls "the most hotly disputed part . . . which requires police to determine the immigration status of someone arrested or detained when there is 'reasonable suspicion' they are not in the U.S. legally" ("Arizona's SB 1070"). The unending messages that focus on black and Latinx criminality and on personal responsibility divert our attention from the Racism Machine, away from systems that create unequal conditions, unequal opportunities, and unequal outcomes. (See Step 5 action #2C and #3B.)

Divide and Conquer: The Census, Again

Step 3 explained the power of the census to define and redefine racial categories, which affirmed the ideology that race is biological and hierarchical. In particular, Step 3 described the creation of the census and how its definition of racial categories changed every decade, every time the census was administered, which presents us with a perfect illustration of how race is socially constructed. The current census government website even acknowledges that race is a social construct, stating, "The racial categories included in the census questionnaire generally reflect a social definition of race recognized in this country and not an attempt to define race biologically, anthropologically, or genetically" ("About Race"). It describes the purpose of continuing to ask residents to self-identify their race for the following reasons: "Information on race is required for many Federal programs and is critical in making policy decisions, particularly for civil rights. States use these data to meet legislative redistricting principles. Race data also are used to promote equal employment opportunities and to assess racial disparities in health and environmental risks" ("About Race").

While for centuries, the census was used as a tool of white supremacy to police the borders of whiteness, the official position now focuses on the opposite purpose, that of "civil rights." While intent and motive may attempt to focus on racial justice rather than oppression, we still need to look at impact (see Step 5 action #1C). In addition to the presence of racial categories on the census today sending a message to native-born Americans and immigrants alike that racial definitions matter, the media's response to census results also sends a powerful message.

Since 1980, there has been one census question devoted solely to the respondent's "origin," often referred to as "ethnicity." However, this question only asked in essentially a yes/no way whether the respondent identified as "Hispanic, Latino, or Spanish." This was a new question starting in 1980 and continued, though the precise language always shifted, to the most recent census of 2010. The question about "race," as Step 3 makes clear, goes back to the creation of the census in 1790. Since 1980, at the same time as the "origin" question was included, a separate question asked for the "race" of the respondent, and though the precise language varied, the basic categories remained: white, black, Asian, American Indian, and Pacific Islander. Starting in 2000, respondents could check more than one racial category. Not only are the questions and categories on the form quite telling, but the media's response to the results also warrants our attention.

The news media's coverage of the 2000 census results in particular sent a very powerful divide-and-conquer message about competition between races. Even though the census questionnaire insists that "Hispanic origins are not races," that message was often ignored in the media's response. There were two major themes in the media's response to the 2000 census data: the sheer number of Latinx people and then the competition between Latinx and black people for "biggest minority." A sampling of newspaper headlines from March 2001 illustrates these themes:

- "Latinos Surge in Census Count Officials Surprised By 2000 Figures" in *Boston Globe* (Rodriguez)
- "Census Shows Greater Numbers of Hispanics" in *USA Today* (Nasser)
- "Number of Hispanics Ballooned in '90s; Group Is About to Become Biggest Minority" in the *Wall Street Journal* (Porter)
- "New Census Shows Hispanics Are Even with Blacks in U.S." in the *New York Times* (Schmitt)
- "Hispanics Close in on No. 2 Fueled by Immigration, Latinos Soon Will Pass Blacks as Largest Minority in U.S." in the *Seattle Post-Intelligencer* (Cox News Service)
- "Hispanics Draw Even with Blacks in New Census; Latino Population Up 60% Since 1990" in the *Washington Post* (Cohn and Fears)
- "Hispanics Match Black Populace in U.S. Census/58 Percent Rise in 10 Years Outpaces Rest of Nation" in the *San Francisco Chronicle* (Ness)
- "Hispanic Population Booming/Dramatic Increase has Sparked Friction with Blacks, Some Demographers Say" in the *Atlanta Journal-Constitution* (Bixler)

Words like "surge," "balloon," and "outpace" emphasize the message that the Latinx population is growing too quickly, that something is not normal, not appropriate, not fair, and not American, which connects to the "illegal" stereotype just discussed. Furthermore, many of these headlines emphasize a competition between Latinx and black people with words like "draw even," "pass," and "match." Why is census data a competition?

We can start to see an answer to this question when we look at additional headlines, which complete the picture:

- "Non-Hispanic Whites May Soon Be a Minority in Texas" in the *New York Times* (Yardley)
- "Non-Hispanic Whites a Minority, California Census Figures Show" in the *New York Times* (Purdum)
- "Whites in Minority in Largest Cities, the Census Shows" in the *New York Times* (Schmitt)

The latter article opens, "For the first time, nearly half of the nation's 100 largest cities are home to more blacks, Hispanics, Asians and other minorities than whites, an analysis of the latest census figures shows. . . . non-Hispanic whites are now a minority of the total population living in the 100 largest urban centers" (Schmitt). The subtext is that this is a warning of what's to come, the impending national white minority predicted to occur within a few decades. The language this article uses, like "vast majority" of cities "losing white residents," reinforces fear, regardless of the intent. It reinforces the idea that the status quo should be maintained, that this "loss" is a problem.

The years that followed saw the same three themes repeat themselves: a quickly growing Latinx population, competition between Latinx people and blacks, and white fear of becoming the minority. For example, a July 31, 2002, *New York Times* article's headline reads, "Latino Population Growth Is Widespread, Study Says" (Clemetson), as if it's a contagious disease. The opening of the article states, "The Hispanic population has spread out across the nation faster and farther than any previous wave of immigrants, with the movement of Latinos from immigrant gateways into the heartland and suburbs" (Clemetson). The words "faster and farther" focus again on the sheer numbers and almost uncontrollable increase. That uncontrollability is exacerbated by the appearance of

Latinx people in "the heartland" rather than in the "immigrant gateways" where they are presumably expected to be. The message is that "heartland," though, is not supposed to be such a space, as if they are violating some understanding meant to protect middle (white) America.

In January 2003, new census data prompted a flurry of more news articles, this time focusing on the idea that no longer are Latinx people getting close to blacks in the competition for the largest minority but that they have actually surpassed blacks to become the largest minority:

- "Hispanics Inch Toward Outnumbering Blacks" in *USA Today* (Overberg)
- "Hispanics Now Largest Minority, Census Shows" in *New York Times* (Clemetson)
- "Hispanics Achieve a Census Pinnacle/They're Now Largest U.S. Minority" in the *Houston Chronicle* (Cobb)

Then, in June 2003, when the census collected more specific evidence that Latinx people were finally the "winner," regardless of how you count blacks, the media again ran with it:

- "Latinos Now Top Minority; Census Bureau Estimates Group's U.S. Population at 38.8 Million, Ahead of blacks for the First Time. Demographers See Even More Growth Ahead" in the *Los Angeles Times* (Alonso-Zaldivar)
- "Hispanic Population Is Rising Swiftly, Census Bureau Says" in the *New York Times* (Clemetson)

In 2005, another flurry of articles reinforced the theme of an increasing Latinx population:

- "Hispanic Growth Surge Fueled by Births in U.S." in the *Washington Post* (Cohn)
- "Census: Hispanics Are Fastest Growing Minority" in the *Star Tribune* (Westphal)
- "Census Reports Rising Growth Rate for Hispanics" in the *New York Times* (Rahimi)

Given these headlines, year after year, from many major news media out-lets, is it any surprise that white people became fearful of immigration? And of Latinx immigration in particular?

Furthermore, there have been several articles predicting the year in which whites will be the statistical minority. For example, in 2008, the *New York Times* ran an article titled "In a Generation, Minorities May Be the U.S. Majority" that identified 2042 as the year in which whites will become the minority (Roberts). Then, in 2009, the same newspaper announced an update from the census with the headline "Projections Put Whites in Minority in U.S. by 2050" (Roberts). More recently, in 2016, this projection became a reality for babies, as NPR reported "Babies of Color Are Now the Majority, Census Says" (Yoshinaga).

While it's hard to know the intent of this type of headline, the impact is certainly one that fuels the tension and even panic connected to anti-immigrant legislation and rhetoric. By the time Trump's presidential campaign emerged as a powerful force in 2016, it should not have been a surprise that his campaign promises to "build a wall" and "ban Muslims" were so popular. The rhetoric surrounding these anti-immigrant measures target whites who feel fearful of becoming the minority. The census has been a mechanism of the Racism Machine since 1790, when it established whiteness as the norm for citizenship. The census has been used for more than two centuries to police that whiteness, and the census results are now being used to provoke whites to protect that whiteness. The census has been a mechanism of the Racism Machine at every stage, which should prompt us to think about the future of the census (see Step 5 action #1C).

The rhetoric of competition seen in the media's response to the cen-sus results just reinforces the mechanism of capitalism within the Racism Machine. The white wealthy elite maintain their power through divide-and-conquer stereotypes that pit groups marginalized by race and class against each other at the same time as we're told that racism is a thing of the past, that the American Dream is available to all who work hard, and that social services should be cut to avoid enabling dependence. This dynamic forces marginalized people (including people of color and poor whites) to compete with each other for resources that are presented as scarce but are in fact reserved almost entirely for the elite. Step 5 will share action steps to begin to address these problems and other aspects of the Racism Machine.

Reflection Questions

1. What part of Step 4 were you already familiar with, and why do you think that might be?
2. Was anything unfamiliar to you, and why do you think that might be?
3. How would you summarize the ideas that stand out to you the most? Why are they important?
4. What reflection question would you create to respond to Step 4, and why?

Recommended Resources

Films

Black America Since MLK: And Still I Rise. McGee Media, LLC and Inwell Films, Inc., 2016.
The Black Panthers: Vanguard of the Revolution. Firelight Films, Inc., 2015.
The Central Park Five. Florentine Films, 2013.
A Day Without a Mexican. Xenon Pictures, Inc., 2004.
FREE CeCe! Jac Gares Media, Inc., 2016.
Inequality for All. Directed by Jacob Kornbluth, created by Robert Reich, 72 Productions, 2013.

Websites

"About Race." United States Census Bureau, 12 January 2017, www.census.gov/topics/population/race/about.html.
Inequality for All. Radius TWC, 2013, inequalityforall.com/.
"Model Minority Stereotype for Asian Americans." Counseling and Mental Health Center, University of Texas, 2017, cmhc.utexas.edu/modelminority.html.
Rise Up North: Newark. riseupnewark.com/.
SNCC Legacy Project. 2017, www.sncclegacyproject.org/.

Articles

Angyal, Chloe. "Affirmative Action Is Great for White Women. So Why Do They Hate It?" *Huffington Post*, 23 June 2016, www.huffingtonpost.com/entry/affirmative-action-white-women_us_56a0ef6ae4b0d8cc1098d3a5.
"Asian Americans and Pacific Islanders: Facts, Not Fiction: Setting the Record Straight." *The College Board*, 2008, secure-media.collegeboard.org/digitalServices/pdf/professionals/asian-americans-and-pacific-islanders-facts-not-fiction.pdf.
Berman, Ari. "Voter Suppression Is a Much Bigger Problem Than Voter Fraud." *The Nation*, 20 October 2016, www.thenation.com/article/voter-suppression-is-a-much-bigger-problem-than-voter-fraud/.
Massie, Victoria M. "White Women Benefit Most From Affirmative Action—and Are Among Its Fiercest Opponents." *Vox*, 23 June 2016, www.vox.com/2016/5/25/11682950/fisher-supreme-court-white-women-affirmative-action.

Velasquez-Manoff, Moises. "What Biracial People Know." *New York Times*, 4 March 2017, nyti.ms/2lr2DOR.

Wingfield, Adia Harvey. "The Professional Burdens of Being a 'Model Minority.'" *Atlantic*, 6 June 2016, www.theatlantic.com/business/archive/2016/06/professional-burdens-model-minority-asian-americans/485492/.

Books

Alexander, Michelle. *The New Jim Crow: Mass Incarceration in the Age of Colorblindness.* The New Press, 2012.

Ancheta, Angelo N. *Race, Rights, and the Asian American Experience.* Rutgers University Press, 1998.

Baldwin, James. *The Fire Next Time.* Vintage Books, 1993.

Bartels, Larry M. *Unequal Democracy: The Political Economy of the New Gilded Age.* Princeton University Press, 2008.

Bell, Derrick. *And We Are Not Saved: The Elusive Quest for Racial Justice.* Basic Books, 1987.

———. *Faces at the Bottom of the Well: The Permanence of Racism.* Basic Books, 1992.

Berman, Ari. *Give Us the Ballot: The Modern Struggle for Voting Rights in America.* Picador, 2015.

Biggers, Jeff. *State Out of the Union: Arizona and the Final Showdown Over the American Dream.* Nation Books, 2012.

Bonilla-Silva, Eduardo. *Racism Without Racists: Color-Blind Racism and the Persistence of Racial Inequality in America.* 4th ed., Rowman & Littlefield Publishers, 2014.

Burrell, Tom. *Brainwashed: Challenging the Myth of Black Inferiority.* Smiley Books, 2010.

Dávila, Arlene. *Latinos, Inc.: The Marketing and Making of a People.* University of California Press, 2001.

Deggans, Eric. *Race-Baiter: How the Media Wields Dangerous Words to Divide a Nation.* Palgrave Macmillan, 2012.

Delgado, Richard and Jean Stefancic, editors. *Critical White Studies: Looking Behind the Mirror.* Temple University Press, 1997.

———, editors. *The Latino/a Condition: A Critical Reader.* New York University Press, 1998.

Dyson, Michael Eric. *The Black Presidency: Barack Obama and the Politics of Race in America.* Houghton Mifflin, 2016.

Glaude, Eddie S., Jr. *Democracy in Black: How Race Still Enslaves the American Soul.* Crown Publishers, 2016.

Guy-Sheftall, Beverly. *Words of Fire: An Anthology of African-American Feminist Thought.* The New Press, 1995.

Hayes, Chris. *A Colony in a Nation.* W.W. Norton & Company, 2017.

Hill, Marc Lamont. *Nobody: Casualties of America's War on the Vulnerable, from Ferguson to Flint and Beyond.* Atria Books, 2016.

Hochschild, Arlie Russell. *Strangers in Their Own Land: Anger and Mourning on the American Right.* The New Press, 2016.

Iyer, Deepa. *We Too Sing America: South Asian, Arab, Muslim, and Sikh Immigrants Shape Our Multiracial Future.* The New Press, 2015.

Kabaservice, Geoffrey. *Rule and Ruin: The Downfall of Moderation and the Destruction of the Republican Party, From Eisenhower to the Tea Party.* Oxford University Press, 2012.

Kennedy, Randall. *The Persistence of the Color Line: Racial Politics and the Obama Presidency.* Pantheon Books, 2011.

Klein, Naomi. *The Shock Doctrine: The Rise of Disaster Capitalism.* Metropolitan Books, 2007.

Krugman, Paul. *The Conscience of a Liberal.* W.W. Norton & Company, 2007.

The Latina Feminist Group. *Telling to Live: Latina Feminist* Testimonios. Duke University Press, 2001.

Lee, Erika. *The Making of Asian America: A History.* Simon & Schuster, 2015.

Lee, Robert G. *Orientals: Asian Americans in Popular Culture.* Temple University Press, 1999.

Lipsitz, George. *The Possessive Investment in Whiteness: How White People Profit From Identity Politics.* Temple University Press, 1998.

López, Ian Haney. *Dog Whistle Politics: How Coded Racial Appeals Have Reinvented Racism & Wrecked the Middle Class.* Oxford University Press, 2014.

Lowe, Lisa. *Immigrant Acts: On Asian American Cultural Politics.* Duke University Press, 1996.

Marable, Manning. *How Capitalism Underdeveloped Black America: Problems in Race, Political Economy, and Society.* Haymarket Books, 2015.

Marrero, Pilar. *Killing the American Dream: How Anti-Immigration Extremists Are Destroying the Nation.* Palgrave Macmillan, 2012.

Matsuda, Mari J. *Where Is Your Body? And Other Essays on Race, Gender, and the Law.* Beacon Press, 1996.

McChesney, Robert W. *The Problem of the Media: U.S. Communication Politics in the 21st Century.* Monthly Review Press, 2004.

Muhammad, Khalil Gibran. *The Condemnation of Blackness: Race, Crime, and the Making of Modern Urban America.* Harvard University Press, 2010.

Omi, Michael and Howard Winant. *Racial Formation in the United States.* 3rd ed., Routledge, 2015.

Perez, William. *We Are Americans: Undocumented Students Pursuing the American Dream.* Stylus, 2009.

Perry, Imani. *More Beautiful and More Terrible: The Embrace and Transcendence of Racial Inequality in the United States.* New York University Press, 2011.

Phillips, Steve. *Brown Is the New White: How the Demographic Revolution Has Created a New American Majority.* The New Press, 2016.

Press, Bill. *The Obama Hate Machine: The Lies, Distortions, and Personal Attacks on the President—And Who Is Behind Them.* Thomas Dunne Books, 2012.

Prewitt, Kenneth. *What Is Your Race? The Census and Our Flawed Efforts to Classify Americans.* Princeton University Press, 2013.

Reid, Joy-Ann. *Fracture: Barack Obama, the Clintons, and the Racial Divide.* Harper Collins Publishers, 2016.

Sharpe, Christina. *In the Wake: On Blackness and Being.* Duke University Press, 2016.

Skocpol, Theda and Vanessa Williamson. *The Tea Party and the Remaking of Republican Conservatism.* Oxford University Press, 2012.

Stevenson, Bryan. *Just Mercy: A Story of Justice and Redemption.* Spiegel & Grau, 2015.

Sugrue, Thomas J. *Sweet Land of Liberty: The Forgotten Struggle for Civil Rights in the North.* Random House, 2008.

Taylor, Keeanga-Yamahtta. *From #BlackLivesMatter to Black Liberation.* Haymarket Books, 2016.

Ward, Jesmyn, editor. *The Fire This Time: A New Generation Speaks about Race.* Scribner, 2016.

Wu, Frank. *Yellow: Race in America Beyond Black and White.* Basic Books, 2002.

Zernike, Kate. *Boiling Mad: Inside Tea Party America.* Henry Holt and Company, 2010.

Zia, Helen. *Asian American Dreams: The Emergence of an American People.* Farrar, Straus and Giroux, 2000.

Works Cited

"About Race." United States Census Bureau, 12 January 2017, www.census.gov/topics/population/race/about.html.

"ALEC." American Legislative Exchange Council, 2017, www.alec.org/.

Alonso-Zaldivar, Ricardo. "Latinos Now Top Minority; Census Bureau Estimates Group's U.S. Population at 38.8 Million, Ahead of Blacks for the First Time. Demographers See Even More Growth Ahead." *Los Angeles Times*, 19 June 2003, *US Newsstream*, ezp.raritanval.edu/login?url=http://search.proquest.com/docview/421824594?accountid=13438.

Angyal, Chloe. "Affirmative Action Is Great for White Women. So Why Do They Hate It?" *Huffington Post*, 23 June 2016, www.huffingtonpost.com/entry/affirmative-action-white-women_us_56a0ef6ae4b0d8cc1098d3a5.

"Arizona's SB 1070." ACLU, 2017, www.aclu.org/feature/arizonas-sb-1070.

Barbaro, Michael. "Donald Trump Clung to 'Birther' Lie for Years, and Still Isn't Apologetic." *New York Times*, 16 September 2016, nyti.ms/2jHUBPM.

Bell, David A. "The Triumph of Asian-Americans." *The New Republic*, 15 and 22 July 1985, pp. 24+.

Bell, Derrick. *And We Are Not Saved: The Elusive Quest for Racial Justice.* Basic Books, 1987.

Benns, Whitney and Blake Strode. "Debtors' Prison in 21st-Century America." *Atlantic*, 23 February 2016, www.theatlantic.com/business/archive/2016/02/debtors-prison/462378/.

Berman, Ari. "Voter Suppression Is a Much Bigger Problem Than Voter Fraud." *The Nation*, 20 October 2016, www.thenation.com/article/voter-suppression-is-a-much-bigger-problem-than-voter-fraud/.

Bixler, Mark. "Hispanic Population Booming. Dramatic Increase Has Sparked Friction With Blacks, Some Demographers Say." *Atlanta Constitution*, 8 March 2001, *US Newsstream*, ezp.raritanval.edu/login?url=http://search.proquest.com/docview/413873003?accountid=13438.

Black America Since MLK: And Still I Rise. McGee Media, LLC and Inwell Films, Inc., 2016.

"Black Lives Matter Stands in Solidarity With Water Protectors at Standing Rock." *Black Lives Matter*, 2016, blacklivesmatter.com/solidarity-with-standing-rock/.

Black, Rachel and Aleta Sprague. "The 'Welfare Queen' Is a Lie." *Atlantic*, 28 September 2016, www.theatlantic.com/business/archive/2016/09/welfare-queen-myth/501470/.

"Brief of the Asian American Legal Foundation as *Amicus Curiae* in Support of Petitioner." *Abigail Noel Fisher v. University of Texas at Austin*, tarlton.law.utexas.edu/ld.php?content_id=19666587.

Chang, Robert S. *Disoriented: Asian Americans, Law, and the Nation-State.* New York University Press, 1999.

Cho, Sumi K. "Korean Americans vs. African Americans: Conflict and Construction." *Reading Rodney King Reading Urban Uprising*, edited by Robert Gooding-Williams, Routledge, 1993, pp. 196–211.

Churchill, Ward and Jim Vander Wall. *The COINTELPRO Papers: Documents From the FBI's Secret Wars Against Dissent in the United States*. South End Press, 2002.

Clemetson, Lynette. "Hispanics Now Largest Minority, Census Shows." *New York Times*, 22 January 2003, nyti.ms/2jGdYZg.

———. "Hispanic Population Is Rising Swiftly, Census Bureau Says." *New York Times*, 19 June 2003, nyti.ms/2rEkfph.

———. "Latino Population Growth Is Widespread, Study Says." *New York Times*, 31 July 2002, nyti.ms/2rEIjbz.

Cobb, Kim. "Hispanics Achieve a Census Pinnacle; They're Now Largest U.S. Minority." *Houston Chronicle*, 22 January 2003, *US Newsstream*, ezp.raritanval.edu/login?url=http://search.proquest.com/docview/395976517?accountid=13438.

Cohn, D'Vera. "Hispanic Growth Surge Fueled by Births in U.S." *Washington Post*, 9 June 2005, www.washingtonpost.com/wp-dyn/content/article/2005/06/08/AR2005060802381.

Cohn, D'Vera and Darryl Fears. "Hispanics Draw Even with Blacks in New Census; Latino Population Up 60% Since 1990." *Washington Post*, 7 March 2001, p. A1, *US Newsstream*, ezp.raritanval.edu/login?url=http://search.proquest.com/docview/409093868?accountid=13438.

Cooper, Helene. "Obama Offers Plan to Cut Deficit by Over $3 Trillion." *New York Times*, 18 September 2011, nyti.ms/2rEkwbN.

Cox News Service. "Hispanics Close in on No. 2 Fueled by Immigration; Latinos Soon Will Pass Blacks as Largest Minority in U.S." *Seattle Post-Intelligencer*, 8 March 2001, p. A3, *US Newsstream*, ezp.raritanval.edu/login?url=http://search.proquest.com/docview/385567487?accountid=13438.

"Criminal Justice Facts." *The Sentencing Project*, 2017, www.sentencingproject.org/criminal-justice-facts/.

"Debunking the Voter Fraud Myth." *Brennan Center for Justice*, 31 January 2017, www.brennancenter.org/analysis/debunking-voter-fraud-myth.

Doerner, William R., et al. "To America with Skills." *Time*, 8 July 1985, pp. 42–44.

Faulders, Katherine and Alexander Mallin. "President Trump Launches Commission on 'Election Integrity'." *ABC News*, 11 May 2017, abcnews.go.com/Politics/president-trump-expected-launch-commission-election-integrity/story?id=47337222.

Geary, Daniel. "The Moynihan Report: An Annotated Edition." *Atlantic*, 14 September 2015, www.theatlantic.com/politics/archive/2015/09/the-moynihan-report-an-annotated-edition/404632/.

Gonzalez, Juan. *Harvest of Empire: A History of Latinos in America*. Viking, 2000.

Gooding-Williams, Robert. "Introduction: On Being Stuck." *Reading Rodney King Reading Urban Uprising*, edited by Robert Gooding-Williams, Routledge, 1993, pp. 1–12.

"A Graphical Look at Economic Inequality in Three Parts." *Inequality for All*, Radius TWC, 2013, inequalityforall.com/wp-content/uploads/2014/12/A_Visual_Story PDF.pdf.

Inequality for All. Directed by Jacob Kornbluth, created by Robert Reich, 72 Productions, 2013.

"Infant Mortality." *Centers for Disease Control and Prevention*, U.S. Department of Health & Human Services, 2016, www.cdc.gov/features/infantmortality/index.html.

"Issue Brief: Criminalizing Undocumented Immigrants." *Immigrants' Rights Project*, ACLU, February 2010, www.aclu.org/files/assets/FINAL_criminalizing_undocumented_immigrants_issue_brief_PUBLIC_VERSION.pdf.

Kasindorf, Martin, et al. "Asian-Americans: A 'Model Minority.'" *Newsweek*, 6 December 1982, p. 39+.

Kim, Kwang Chung and Shin Kim. "The Multiracial Nature of Los Angeles Unrest in 1992." *Koreans in the Hood: Conflict With African Americans*, edited by Kwang Chung Kim, The Johns Hopkins University Press, 1999, pp. 17–38.

Kochhar, Rakesh and Richard Fry. "Wealth Inequality Has Widened Along Racial, Ethnic Lines Since End of Great Recession." *Fact Tank: News in the Numbers*, Pew Research Center, 12 December 2014, www.pewresearch.org/fact-tank/2014/12/12/racial-wealth-gaps-great-recession/.

Krugman, Paul. "Moochers Against Welfare." *New York Times*, 16 February 2012, nyti.ms/2jOqVjS.

Liptak, Adam. "Supreme Court Upholds Affirmative Action Program at University of Texas." *New York Times*, 23 June 2016, nyti.ms/2k5vsLT.

López, Ian Haney. *Dog Whistle Politics: How Coded Racial Appeals Have Reinvented Racism & Wrecked the Middle Class*. Oxford University Press, 2014.

Luntz, Maslansky Strategic Research. "Respect for the Law & Economic Fairness: Illegal Immigration Prevention." *Luntz Research & Strategic Services*, October 2005, images.dailykos.com/images/user/3/Luntz_frames_immigration.pdf. Accessed 17 May 2017.

Marquardt, Marie Friedmann, et al. *Living "Illegal": The Human Face of Unauthorized Immigration*. The New Press, 2013.

Massie, Victoria M. "White Women Benefit Most From Affirmative Action—and Are Among Its Fiercest Opponents." *Vox*, 23 June 2016, www.vox.com/2016/5/25/11682950/fisher-supreme-court-white-women-affirmative-action.

Mathews, T. J. and Anne K. Driscoll. "Trends in Infant Mortality in the United States, 2005–2014." *NCHS Data Brief*, U.S. Department of Health & Human Services, March 2017, www.cdc.gov/nchs/data/databriefs/db279.pdf.

Medsger, Betty. *The Burglary: The Discovery of J. Edgar Hoover's Secret FBI*. Vintage Books, 2014.

"Model Minority Stereotype for Asian Americans." Counseling and Mental Health Center, University of Texas, 2017, cmhc.utexas.edu/modelminority.html.

Nasser, Haya E. "Census Shows Greater Numbers of Hispanics." *USA Today*, 8 March 2001, *US Newsstream*, ezp.raritanval.edu/login?url=http://search.proquest.com/docview/408839126?accountid=13438.

Ness, Carol. "Hispanics Match Black Populace in U.S. Census; 58 Percent Rise in 10 Years Outpaces Rest of Nation." *San Francisco Chronicle*, 8 March 2001, *US Newsstream*, ezp.raritanval.edu/login?url=http://search.proquest.com/docview/411502970?accountid=13438.

Oh, Angela E. "Race Relations in Los Angeles: 'Divide and Conquer' Is Alive and Flourishing." *Southern California Law Review*, vol. 66, 1992–1993, pp. 1647–1651.

Orfield, Gary, et al. "Brown at 62: School Segregation by Race, Poverty and State." *The Civil Rights Project*, UCLA, 16 May 2016, www.civilrightsproject.ucla.edu/research/k-12-education/integration-and-diversity/brown-at-62-school-segregation-by-race-poverty-and-state.

Overberg, Paul. "Hispanics Inch Toward Outnumbering Blacks." *USA Today*, 22 January 2003, *US Newsstream*, ezp.raritanval.edu/login?url=http://search.proquest.com/docview/408882495?accountid=13438.

Oxnam, Robert B. "Why Asians Succeed Here." *New York Times Magazine*, 30 November 1986, pp. 72+.

Park, Kyeyoung. "Use and Abuse of Race and Culture: Black-Korean Tension in America." *Koreans in the Hood: Conflict with African Americans*, edited by Kwang Chung Kim, The Johns Hopkins University Press, 1999, pp. 60–74.

Pearson, Matthew R. "How 'Undocumented Workers' and 'Illegal Aliens' Affect Prejudice Toward Mexican Immigrants." *Social Influence*, vol. 5, no. 2, April 2010, pp. 118–132. *EBSCOhost*, doi:10.1080/15534511003593679.

Petersen, William. "Success Story, Japanese Style." *New York Times Magazine*, 9 January 1966, pp. 20+.

Porter, Eduardo. "Number of Hispanics Ballooned in '90s; Group Is About to Become Biggest Minority." *Wall Street Journal*, 8 March 2001, *US Newsstream*, ezp.raritanval.edu/login?url=http://search.proquest.com/docview/398811222?accountid=13438.

Purdum, Todd S. "Non-Hispanic Whites a Minority, California Census Figures Show." *New York Times*, 30 March 2001, nyti.ms/2qG9llx.

Rahimi, Shadi. "Census Reports Rising Growth Rate for Hispanics." *New York Times*, 9 June 2005, nyti.ms/2rEmLvC.

Ramirez, Anthony. "America's Super Minority." *Fortune*, 24 November 1986, pp. 148+.

"Report: The War on Marijuana in Black and White." ACLU. June 2013, www.aclu.org/report/report-war-marijuana-black-and-white?redirect=criminal-law-reform/war-marijuana-black-and-white.

Roberts, Sam. "In a Generation, Minorities May Be the U.S. Majority." *New York Times*, 13 August 2008, nyti.ms/2rEhIeD.

———. "Projections Put Whites in Minority in U.S. by 2050." *New York Times*, 17 December 2009, www.nytimes.com/2009/12/18/us/18census.html.

Rodriguez, Cindy. "Latinos Surge in Census Count Officials Surprised by 2000 Figures." *Boston Globe*, 8 March 2001, *US Newsstream*, ezp.raritanval.edu/login?url=http://search.proquest.com/docview/405382746?accountid=13438.

Romney, Mitt. "What Kind of Society Does America Want?" *USA Today*, 19 December 2011, usatoday30.usatoday.com/news/opinion/forum/story/2011–12–19/romney-us-economy-entitlements/52076252/1.

Rubin, Rachel Lee and Jeffrey Melnick. *Immigration and American Popular Culture: An Introduction*. NYU Press, 2006.

Schmitt, Eric. "New Census Shows Hispanics Are Even With Blacks in U.S." *New York Times*, 8 March 2001, nyti.ms/2qGF9qp.

———. "Whites in Minority in Largest Cities, the Census shows." *New York Times*, 30 April 2001, *US Newsstream*, ezp.raritanval.edu/login?url=http://search.proquest.com/docview/431714948?accountid=13438.

Schnurer, Eric. "Just How Wrong Is Conventional Wisdom About Government Fraud?" *Atlantic*, 15 August 2013, www.theatlantic.com/politics/archive/2013/08/just-how-wrong-is-conventional-wisdom-about-government-fraud/278690/.

Semuels, Alana. "The End of Welfare as We Know It." *Atlantic*, 1 April 2016, www.theatlantic.com/business/archive/2016/04/the-end-of-welfare-as-we-know-it/476322/.

Stone, Chad. "The Facts About Food Stamps Conservatives Don't Want You to Hear." *U.S. News & World Report*, 16 May 2013, www.usnews.com/opinion/blogs/economic-intelligence/2013/05/16/facts-show-food-stamp-program-has-a-strong-record-of-efficienty.

"Success Story of One Minority Group in U.S." *U.S. News & World Report*, 26 December 1966, pp. 73–76.

Taylor, G. Flint. "The FBI COINTELPRO Program and the Fred Hampton Assassination." *Huffington Post*, 3 December 2013, www.huffingtonpost.com/g-flint-taylor/the-fbi-cointelpro-progra_b_4375527.html.

"Transcript: GOP Response From Rep. Paul Ryan." NPR, 25 January 2011, www.npr.org/2011/01/26/133227396/transcript-gop-response-from-rep-paul-ryan.

"Transcript: Rep. Paul Ryan's Convention Speech." NPR, 29 August 2012, www.npr.org/2012/08/29/160282031/transcript-rep-paul-ryans-convention-speech.

"Voices of the Tea Party." *New York Times*, www.nytimes.com/interactive/2010/04/14/us/teaparty.html. Accessed 17 May 2017.

"Voting Rights Act: Major Dates in History." ACLU, www.aclu.org/timelines/history-voting-rights-act. Accessed 17 May 2017.

Weller, Christian E. and Jeffrey Thompson. "Wealth Inequality Among Asian Americans Greater Than Among Whites." *Center for American Progress*, 20 December 2016, www.americanprogress.org/issues/race/reports/2016/12/20/295359/wealth-inequality-among-asian-americans-greater-than-among-whites/.

Westphal, David. "Census: Hispanics Are Fastest-Growing Minority; Birth Rates More Than Immigration Are Credited for the Jump, New Numbers Show." *Star Tribune*, 9 June 2005, p. 11A, *US Newsstream*, ezp.raritanval.edu/login?url=http://search.proquest.com/docview/427718065?accountid=13438.

Williams, Dennis A., et al. "A Formula for Success." *Newsweek*, 23 April 1984, pp. 77–78.

Wingfield, Adia Harvey. "The Professional Burdens of Being a 'Model Minority.'" *Atlantic*, 6 June 2016, www.theatlantic.com/business/archive/2016/06/professional-burdens-model-minority-asian-americans/485492/.

Wu, Frank. *Yellow: Race in America Beyond Black and White*. Basic Books, 2002.

———. "Why Vincent Chin Matters." *New York Times*, 22 June 2012, nyti.ms/2k2hBG4.

Yardley, Jim. "Non-Hispanic Whites May Soon Be a Minority in Texas." *New York Times*, 25 March 2001, nyti.ms/2qG9gOL.

Yoshinaga, Kendra. "Babies of Color Are Now the Majority, Census Says." NPR, 1 July 2016, www.npr.org/sections/ed/2016/07/01/484325664/babies-of-color-are-now-the-majority-census-says.

Zernike, Kate and Megan Thee-Brenan. "Poll Finds Tea Party Backers Wealthier and More Educated." *New York Times*, 14 April 2010, www.nytimes.com/2010/04/15/us/politics/15poll.html.

Zia, Helen. *Asian American Dreams: The Emergency of an American People*. Farrar, Straus and Giroux, 2000.

Zucchino, David. *Myth of the Welfare Queen*. Touchstone, 1999.

STEP 5

TAKE APART THE RACISM MACHINE

What specific actions can we take to dismantle the Racism Machine?

Steps 1 through 4 provided an introductory foundation to understanding the creation of a racial ideology in colonial America and its persistence throughout US history. The metaphor of the Racism Machine revealed how humans have constructed racism, strengthened it, maintained it, and recalibrated it at various times. Activists have been working on taking apart this machine ever since it was built. However, this machine is very powerful, and if one wheel is removed, another takes its place. As Step 1 explained, many people in the US today are unfamiliar with the Racism Machine because they were taught to ignore it. We can only take it apart if we involve more people and if they learn how this machine operates and that it only serves the interests of a tiny, wealthy, white elite. The machine has divided and conquered us for centuries in order to protect this white elite. What can we do to resist that dividing and conquering? The final part of this manual is an attempt to answer that question. These actions are also presented for a wide variety of audiences, both individuals and groups, with different relationships to systems and power. Step 5 includes names of many organizations, activists, writers, and scholars, and there are many ways to engage their work. Please listen to their podcasts, watch their videos and films, read their books and articles, visit their websites, and/or follow them on Twitter, Facebook, and other social media platforms.

1. Start at the Beginning

In order to understand what action to take today, we need to understand how we got here. As Steps 1 and 2 explained, race is a relatively recent belief system, and racism is a relatively recent system of oppression. Many people think that racism has always existed and is a natural part of the human condition, so they don't question it and don't fight it. I began Step 1 by focusing on how race is a social construct, and we need to understand this idea in order to begin to address racism. As Step 1 explained, this approach includes an examination of the false ideology that race is biological. Therefore, one of the actions I'm recommending here focuses on raising awareness about the creation of race and racism.

1A) **Learn about and teach others that race is not biological but rather a human invention created to divide and conquer the masses and protect a small, wealthy, white elite.** Depending on the type of resources you prefer (books, videos, websites, etc.), pick as a starting place one of the Recommended Resources listed in Step 1, strengthen your understanding, and share that understanding.

- Individuals: Teach others, even if you're not a teacher. There are still people you engage with in your circle of friends, family, and/or coworkers. Bring people together to watch the first episode ("The Difference Between Us") of the documentary *Race: The Power of an Illusion*, which does an excellent job of establishing an introduction to these ideas. You can organize an informal screening of the film in your home with people you know. You can ask your local library, community center, place of worship, and/or school to host a screening.
- Educators and parents: There are many age-appropriate and discipline-appropriate ways of teaching students that race is not biological. (See action #5.) By the time I teach this at the college level, most of my students say that they did not learn this in K–12 and wish they had. The film *Race: The Power of*

an Illusion is appropriate for high school audiences. In fact, it features a group of high school students. Furthermore, the film's website (www.pbs.org/race) includes a downloadable discussion guide as well as resources for teachers and grades 9–12 teaching recommendations. Resources for parents include the online group Embrace Race.

- Community groups: It can be very effective to read and discuss an article together or watch a documentary together that introduces the concept that race is a social construct. Pick one recommended film or text as a common starting point.

- Consider supplementing a discussion for teens and/or adults with one of the supplementary one-page handouts developed by the creators of *Race: The Power of an Illusion.* This helpful overview, "Ten Things Everyone Should Know About Race," is available at newsreel.org/guides/race/10things.htm.

- Keep in mind that furthering your own education and educating others are only the beginning.

1B) Support #BlackLivesMatter. This movement speaks directly against the antiblack racial ideology and racial hierarchy that positions black people as inferior. This movement focuses on the recognition of the humanity of black people. The fact that some people today, including government officials, want to label it a terrorist organization just reinforces how threatening it is to the status quo to disrupt the racial hierarchy. The official website for #BlackLivesMatter, founded by Patrisse Cullors, Opal Tometi, and Alicia Garza, includes thirteen Guiding Principles that we should all read carefully, share, discuss, and support. Also learn how you can support local chapters in your area. See blacklivesmatter.com/ and blacklivesmatter.com/guiding-principles/.

- Learn more about the creation of #BlackLivesMatter in order to recognize the need for this movement and to support it. Watch, read, share, and discuss the following resources, especially with people unfamiliar with the movement or who question it:

- The 2016 Facing Race conference featured a plenary session titled "Multiracial Movements for Black Lives" on November 11, 2016. This panel included Michelle Alexander (*The New Jim Crow*), Alicia Garza (cofounder of #BlackLivesMatter), Zon Moua, (Freedom, Inc.), Judith LeBlanc (Native Organizers Alliance), Isa Noyola (Transgender Law Center), and Chris Crass (educator and author). The video is available here: www.colorlines.com/articles/watch-multiracial-movements-black-lives-plenary-facing-race-2016.
- #BlackLivesMatter cofounders Alicia Garza, Patrisse Cullors, and Opal Tometi participated in a powerful introductory interview for *TED Talks*, recorded in October 2016.
- Alicia Garza wrote a reflection about her role in the movement: "A Herstory of the #BlackLivesMatter Movement." *Feminist Wire*, 7 October 2014, thefeministwire.com/2014/10/blacklivesmatter-2/.
- Spoken word artist, attorney, and #BlackLivesMatter activist Nikkita Oliver performs her original work: "Black Lives Matter." *KCTS9*, 28 October 2015, kcts9.org/programs/in-close/why-black-lives-matter-nikkita-oliver.
- Roberts, Frank Leon. *Black Lives Matter Syllabus*. 2017, www.blacklivesmattersyllabus.com/.
- Taylor, Keeanga-Yamahtta. *From #BlackLivesMatter to Black Liberation*. Haymarket Books, 2016.
- *A Vision for Black Lives: Policy Demands for Black Power, Freedom & Justice*. The Movement for Black Lives, policy.m4bl.org/.

1C) Question the census. As Steps 3 and 4 explained, the census has been used since the founding of this nation every ten years to construct and reconstruct racial categories. We cannot forget that the census originally contributed to the institution of slavery, as outlined in the Constitution's Three-Fifth's Compromise (see Step 3). And the census also contributed to the ideology that races are biologically distinct and hierarchical. The language of the census affects a cascade of forms that many people regularly encounter when they apply for employment, government services, schools, and more. Read and consider the work of former director of the Census Bureau Kenneth Prewitt in his 2013 book *What Is Your Race? The Census and Our Flawed Efforts to Classify Americans*. The recommended actions here focus on the challenging questions we need to ask about the continued use of the census:

- What effect does the continued use of racial categories in the census have on the people who fill out the forms? For example, when I teach the idea that race is a social construct, students often ask, "If race is made up, then why are there so many forms that ask me for my race?"
- What effect does the language of those racial categories in the census have on the people who fill out the forms?
- What happens when people don't know how to answer these questions?
- Can a tool used for something so devastating in the past be used today to protect civil rights (as the current census website states)?
- If the purpose of racial categories in the census today is to protect civil rights, what alternatives do we have to protect those rights aside from the use of the census? In other words, if the purpose is to protect marginalized communities, why not just work directly with those communities and have them determine their needs?
- Is it possible that the persistent use of racial categories in the census lends legitimacy to a racial hierarchy?
- How do questions in the census about race relate to its purpose of providing information for mapping Congressional districts? If we get greater Congressional representation by filling out the census but don't want to support the persistent use of questions about race, how do we reconcile that?
- What should the 2020 census look like? For example, as Step 4 explained, the 2010 census had one question on the respondent's "origin," but it was essentially just a yes/no question

on whether the respondent identified as "Hispanic, Latino, or Spanish." Then a separate question asked for the respondent's "race" and included options related to the categories of white, black, Asian, American Indian, and Pacific Islander, but not to Latinx identity. There were no separate categories for Middle Eastern or North African, which the census website says is included in "White" (see www.census.gov/topics/population/race/about.html). On October 4, 2016, the Pew Research Center shared a proposal for the 2020 census that makes several changes to these categories (see www.pewresearch.org/fact-tank/2016/10/04/federal-officials-may-revamp-how-americans-identify-race-ethnicity-on-census-and-other-forms/). It combines the "origin" and "race" questions together. It also adds a new category, "Middle Eastern or North African." The proposal keeps all of the original five racial categories and, by adding the "origin" question and one new category, there are now seven categories, and the respondent can check one or multiple boxes. Furthermore, the proposal indicates the Census Bureau is deciding whether to use the word "race," "origin," or "category" for this question.

- Does anything really change if the word "race" is removed and replaced with "category"? Is that like taking down the "Whites Only" sign from an institution in the 1950s but keeping everything else the same?

- How does this proposal or any future proposals for the census relate to the "1997 Office of Management and Budget (OMB) standards on race and ethnicity," to which, as the census website states, it "must adhere" (see www.census.gov/topics/population/race/about.html)?

- What happens when an organization representing a marginalized group works with the Census Bureau to get that group added as a category but then some individuals from that marginalized group feel targeted when they fill out the form? For example, several decades ago, "Mexican-American leaders worked to get a Hispanic-ethnicity question added to the census" (Goodman et al. 168). That work led to the "origin" question previously described, which has been on the census for the past four census cycles. More recently, "Arab Americans asked that a separate Arab category be included. They hoped for data to be collected that would help monitor discrimination against them as a minority group" (Goodman et al. 160). The 2020 census proposal described earlier appears to carry that out. However, there seems to be a disconnect between community leaders advocating for a separate category to represent their community and individuals who feel that a separate category targets them. For example, in my workshops and classes, when members of marginalized communities analyze the history of the census, the 2010 census, and the 2020 census proposal, they express concern about how these categories make them feel confused, targeted, and exploited.

2. Resist the Divide-and-Conquer Strategies That Created Race and Racism

For centuries, we have been manipulated to support divide-and-conquer strategies that protect the interests of a small, white, wealthy elite, as this manual has explained. We need to recognize and resist the many ways that capitalism, patriarchy, and colonialism operate within the Racism Machine to divide and conquer us and to teach us to compete with each other for resources that are supposedly scarce, all the while the white elite protect their wealth and status quo. The media, criminal justice system, education, and many other systems perpetuate powerful stereotypes and ideologies that block potential coalition building.

2A) **Support indigenous rights.** As Step 1 explains, the construction of the Racism Machine depended on creating a belief that persists today that indigenous people are uncivilized and that their land doesn't belong to them, which is part of the divide-and-conquer mentality.

- For those who are not familiar with indigenous history and activism, learn the history that many nonnatives don't learn.
  - Read the #StandingRockSyllabus (see nycstandswith standingrock.wordpress.com/standingrocksyllabus/).

- Follow indigenous media, like Indian Country Media Network (see indiancountrymedianetwork.com/) and The 90%: Stories of Diaspora from Indian Country (www. nativeninetypercent.com/).
- Follow the work of Jacqueline Keeler and Judith LeBlanc.
- Read *An Indigenous Peoples' History of the United States* by Roxanne Dunbar-Ortiz. See also:
  - Kuo, Rachel. "Why Racial Justice Work Needs to Address Settler Colonialism and Native Rights." *Everyday Feminism*, 16 August, 2015, everydayfeminism.com/ 2015/08/racial-justice-native-rights/.
- Learn more about indigenous children forcibly removed to boarding schools (described briefly in Step 3). See, for example:
  - *The National Native American Boarding School Healing Coalition*. www.boardingschoolhealing.org/.
  - Walker, Taté. "The Horrifying Legacy of Indian Boarding Schools Hasn't Ended—Here's What You Need to Know." *Everyday Feminism*, 11 October, 2015, everydayfeminism.com/2015/10/indian-boarding-school-legacy/.
  - Kilgore, James. "Mass Incarceration Since 1492: Native American Encounters With Criminal Injustice." *Truthout*. 7 February 2016. www.truth-out.org/news/ item/34725-mass-incarceration-since-1492-native-american-encounters-with-criminal-injustice.
- Find out how treaties with indigenous nations can be honored.
- Support indigenous activism (Native Organizers Alliance, Association of American Indian Farmers, and Indigenous Environmental Network, for example).
- Support campaigns to resist the building of pipelines that enter or impact indigenous lands (like the Dakota Access Pipeline and PennEast).
- Find out how to support campaigns by indigenous communities in your area.

- Support campaigns to change offensive mascot names that dehumanize indigenous peoples (see, for example, Eradicating Offensive Native Mascotry).
- Recognize that the land that most of us occupy in the US is stolen land.

2B) Learn about and resist the extreme capitalism that has developed over the past decades that maintains a divide-and-conquer mentality.

- Watch Robert Reich's documentary *Inequality for All*, as Step 4 briefly describes, and explore the film's website for its graphics and action items. Organize a film screening and discussion to raise awareness and take action on the damage caused by an extreme gap between the rich and the poor, deregulation, stagnant wages, corporate lobbying power, union busting, and more.
- Read: Hacker, Jacob S. and Paul Pierson. *Winner-Take-All Politics: How Washington Made the Rich Richer—and Turned Its Back on the Middle Class*. Simon & Schuster, 2010. Watch the documentary *Inside Job*, 2010.
- Work to get money out of politics. Learn more about specific campaign finance reform proposals. Corporations are not people, and in a democracy, it is not acceptable for big business to have political influence, as Step 4 briefly explains. Learn about ALEC, the *Citizens United* Supreme Court decision, and the role of the Koch brothers.
  - Navigate the "Kochtopus," a powerful info-graphic that reveals the relationships between the Koch brothers, corporations, politics, and many other systems. Figure out how you can boycott products and companies and otherwise resist their power (see kochcash.org/the-kochtopus/).
  - Read and organize a discussion about Jane Mayer's book *Dark Money: The Hidden History of the Billionaires Behind the Rise of the Radical Right*.
- Support local businesses that have racially just policies and practices.

- Support national businesses that are independent and have racially just policies and practices.

- Participate in local and national boycotts of products and companies when their policies and practices conflict with racial justice. Sometimes these campaigns begin on social media, and sometimes it's word of mouth. As consumers, we have a lot more power than we think we do.

- When political candidates focus on economic justice alone as the solution, push them to prioritize racial justice and develop an intersectional approach.

- Recognize the danger of corporate consolidation of media (meaning that only a handful of large media corporations own almost all networks, stations, production companies, and other media-related companies). This interactive infographic helps illustrate this consolidation of power and the massive profit involved: www.freepress.net/ownership/chart.

2C) Resist narratives and racial stereotypes from all of our systems that support divide-and-conquer strategies.

- Watch, share, and discuss MTV's web series *Decoded* by Franchesca Ramsey. These videos are usually less than ten minutes, and they each tackle a particular racial justice issue with an intersectional approach, using humor, pop culture references, and some history. (Educators, these short videos are a great way to kick-start a discussion.) There are now several seasons' worth of episodes, but here are a few of the most notable episodes (see youtube.com):
  - "Why Does MTV's Decoded Hate White People?!?"
  - "The Surprisingly Racist History of 'Caucasian'"
  - "10 Excuses Used To Deny Racism DEBUNKED!"
  - "Where Are You REALLY From???"
  - "You CAN'T Sound White!"
  - "7 Myths about Cultural Appropriation DEBUNKED!"
- Support campaigns that represent undocumented people as human beings, not as "illegal." Find out how you can

best support undocumented people in your community (see action #3B).

- Recognize the wide diversity within the Asian American community so you don't perpetuate the "model minority" stereotype of Asian Americans. Keep in mind the danger of a good minority-versus-bad minority dichotomy that serves the status quo. Resisting it can include many strategies, like not assuming that all Asian American students are inherently good at math and don't need help.
    - ○ Learn more about the extensive research on the model minority myth described in Step 4. See, for example:
        - − "Asian Americans and Pacific Islanders: Facts, Not Fiction: Setting the Record Straight." *The College Board*, 2008, secure-media.collegeboard.org/digitalServices/ pdf/professionals/asian-americans-and-pacific-islanders-facts-not-fiction.pdf.
        - − Wingfield, Adia Harvey. "The Professional Burdens of Being a 'Model Minority.'" *Atlantic*, 6 June 2016, www.the-atlantic.com/business/archive/2016/06/professional-burdens-model-minority-asian-americans/485492/.
        - − "Model Minority Stereotype for Asian Americans." *Counseling and Mental Health Center*, University of Texas, 2017, cmhc.utexas.edu/modelminority.html.
- Watch the video "Dear Mom, Dad, Uncle, Auntie: Black Lives Matter to Us, Too." This "Open Letter Project on Anti-Blackness" is a powerful rejection of the model minority stereotype and a powerful statement of support for #Black-LivesMatter. See lettersforblacklives.com/dear-mom-dad-uncle-auntie-black-lives-matter-to-us-too-7ca577d59f4c.
- Reject the criminalization of black and Latinx people (see actions #3A, #3B, and #3C). Consider how the rise of the criminalization of black and Latinx people corresponds to the rising popularity of TV shows and film featuring police and government agents (FBI, CIA, etc.) as the heroes. Activist, filmmaker, and writer dream hampton suggested at a Facing Race conference in 2014 that this increasingly popular "agent of the state"

character has contributed to the normalization of the criminal justice system, mass incarceration, and actions by the police and other government agencies over the past few decades, even when such characters were played by actors of color.

- If you work in advertising or marketing, use a lens of racial justice to examine the messages that your company's images and words potentially send to viewers, readers, and customers. How might these words and images be inadvertently reinforcing racial stereotypes? How diverse are the people in your ads? What kinds of assumptions related to race are being made during the production of these words and images? Recognize the long history of racism in advertising, and work to resist that history. (See action #3C.)

2D) Support interracial and intersectional coalitions where those with more power are held accountable to those with less power.

- Recognize how divide-and-conquer strategies can operate within interracial coalitions, especially how members of dominant groups (like white men and white women) can consciously or unconsciously support patriarchy and white supremacy. Develop strategies to address this.
- Learn about and support the work of coalitions, including: Southerners On New Ground (SONG), Freedom, Inc., EBASE, Grassroots Global Justice Alliance, South Asian Americans Leading Together (SAALT), Enlace, DRUM—South Asian Organizing Center, Council on American-Islamic Relations (CAIR), #Our100, National Domestic Workers Alliance, Forward Together, Mijente, Black Alliance for Just Immigration, National Latina Institute for Reproductive Health, Anna Julia Cooper Center, and Committee Against Anti-Asian Violence (CAAAV).
- Students: Cultural clubs and organizations can partner together to form an interracial coalition to create events that educate the larger student body about the issues described in this manual. They could also partner together to work on campaigns to address racial justice at the school and/or in

the community. For strategies on getting started, consider Boston College's "Eradicate Institutional Racism Campus Toolkit" (see bostoncollegeracism.tumblr.com/Toolkit).

- Community groups: Religious communities and civic organizations, which are often racially segregated, can partner together to form interracial coalitions to create events, host discussions, and take action on racial justice issues.

2E) Support social justice theater that engages the audience in intersectional and experiential performance and analysis. The Meta Theatre Company of New Jersey is a great example (see www.themetatheatrecompany.org/). Learn about Theatre of the Oppressed, based on Paulo Freire's *Pedagogy of the Oppressed.*

2F) Read recent work that examines systemic racism today, organize book discussions, and create action plans. Here are some examples of such recent work:

- Anderson, Carol. *White Rage: The Unspoken Truth of Our Racial Divide.* Bloomsbury, 2016.
- Davis, Angela Y. *Freedom Is a Constant Struggle: Ferguson, Palestine, and the Foundations of a Movement.* Haymarket Books, 2016.
    - See this published excerpt of her book: www.truth-out.org/opinion/item/35355-black-liberation-the-ghosts-of-the-past-the-potential-of-the-future.
- Glaude, Eddie S., Jr. *Democracy in Black: How Race Still Enslaves the American Soul.* Crown Publishers, 2016.
    - See Glaude's interview with Bill Moyers: www.newblackmaninexile.net/2016/05/bill-moyers-in-conversation-eddie.html.
- Hill, Marc Lamont. *Nobody: Casualties of America's War on the Vulnerable, from Ferguson to Flint and Beyond.* Atria Books, 2016.
- Kendi, Ibram X. *Stamped from the Beginning: The Definitive History of Racist Ideas in America.* Nation Books, 2016.

    ○ See this published excerpt of his book: www.alternet.
org/books/how-colorblind-rhetoric-and-multicultural-
ideology-made-america-more-racist.

- Smith, Mychal Denzel. *Invisible Man, Got the Whole World Watching: A Young Black Man's Education.* Nation Books, 2016.
- Taylor, Keeanga-Yamahtta. *From #BlackLivesMatter to Black Liberation.* Haymarket Books, 2016.
  - ○ Note that Haymarket Books sponsored a conversation with Angela Davis and Keeanga-Yamahtta Taylor on November 16, 2016, and a conversation that Keeanga-Yamahtta Taylor moderated with Michelle Alexander and Naomi Klein on May 9, 2017. Videos of these events are available online, especially via Haymarket's website and Facebook page.

2G) Read work from the civil rights movement that examines systemic racism, organize book discussions, and create action plans that connect this work to the present. Consider, for example:

- Baldwin, James. *The Fire Next Time.* Vintage, 1993. Watch *I Am Not Your Negro.*
- Davis, Angela. *An Autobiography.* International Publishers, 1988.
- Davis, Angela. *Women, Race & Class.* Vintage Books, 1983.
- While many people are familiar with Martin Luther King's "Letter from a Birmingham Jail" and his "I Have a Dream Speech," many of his other more radical speeches demand our attention, including "Beyond Vietnam" and "Where Do We Go From Here?"
- "The Combahee River Collective Statement."
- Lorde, Audre. "The Master's Tools Will Never Dismantle the Master's House."

3. Focus on Systems. (Find additional context in Step 4.)

3A) End mass incarceration.

- Learn about and support the work and actions of specific organizations (Equal Justice Initiative, Hands Up United, the ACLU, Campaign Zero, the Sentencing Project, the Innocence Project, WeCopwatch, Amnesty International, Justice Policy Institute and the Vera Institute of Justice, for example).

- If you haven't seen Ava DuVernay's documentary *13th*, watch it (available on Netflix). The film brilliantly explains how the Thirteenth Amendment did not abolish slavery for those labeled "criminal," as Steps 3 and 4 describe. Once you see this film, encourage more people to see it. Host an informal screening at your house with family and/or friends. Work with a local library, community center, your place of employment, and/or school to host a screening and discussion.

- Another related and powerful documentary is *Slavery by Another Name*, based on the book of the same title by Douglas Blackmon, which focuses on how post–Civil War blacks were criminalized and forced to labor through convict leasing. This PBS documentary can be viewed and discussed in local film screenings.

- Support the latest criminal justice campaigns by Color of Change (see colorofchange.org/campaigns/). They create powerful racial justice campaigns that address a variety of systems.

- Color of Change also put together an exceptional report titled "Not to Be Trusted: Dangerous Levels of Inaccuracy in TV Crime Reporting in NYC," which is an excellent resource for connecting different systems together and showing how individuals interact with these systems. The report includes an info-graphic (p. 11) that shows how the police overtarget black people in NYC, which leads to a disproportionate arrest rate, which the media then exaggerate in their crime reporting, which in turn leads TV viewers to believe in black criminality, which in turn affects these viewers' decisions about black people at work (as a judge or a potential employer) or in their personal life (when riding a subway). This very powerful info-graphic can be a great focus of discussion for classes and community groups. Find the full report, including this info-graphic, here: s3.amazonaws.com/s3.colorofchange.org/images/ColorOfChangeNewsAccuracyReportCardNYC.pdf.

- Watch and share the following introductory videos and info-graphics. Consider how you can integrate them into your classroom or community-based discussion.
  - ○ "Mass Incarceration, Visualized." *Atlantic*, 11 September 2015, www.theatlantic.com/video/index/404890/prison-inherited-trait/.
  - ○ "The Enduring Myth of Black Criminality." *Atlantic*, 10 September 2015, www.theatlantic.com/video/index/404674/enduring-myth-of-black-criminality/.
  - ○ "Criminal Justice Facts." *The Sentencing Project*, 2017, www.sentencingproject.org/criminal-justice-facts/.
  - ○ "Racial Disparity." *The Sentencing Project*, 2017, www.sentencingproject.org/issues/racial-disparity/.
  - ○ Kahn, Andrew and Chris Kirk. "What It's Like to Be Black in the Criminal Justice System." *Slate*, 9 August 2015, www.slate.com/articles/news_and_politics/crime/2015/08/racial_disparities_in_the_criminal_justice_system_eight_charts_illustrating.html.
- Develop an intersectional understanding of mass incarceration, especially how mass incarceration affects women of color, particularly transwomen of color. See, for example:
  - ○ *FREE CeCe!* Jac Gares Media, Inc., 2016. [This documentary features CeCe McDonald, a transwoman of color who was incarcerated in a men's prison for defending herself against a racist and transphobic attack.]
  - ○ Williams, Timothy. "Number of Women in Jail Has Grown Far Faster Than That of Men, Study Says." *New York Times*, 17 August 2016, nyti.ms/2k52Ke7.
- Learn how plea bargains are overused to the detriment of justice. Michelle Alexander discusses this in *The New Jim Crow*, and the PBS documentary series *Frontline* created an excellent episode on this issue titled "The Plea," which

originally aired on June 17, 2004, and is currently available at www.pbs.org/video/2216784391/.

- Consider the recommendations in the following reports:
  - "Reducing Racial Disparity in the Criminal Justice System: A Manual for Practitioners and Policymakers." The Sentencing Project, 2008, www.sentencingproject. org/wp-content/uploads/2016/01/Reducing-Racial-Disparity-in-the-Criminal-Justice-System-A-Manual-for-Practitioners-and-Policymakers.pdf.
  - "Final Report of the President's Task Force on Twenty-First Century Policing." Office of Community Oriented Policing Services, May 2015, cops.usdoj.gov/pdf/taskforce/taskforce_finalreport.pdf.
  - "Investigation of the Ferguson Police Department." United States Department of Justice Civil Rights Division, 4 March 2015, www.justice.gov/sites/default/files/opa/press-releases/attachments/2015/03/04/ferguson_police_department_report.pdf.
- Learn and take action to end overpolicing of communities of color (stop-and-frisk, racial profiling, high arrest rates, and more).
  - Learn how the fees and fines collected lead to debtors' prison. Read the following articles, share, and discuss them:
    - Burdeen, Cherise Fanno. "The Dangerous Domino Effect of Not Making Bail." *Atlantic*, 12 April 2016, www.theatlantic.com/politics/archive/2016/04/the-dangerous-domino-effect-of-not-making-bail/477906/.
    - Benns, Whitney and Blake Strode. "Debtors' Prison in 21st-Century America." *Atlantic*, 23 February 2016, www.theatlantic.com/business/archive/2016/02/debtors-prison/462378/.
  - Support the ACLU's campaign to "end modern-day debtors' prisons" (see www.aclu.org/feature/ending-modern-day-debtors-prisons).

- ○ Support Color of Change's campaign that focuses on passing bail reform in California (in coordination with the Essie Justice Group), because the bail bond industry makes a massive profit from incarceration (see act. colorofchange.org/sign/ca-bail-reform).
- End the privatization of prisons (which creates enormous profits for shareholders).
  - ○ Support the Prison Divestment Movement (see prison-divest.com/).
  - ○ Support the National Prison Divestment Campaign (see www.enlaceintl.org/prison-divestment and the corresponding Toolkit for Campus Organizers at media.wix.com/ugd/3e7183_00a8fc17c2ac4b0f9eae8c8090e8382f.pdf).
- Find out how you can support reentry programs in your community.
  - ○ See, for example, *A New Way of Life Re-Entry Project*. 2017, www.anewwayoflife.org/.
- Support restorative justice.
- Support legislation and their sponsoring elected officials that seek to reverse the criminalization of drug use and the harsh sentencing laws that were part of the War on Drugs.
  - ○ Support Color of Change's campaign (begun in May 2017) that resists Attorney General Jeff Sessions's recent mandate to strengthen the War on Drugs (see act. colorofchange.org/sign/no_sessions_war_on_drugs).
  - ○ See evidence and recommendations from the ACLU, like their report, "The War on Marijuana in Black and White," available at www.aclu.org/files/assets/aclu-thewaronmarijuana-rel2.pdf. It breaks down evidence state by state of racial disparities in arrest rates.
- Support rights for ex-offenders, including employment opportunities ("ban the box"), educational opportunities, voting, jury duty, and access to social services and resources. See, for example:

- ○ Turner, Nicholas. "A Home After Prison." *New York Times*, 21 June 2016, nyti.ms/2nxkXn6.
- Hold prosecutors accountable when they campaign, and support candidates who have a racial justice approach (if the position of prosecutor is an elected position in your state).
- End police brutality. Support protests to raise awareness. Speak out about these issues at your local town council meetings, and hold your local elected officials accountable for decisions they make regarding police departments. Many of the organizations (like Campaign Zero, #BlackLivesMatter, and Hands Up United) included in this section offer specific recommendations.
- End widespread sexual assault by officers inside prisons. See, for example:
  - ○ Goldstein, Joseph. "Brooklyn Prison Supervisors Charged With Sexually Assaulting Inmates." *New York Times*, 25 May 2017, nyti.ms/2s136WL.
- End the school-to-prison pipeline (see action #3D).
- Work to abolish the death penalty.
  - ○ See Amnesty International's extensive resources and actions at www.amnestyusa.org/issues/death-penalty/.
- Learn about the prison abolition movement. (See, for example, Angela Davis's *Are Prisons Obsolete?* Seven Stories Press, 2003.)
- Organize reading groups to discuss the following, and develop action plans:
  - ○ Alexander, Michelle. *The New Jim Crow: Mass Incarceration in the Age of Colorblindness.* The New Press, 2012.
    - – Alexander's *TED Talk* "The Future of Race in America" is a great introduction to her work.
    - – Also see the action guides that were developed in response to Alexander's books:
      - → The New Jim Crow *Study Guide and Call to Action.* The Veterans of Hope Project, 2013.

→ Hunter, Daniel. *Building a Movement to End the New Jim Crow: An Organizing Guide.* The Veterans of Hope Project, 2015.

○ Benforado, Adam. *Unfair: The New Science of Criminal Injustice.* Crown Publishers, 2015.

○ Camp, Jordan T. and Christina Heatherton, editors. *Policing the Planet: Why the Policing Crisis Led to Black Lives Matter.* Verso, 2016.

○ Kilgore, James. *Understanding Mass Incarceration: A People's Guide to the Key Civil Rights Struggle of Our Time.* The New Press, 2015.

○ Stevenson, Bryan. *Just Mercy: A Story of Justice and Redemption.* Spiegel & Grau, 2015.

– Stevenson's *TED Talk* "We Need to Talk about an Injustice" is an excellent introduction to his book. He also did a short video for *History Now* called "Bryan Stevenson Wants Us to Talk More About Slavery" that is a valuable introduction (available on YouTube).

3B) End mass deportations and immigrant detention.

• Learn more about immigration with the reading list of the #ImmigrationSyllabus at editions.lib.umn.edu/immigration syllabus/.

• Organize reading groups to discuss relevant books, including:

○ Chomsky, Aviva. *Undocumented: How Immigration Became Illegal.* Beacon Press, 2014.

– Her interview on *Democracy Now* is a great introduction. See www.democracynow.org/2014/5/30/how_ immigration_became_illegal_aviva_chomsky.

○ Perez, William. *We ARE Americans: Undocumented Students Pursuing the American Dream.* Stylus, 2009.

• Learn the damage of calling a human being "illegal." Join the campaign to "drop the I word." Find tools and resources here: www.raceforward.org/practice/tools/drop-i-word-campaign.

• Follow current federal policy changes and contact elected officials to share concerns. See, for example:

- o Davis, Julie Hirschfeld and Ron Nixon. "Trump Budget Takes Broad Aim at Undocumented Immigrants." *New York Times*, 25 May 2017, nyti.ms/2qZHc94.
- o Dickerson, Caitlin. "Immigration Arrests Rise Sharply as a Trump Mandate Is Carried Out." *New York Times*, 17 May 2017, nyti.ms/2rsOCyO.
- Keep up with actions recommended to address federal policy changes and actions. See, for example:
  - o Cárdenas, Ariana Rosas. "How to Fight Trump's Racist Immigration Policies." *The Nation*, 27 January 2017, www.thenation.com/article/how-to-fight-trumps-racist-immigration-policies/.
- Watch the documentary *Harvest of Empire*, which provides valuable background on immigration. It's based on the book of the same title by journalist Juan González. Organize a film screening and discussion about the film.
- Follow and support organizations that seek to end mass deportation and immigrant detention, including: Detention Watch Network, #Not1More, Black Alliance for Just Immigration, United We Dream, National Immigration Law Center, and Immigrant Legal Resource Center.
- Use the resources of Amnesty International to organize protests (like #NoBanNoWall) and learn more about their campaigns.
- Learn about "sanctuary city" status and "fair and welcoming community" status. Support local immigrant communities in whatever ways they would find most valuable.

3C) Recognize that representation matters.

- Learn more about fundamental aspects of why representation matters, whether it's in news media, popular culture, policy, or other systems.
  - o Read the thorough reports "Moving the Race Conversation Forward" created by Race Forward, downloadable here: www.raceforward.org/research/reports/moving-race-conversation-forward. They include Part 1, "How the

Media Covers Racism, and Other Barriers to Productive Racial Discourse," and Part 2, "Racial Discourse Change in Practice," which uses case studies to analyze action.

- Support networks and entertainment companies that feature a wide range of racially diverse, three-dimensional characters in their popular culture.
  - Share and discuss sources that explain why this work is so important. See, for example:
    - Harris, Aisha. "Same Old Script: On screen, TV is more diverse than ever. Why aren't writing staffs catching up?" *Slate*, 18 October 2015, www.slate.com/articles/arts/culturebox/2015/10/diversity_in_the_tv_writers_room_writers_and_showrunners_of_color_lag_far.html.
    - "The Diversity Gap in the Academy Awards." Lee & Low Books, 2015. i1.wp.com/blog.leeandlow.com/wp-content/uploads/2015/02/Academy_Awards_Infographic-2015-lg.jpg.
    - Singh, Maanvi. "How Shows Like 'Will & Grace' And 'Black-ish' Can Change Your Brain." *Code Switch*, NPR, 31 August 2015. www.npr.org/sections/codeswitch/2015/08/31/432294253/how-shows-like-will-grace-and-black-ish-can-change-your-brain.
    - "Viola Davis Gives Powerful Speech About Diversity and Opportunity: Emmys 2015." 20 September 2015, www.youtube.com/watch?v=OSpQfvd_zkE.
    - Chow, Keith. "Why Won't Hollywood Cast Asian Actors?" *New York Times*, 22 April 2016, nyti.ms/2jOuHqG. See also the corresponding slideshow: "Whitewashing, a Long History." *New York Times*, www.nytimes.com/slideshow/2016/04/22/opinion/whitewashing-a-long-history/s/chow-ss-slide-HTTQ.html?_r=0.
    - Rice, Zak Cheney. "7 Things About Native Americans You'll Never Learn From the Mainstream Media." *Mic*, 21 August 2015, mic.com/articles/124160/7-things-about-native-americans-you-ll-never-learn-from-the-mainstream-media#.NZev6QPQ4.

– Nittle, Nadra Kareem. "5 Common Native American Stereotypes in Film and Television." *ThoughtCo*, 2 March 2017, www.thoughtco.com/native-american-stereotypes-in-film-television-2834655.

– "The Impact of Media Stereotypes on Opinions and Attitudes Towards Latinos." *National Hispanic Media Coalition*, September 2012, www.nhmc.org/wp-content/uploads/2014/01/LD_NHMC_Poll_Results_Sept.2012.pdf.

– Leguizamo, John. "'Too Bad You're Latin.'" *New York Times*, 21 October 2016, nyti.ms/2ksR9cT.

– Bahr, Anna. "Latinos Onscreen, Conspicuously Few." *New York Times*, 18 June 2014, nyti.ms/2s8k6e1.

– "Media and Art Activism." *Popular Culture*. Cultural Politics, 2017, culturalpolitics.net/popular_culture.

– I'm also including my own article on the TV show *Scandal* to provide strategies for applying critical race theory to television and audience reception: Gaffney, Karen. "'Standing in the Sun': 'Scandal' in the Age of 'The New Jim Crow.'" 24 May 2016, www.popmatters.com/feature/standing-in-the-sun-scandal-in-the-age-of-the-new-jim-crow/.

• Learn how tokenism, whitewashing, and the white savior can serve as obstacles to racial justice. The above sources (and many others) explain these problems that we need to keep in mind as we advocate for three-dimensional characters that represent marginalized people as fully human.

• Contact producers, networks, and media companies to advocate for racial diversification at every level (from behind-the-scenes crew to writers to directors to actors). Advocate for three-dimensional roles for people of color and complain and boycott when you don't see them.

• Support organizations that work on media activism, like the Center for Media Justice, Color of Change, and Unbound: Pop Culture for Social Change.

- Support artists who explicitly address racial justice, like founder of 1Hood Media Jasiri X, founder of RAPtivism Aisha Fukushima, director Ava DuVernay, and performers/creators Hari Kondabolu, Hasan Minhaj, Keegan-Michael Key, Jordan Peele, Issa Rae, Aziz Ansari, and many more.
- Support organizations that increase opportunities for people of color in the media (CoCre.TV and Weird Enough Productions, for example).
- Support independent media.
- Recognize the need to analyze all forms of popular culture. Saying it's "just entertainment" often blocks much-needed discussion and analysis.

3D) Support liberation-based education. (Note that these suggestions are for parents, community members, educators, and students alike. For more specific suggestions for educators, see action #5.)

- Learn about patterns of racial school segregation in your region. For example, in 2013, Rutgers University published a report titled "New Jersey's Apartheid and Intensely Segregated Urban Schools," which identified New Jersey as one of the most racially segregated states in the country, with one of the most racially segregated school systems. Those of us living in the North need to acknowledge the seriousness of racial segregation in our region and abandon the mentality that we're the "good guys" (see ielp.rutgers.edu/docs/IELP%20final%20report%20on%20apartheid%20schools%20101013.pdf).
  - Work with communities of color to determine effective strategies to address racial segregation and gentrification.
- Support organizations that advocate liberation-based education (Teaching for Change, Teaching Tolerance, Zinn Education Project, Badass Teachers Association, Journey for Justice Alliance, Courageous Conversations, Border Crossers, National Opportunity to Learn Network, and the Alliance

to Reclaim Our Schools, for example). Note that some of these include great resources for parents.

- End the school-to-prison pipeline.
  - Learn the serious impact of this pipeline:
    - Morris, Monique W. *Pushout: The Criminalization of Black Girls in Schools.* The New Press, 2016.
    - Nelson, Libby. "The Hidden Racism of School Discipline, in 7 Charts." Vox, 31 October 2015, www.vox.com/2015/10/31/9646504/discipline-race-charts.
    - "School-to-Prison Pipeline." ACLU, 2017, www.aclu.org/issues/racial-justice/race-and-inequality-education/school-prison-pipeline.
    - Nelson, Libby and Lind, Dara. "The School to Prison Pipeline, Explained." *Justice Policy Institute*, 24 February 2015, www.justicepolicy.org/news/8775.
  - Advocate for restorative justice positions rather than police in your local schools.
  - Learn how antibullying policies and zero-tolerance policies can inadvertently support the school-to-prison pipeline by neutralizing the power dynamics of an incident. Conduct a power analysis of existing policies, and revise them to support racial justice.
  - Advocate for schools to examine their data on suspensions and expulsions and to take action (since children of color tend to be penalized more harshly than white children for similar behavior). See, for example:
    - Jacobs, Tom. "Racism in the Kindergarten Classroom." *Pacific Standard*, 2 February 2016, psmag.com/social-justice/racism-in-the-kindergarten-classroom.
    - Klein, Rebecca. "Black Students in the U.S. Get Criminalized While White Students Get Treatment." *Huffington Post*, 28 July 2015, www.huffingtonpost.com/entry/racial-disparities-american-schools_us_55b67572e4b0074ba5a576c1?67pvte29=&utm_hp_ref=black-voices.
    - "Racial Profiling in Preschool." *New York Times*, 8 October 2016, nyti.ms/2jDOxHX.

- Support school curricula that teach about race, racism, and racial justice.
  - Support professional development for teachers to help them with these curricula.
- Read Paulo Freire's *Pedagogy of the Oppressed* and engage with others about the need for liberation-based education.
- Support the creation of ethnic studies courses and programs in K–12 schools.
  - Organize a screening and discussion of the documentary film *Precious Knowledge*, which focuses on a high school Mexican American studies program that the state of Arizona banned.
  - Read and discuss articles that advocate for ethnic studies courses and programs, including:
    - "At-risk students improve when they take a race and ethnicity class—study." *The Guardian*, 14 January 2016, www.theguardian.com/education/2016/jan/14/stanford-study-at-risk-students-race-ethnicity-class-performance.
    - Klein, Rebecca. "These Underrepresented Students Are Tired of School Curriculums That Make Them Invisible." *Huffington Post*, 20 November 2015, www.huffingtonpost.com/entry/portland-ethnic-studies-campaign_us_564e41c3e4b0879a5b0a438c?ir=Education&section=education&utm_hp_ref=education.
    - Phippen, J. Weston. "How One Law Banning Ethnic Studies Led to Its Rise." *Atlantic*, 19 July 2015, www.theatlantic.com/education/archive/2015/07/how-one-law-banning-ethnic-studies-led-to-rise/398885/.
    - Anderson, Melinda D. "The Ongoing Battle Over Ethnic Studies." *Atlantic*, 7 March 2016, www.theatlantic.com/education/archive/2016/03/the-ongoing-battle-over-ethnic-studies/472422/.
    - Rich, Motoko. "For Young Latino Readers, an Image Is Missing." *New York Times*, 4 December 2012, nyti.ms/2kCBNyP.

- Attend local school board meetings to find out what is being done to address racial justice. Support educators and parents who are engaging in this work.
- Learn more about the negative impact of standardized testing in K–12 in recent years, especially in the context of race. See, for example:
  - Taylor, Kate. "Race and the Standardized Testing Wars." *New York Times*, 23 April 2016, nyti.ms/2jKUt1Q.
- Learn more about how gifted and talented programs in K–12 tend to overlook children of color, and take action. See, for example:
  - Dynarski, Susan. "Why Talented Black and Hispanic Students Can Go Undiscovered." *New York Times*, 8 April 2016, nyti.ms/2k9hA30.
- Recognize and discuss the serious concerns about charter schools. Read the NAACP's "Resolution on a Moratorium on Charter Schools" (see www.naacp.org/latest/statement-regarding-naacps-resolution-moratorium-charter-schools/).

3E) End the racial wealth gap and persistent racial segregation.

- Recognize the significance of the racial wealth gap.
  - See, for example: Kochhar, Rakesh and Richard Fry. "Wealth Inequality Has Widened along Racial, Ethnic Lines since End of Great Recession." *Fact Tank: News in the Numbers*, Pew Research Center, 12 December 2014, www.pewresearch.org/fact-tank/2014/12/12/racial-wealth-gaps-great-recession/.
  - Examining the issue of race and wealth helps reinforce the need for an intersectional analysis. For example, the commonly quoted statistic is that women make $.75 for every $1 a man makes, but that is only if the man and woman are white. If we compare the income of black women to white men, we see that it goes down to $.63. For indigenous women, it's $.58, and for Latinas, $.54. (See "How Does Race Affect the Gender Wage Gap?" *Economic* Justice, AAUW, 25 October 2016, www.aauw.org/2014/04/03/

race-and-the-gender-wage-gap/.) Furthermore, the African American Policy Forum reports that "The median
wealth for single Black women is $5.00" (see www.aapf.
org/healthdisparities).

- ○ Watch the short film *Black Heirlooms* available at "Watch:
  'Black Heirlooms' Examines the Toll of the Racial Wealth
  Gap on Black Families." *Shine*, For Harriet, 7 December 2014,
  shine.forharriet.com/2014/12/watch-black-heirlooms-
  examines-toll-of.html#axzz4iD43I7iu.
- If you haven't done so, read "The Case for Reparations" by
  Ta-Nehisi Coates, and organize discussions and actions
  based on this reading.
- Read and organize discussions and actions around Richard
  Rothstein's 2017 book *The Color of Law: A Forgotten History
  of How Our Government Segregated America*. Look for inter-
  views with Rothstein, including one on NPR's *Fresh Air*.
  Also see articles like:
  - ○ Eligon, John and Robert Gebeloff. "Affluent and Black,
    and Still Trapped by Segregation." *New York Times*, 20
    August 2016, nyti.ms/2k2FCNb.
- Support investment in communities of color.
- Find out what local, state, and federal legislation allows the
  racial wealth gap and segregation to persist, and advocate for
  change.
- Find out how redlining has affected your community. Was
  there a color-coded map of your city or town to identify
  black neighborhoods in red as "risky"? If so, raise awareness by organizing community-based discussions and
  actions.
  - ○ See, for example: *Mapping Inequality: Redlining in New
    Deal America*. dsl.richmond.edu/panorama/redlining.

3F) Engage in the political process.

- Get informed by reading about and/or attending trainings
  about strategies for making the political process more fair

(Demos, Democracy for America, MoveOn.org, and Citizen University, for example).

- Learn how you can become more politically engaged in order to take action. See, for example:
  ○ Chen, Brian X. "A Low-Tech Guide to Becoming More Politically Active." *New York Times*, 8 February 2017, nyti. ms/2kPrsTI.
- Meet with your elected officials to discuss your concerns about racially unjust laws and policies.
- Run for local office on a racial justice platform.
- Support local candidates who advocate for racial justice.
- Support voter registration drives.
- Recognize that the right to vote is seriously under attack, especially for people of color. Work to protect that right and to end voter identification laws. Step 4 briefly highlights how these rights have been rolled back since the Voting Rights Act was passed in 1965.
  ○ Follow campaigns on voting rights from Color of Change at colorofchange.org/campaigns/.
    – For example, as of May 2017, there is a campaign to "Oppose Presidential Commission on Election Integrity" (run by Vice President Mike Pence and Kansas Secretary of State Kris Kobach, who both have led efforts to disen-franchise communities of color).
  ○ Read and organize discussions and actions around Ari Berman's 2015 book *Give Us the Ballot: The Modern Struggle for Voting Rights in America*. Look for his many interviews, too.

3G) Support healthcare for everyone and a healthy environment for everyone.

- Confront the history of racism in medicine.
- Learn more about how race and racism affect health. Read, for example:

- o Varagur, Krithika. "How Can We Close The Black-White Sleep Gap?" *Huffington* Post, 29 February 2016, www. huffingtonpost.com/entry/black-white-sleep-gap_us_ 56c64123e4b0ec6725e20e4a?.
- o Silverstein, Jason. "How Racism Is Bad for Our Bodies." *Atlantic*, 12 March 2013 www.theatlantic.com/health/ archive/2013/03/how-racism-is-bad-for-our-bodies/ 273911/.
- Support organizations and campaigns that address environmental racism.
  - o Read, for example: Covert, Bryce. "Race Best Predicts Whether You Live Near Pollution." *The Nation*, 18 February 2016, www.thenation.com/article/race-best-predicts-whether-you-live-near-pollution/.
- Support organizations and campaigns that address food deserts.

4. Actions for Specific Audiences: White People

I want to take time here to speak directly to white people about action. Many white people tell me they don't know where to begin, and I think the first step is to recognize the history that got us to where we are. We live in an intensely racially segregated nation, and even states that pride themselves on being very diverse can be very racially segregated, like my own state of New Jersey. You'll find in what follows a series of general principles that I think are important for white people to keep in mind, followed by specific recommendations.

Principles

- Start by educating yourself. Read history, sociology, news, articles, and novels by people of color, and watch documentaries and feature films by people of color. That's a necessary education that should never come to an end. (The Action section that follows offers specific suggestions.)
- Before you take a racial justice action in your community or at your place of work, make sure you understand how this action

was decided upon. Were people of color involved in that decision? Figure out how you can be held accountable to people of color in the action you take.

- It's not fair to people of color if they must bear the burden of teaching white people that racism is a problem, that black lives really do matter. White people need to do the work of talking to other white people about racism, especially family and friends.
- Always keep an intersectional framework in mind. Recognize that it is only when the most marginalized are free that we are all free. The word "intersectionality" has recently become a popular term, but it goes back decades (see more in this section for resources).
- It's never too late to begin this work. I've been working with white members of my community who worry it's too late for them to begin a journey of education and activism for racial justice. I tell them no one is too young or too old to do this work. The more people we engage, the more powerful the change can be.
- The work is never over. I've also heard white people say that they don't need to attend another discussion or workshop about racial justice because "they're done," or "they got this." There is always more to learn, and there are always ways to grow. For white people to be the most effective at challenging white supremacy, we need to be able to recognize that we are never finished examining our own white privilege, that we are never finished learning how racism continues to affect people of color today. Actively resist the narratives we are told that support the Racism Machine. Ask yourself on a daily basis, how am I complicit in patterns of injustice? And what can I do to be less complicit? In other words, as white people, we need to become actively conscious that every day we breathe in the pollution of the Racism Machine (as Step 1 described) and question how it is affecting our decisions and our actions.
- Resist the dominant narratives that allow white people to perpetuate racism. These include myths like racism is over, reverse racism is the only real racism, people of color who are hired are not qualified, and black people are inherently criminal. These false ideologies are perpetuated throughout media and many other systems, and they allow white people to justify current levels of racial

inequality. Don't let the people you know get away with perpetuating these myths. Call them out on it by asking questions.

- Use the power analysis questions (and others like them) presented in the Introduction to help you determine if a bias is individual or systemic. Furthermore, if you're unsure how to handle a situation in which you have identified systemic racism, ask yourself more questions, like: Who has the power in this situation? How do you know? What are they doing with that power? Where are the voices of people of color? What is happening to those voices? How can you address intersectionality in your power analysis? How can you support justice?

- Resist the current narrative that our society is "colorblind" or that individuals can live in this country and be "colorblind." This entire manual explains how for centuries colonial America and then the US itself has been anything but colorblind. White people today may be taught that they are supposed to be colorblind and may be taught to treat everyone the same, but recognizing everyone's full humanity also means recognizing the systems of oppression that impact them. Telling a person of color "I don't see color" is not a compliment. It's an erasure of identity and a denial of current and past injustices. If you're not sure how to reconcile being told that being colorblind was the "good" or "polite" thing to do with all of the concern raised about a colorblind approach today, understanding this history can be very helpful. Legal scholar Ian F. Haney López wrote an insightful article for *Salon* in which he explains that during the civil rights movement, a colorblind approach was used effectively by racial justice activists, but after overt signs of racism were removed (the "whites only" sign), this colorblind approach was coopted by opponents of civil rights.
  - See "How Conservatives Hijacked 'Colorblindness' and Set Civil Rights Back Decades." *Salon*, 20 January 2014, www.salon.com/2014/01/20/how_conservatives_hijacked_color blindness_and_set_civil_rights_back_decades/.

- Over the past several years, there has been a lot of discussion of **micro-aggressions,** comments or slights that reinforce the larger system of oppression. For example, many black women have described instances in which white women make comments about black women's hair and even touch it, and this violation of personal space echoes a history that objectifies black women. White women often don't understand why this is not a compliment. That's where a power analysis is needed, which can reveal a seemingly innocuous action or comment as something that reinforces a larger system of oppression. It's important for white people to become more aware of this power (intent vs. impact). The white woman who makes a comment or touches the black woman's hair thinks of her own intention as positive, as a compliment, without recognizing how this comment reinforces white supremacy and can cause pain, anger, and frustration. The disconnect between intent and impact can lead to white people thinking that black people are angry all the time and overly sensitive. However, again, doing a power analysis is critical. The power analysis reveals that impact matters and that the impact relates to a much larger system of oppression that has been carried out for centuries. A white woman might say that people touch her hair, too, but it's not the same thing. White women have historically been identified as holding the female beauty standard, and white women were never put on the auction block as slaves in this country. Yes, one could say that any stranger touching another person is a violation of personal space, but it's so much more than that if the people involved replicate a power structure and pattern of oppression.

- Avoid **cultural appropriation**. Whether or not it's Halloween, wearing the clothes or hairstyle of a marginalized group can be a violation rather than appreciation. Do a power analysis to understand.
- Dismantling white supremacy is not the same as hating white people. Push back when you hear otherwise, and explain that we are focusing on a system. As white people, we have inherited a system of white supremacy that, for centuries, has perpetuated a racial hierarchy to protect a small, white, wealthy elite. The majority of white people are not part of that elite, yet many still work hard to protect the elite. Why? In hopes that someday they will join

the elite? Because at least they aren't at the bottom? Why would we want to accept a system that has caused centuries of genocide, slavery, and trauma? Wouldn't we want to dismantle this system? And build a fair and equitable society?

- One response to raising awareness about racism that appears throughout social media and sometimes in class or community discussions goes something like this: "I'm Irish [or substitute with another white ethnic identity], and my people were oppressed too. But we just worked hard, and we made it." I've seen historically inaccurate photos posted in social media trying to "prove" that Irish people were treated worse than black people. These beliefs reflect the same racial ideology at work in statements like "Racism is a thing of the past" or "Just work hard, and you'll be successful." Many people who make these statements are completely unfamiliar with the history and concepts presented in this book. In other words, they don't understand that the Racism Machine exists. See resources like:
  - Ignatiev, Noel. *How the Irish Became White*. Routledge, 1995.
  - Stack, Liam. "Debunking a Myth: The Irish Were Not Slaves, Too." *New York Times*, 17 March 2017, https://nyti.ms/2nz 747S.

- Another response to raising awareness about racism is that people of color just need to assume "personal responsibility." This response is another way of saying, "Just work hard, and you'll be successful." This focus on individuality takes all of the emphasis away from the systems and structures of the Racism Machine that cause inequality. **Respectability politics** can also be a similarly damaging narrative of personal responsibility because it sends the message that black people in particular just need to behave better and they'll be successful. Scholar and activist Brittney Cooper as well as #BlackLivesMatter activists have highlighted the problem of respectability politics.

Actions

- If you're new to these principles, start with the Recommended Resources listed in the Introduction.

- Read, follow, and listen to online media about racial justice on a daily basis created by people of color.
  - A few examples include Colorlines, This Week in Blackness, Center for Asian American Media, NPR's Code Switch, Latino USA, The Root, For Harriet, Hyphen, Feministing, Culture-Strike, Everyday Feminism, #EmergingUS, MPower Change, Indian Country Media Network, and Black Girl Nerds.
- Read and follow racial justice activists and writers of color like Keeanga-Yamahtta Taylor, Angela Davis, john a. powell, DiDi Delgado, Imani Gandy, Linda Sarsour, Kimberlé Crenshaw, Rinku Sen, Dorothy Roberts, Brittney Cooper, Jamelle Bouie, Jamilah King, Alicia Garza, Ta-Nehisi Coates, Melissa Harris-Perry, Tressie McMillan Cottom, Jacqueline Keeler, Roxane Gay, L. Joy Williams, Deepa Iyer, Dr. Goddess, Malkia Cyril, Eddie Moore, Jr., Elon James White, Amer F. Ahmed, Eric Liu, Maria Hinojosa, Kat Blaque, Rashad Robinson, Eddie S. Glaude, Jr., bell hooks, Issa Rae, Sister Outsider, Salamishah Tillet, Ileana Jiménez, Akiba Solomon, Lori Adelman, and Brittany Packnett.
- Read the books and articles in the Recommended Resources sections at the end of each chapter, but keep in mind these lists only include nonfiction. Also read literature by people of color.
- Attend conferences, workshops, and trainings about racial justice. A few examples include Undoing Racism (People's Institute for Survival and Beyond), Race Forward's conference Facing Race (held every two years) and their Racial Justice Leadership Institute trainings held periodically throughout the country, Citizen University in Seattle, the Privilege Institute's White Privilege Conference and Leadership Institute trainings, Crossroads Anti-racism Organizing & Training, Anti-Oppression Resource and Training Alliance (AORTA), NJ's Center for the Study of White American Culture, and an online program called "Healing from Toxic Whiteness." Participate in the Safety Pin Box (note that there is now a version for kids).
- Learn about and support the campaigns of racial justice organizations. See, for example: Race Forward, the Southern Poverty Law Center, Color of Change, the African American Policy Forum,

Black Lives Matter, Showing Up for Racial Justice, AWARE-LA, Black Youth Project and Black Youth Project 100, #Our100, the Ella Baker Center for Human Rights, INCITE!, South Asian Americans Leading Together (SAALT), the Dream Defenders, the Center for Social Inclusion, Dream Corps, the Arab American Association of NY, the Movement Strategy Center, Center for New Community, Advancement Project, Demos, 18 Million Rising, Higher Heights, People's Organization for Progress, and Haas Institute for a Fair and Inclusive Society.

- Talk to white friends and family about race and racism. This is an area about which I hear a lot of concern. Especially since the November 2016 election, many white people who care about racial justice do not want to talk to their friends and family who disagree with them. While I would not recommend engaging a self-proclaimed racist, most white people do not identify as racist. Systemic racism has persisted in part because white people are taught to believe that it doesn't exist. No one likes to be called out on being manipulated, but there are strategies for navigating these conversations, including asking questions rather than lecturing. It can also be helpful to reveal your own process of growth with an approach like: I never knew ___ until recently, when I read/watched ___.

- If you're a white parent of white children, it's never too early to start talking about race. Consider the following sources:
  - Dell'Antonia, KJ. "Talking About Racism With White Kids." *New York Times*, 25 November 2014, https://nyti.ms/2j GpAbx.
  - Harvey, Jennifer. "Are We Raising Racists?" *New York Times*, 14 March 2017, nyti.ms/2mFLdeL.
  - Howerton, Kristen. "Resources for Talking to Kids About Race and Racism." *Huffington Post*, 30 April, 2013, www.huffington post.com/kristen-howerton/talking-to-kids-race-racism-books_b_2618305.html.
  - Lormand, Stephanie. "Why White Parents Need to Talk About Race." *Mom's Rising*, 28 September 2016, www.momsrising. org/blog/why-white-parents-need-to-talk-about-race.

- ○ Moyer, Melinda Wenner. "Teaching Tolerance: How White Parents Should Talk to Their Young Kids about Race." *Slate*, 30 March 2014, www.slate.com/articles/double_x/the_kids/2014/03/teaching_tolerance_how_white_parents_should_talk_to_their_kids_about_race.html.
  - ○ Sanders, Topher. "'Only White People,' Said the Little Girl." *New York Times*, 13 October 2016, nyti.ms/2jCl925.
- Take "The 21-Day Racial Equity Habit Building Challenge." Note that the website has a wide range of resources (see www.debbyirving.com/21-day-challenge/).
- Recognize how you are invested in the Racism Machine (emotionally, financially, psychologically, etc.). This recognition requires daily attention. What would it take for you to divest? In other words, how are you a cog in the wheel in the Racism Machine?
- Support racial justice discussions, book talks, and events at your local libraries, houses of worship, schools, and community centers.
- Engage your friends, family members, and/or neighbors in an informal discussion about racial justice by watching a film together and discussing it.
- Help organize a more formal discussion about racial justice by working with a local organization to host a film screening and discussion or a common reading and discussion.
- Find out what racial justice issues people of color in your community are concerned about. Find out how you can support them, whether it's through going to town council meetings, talking to a local business, etc.
- If you attend a house of worship, encourage the leadership to organize book talks and film discussions that address racial justice.
- If you work outside of the home, consider how you can encourage your workplace to host a formal or informal book discussion or other type of event that addresses racial justice. It could even be an informal brown bag lunch.
- Strengthen your understanding of intersectionality, and keep an intersectional framework in mind throughout your daily life, work, and activism. There's always more to learn. If you need direction,

consider these resources, with a focus on the black feminist legal scholar who created the term "intersectionality," Kimberlé Crenshaw:

- Crenshaw, Kimberlé. "The Urgency of Intersectionality." *TED*, October 2016, www.ted.com/talks/kimberle_crenshaw_ the_urgency_of_intersectionality.
- Smooth, Jay. "Our New Video Series '#RaceAnd' Captures the Essence of Intersectionality." *Colorlines*. Race Forward, 4 May 2016, www.colorlines.com/articles/our-new-video-series- raceand-captures-essence-intersectionality.
- Crenshaw, Kimberlé. "Mapping the Margins: Intersectional- ity, Identity Politics, and Violence Against Women of Color." *Stanford Law Review*, vol. 43, July 1991, pp. 1241–1299; social difference.columbia.edu/files/socialdiff/projects/Article__ Mapping_the_Margins_by_Kimblere_Crenshaw.pdf.
- Collins, Patricia Hill and Sirma Bilge. *Intersectionality*. Polity, 2016.
- Recognize the long history of this concept by reading Sojourner Truth's "Ain't I A Woman?" speech delivered in 1851.
- Strengthen your understanding of how women of color have cri- tiqued feminism for normalizing whiteness and ignoring women of color. Consider these key texts from the 1980s and 1990s:
  - Anzaldúa, Gloria, editor. *Making Face, Making Soul, Haciendo Caras: Creative and Critical Perspectives by Feminists of Color*. Aunt Lute Books, 1990.
  - Hull, Gloria T., Patricia Bell Scott, and Barbara Smith, editors. *All the Women Are White, All the Blacks Are Men, But Some of Us Are Brave: Black Women's Studies*. The Feminist Press, 1982.
  - Matsuda, Mari J. *Where Is Your Body? And Other Essays on Race, Gender, and the Law*. Beacon Press, 1996.
  - Moraga, Cherríe and Gloria Anzaldúa, editors. *This Bridge Called My Back: Writings by Radical Women of Color*. Kitchen Table: Women of Color Press, 1983.
  - Smith, Barbara, editor. *Home Girls: A Black Feminist Anthology*. Kitchen Table: Women of Color Press, 1983.

- Take an implicit bias test on race, and reflect on the results. For example, as the Introduction explained, Harvard's Project Implicit has many Implicit Association Tests available here: implicit. harvard.edu/implicit/takeatest.html. This is an activity that can be done and reflected on individually, or it can be done in a group setting.
- Pay more attention to the words you use.
  - See, for example: Brown, Yawo. "The Subtle Linguistics of Polite White Supremacy." *Medium*, 14 August 2015, medium. com/@YawoBrown/the-subtle-linguistics-of-polite-white-supremacy-3f83c907ffff.
  - If you get called out on saying something racist, don't get defensive. Don't make it worse by trying to explain yourself. Accept that you're an imperfect human being, apologize, and learn.
  - Learn more about racial micro-aggressions, and avoid them.
- Pay more attention to how you respond to other people's names. Recent research shows that employers and teachers alike respond much more positively to a name that sounds white than those that sound black. Consider the following sources:
  - "Are Emily and Greg More Employable than Lakisha and Jamal? A Field Experiment on Labor Market Discrimination." *The National Bureau of Economic Research*, July 2003, www.nber. org/papers/w9873. [Note that this page has a link to a short summary as well as to the lengthy scholarly article.]
  - Hing, Julianne. "Experiment Shows Teachers View 'Deshawns' More Harshly Than 'Gregs.'" *Colorlines*, 20 April 2015, www. colorlines.com/articles/experiment-shows-teachers-view-deshawns-more-harshly-gregs.
- Recognize that while poverty crosses racial lines, white people in poverty still benefit from white privilege. This can be a major hurdle for white people to understand, so here are a few resources to consider:
  - Coates, Ta-Nehisi. "The Enduring Solidarity of Whiteness." *Atlantic*, 8 February 2016. www.theatlantic.com/politics/archive/ 2016/02/why-we-write/459909/.
  - Crosley-Corcoran, Gina. "Explaining White Privilege To A Broke White Person." *Huffington Post*, 14 July 2016, www.

huffingtonpost.com/gina-crosleycorcoran/explaining-white-privilege-to-a-broke-white-person_b_5269255.html.

- ○ Fletcher, Michael. "Poor Whites Live in Richer Neighborhoods than Middle-Class Blacks and Latinos." *Washington Post*, 24 June 2015, www.washingtonpost.com/news/wonk/wp/2015/06/24/poor-whites-live-in-richer-neighborhoods-than-middle-class-blacks-and-latinos/?utm_term=.dcfb62c10db1.
- ○ White, Gillian B. "How Black Middle-Class Kids Become Poor Adults." *Atlantic*, 8 February 2015, www.theatlantic.com/business/archive/2015/02/how-black-middle-class-kids-become-poor-adults/425253/.

- Create reading groups on the following books that specifically focus on how white people can develop a critical consciousness about race and racism and how to take action:
  - ○ Cushing, Bonnie Berman, et al., editors. *Accountability and White Anti-Racist Organizing: Stories from Our Work*. Crandall, Dostie & Douglass Books, Inc., 2010.
  - ○ Irving, Debby. *Waking Up White: And Finding Myself in the Story of Race*. Elephant Room Press, 2014.
    - – Irving's *Ted Talk* "Finding Myself in the Story of Race" is a great introduction to her work.
  - ○ Kaolin. *Talking About Race: A Workbook About White People Fostering Racial Equality in Their Lives*. Crandall, Dostie & Douglass Books, Inc., 2010.
  - ○ Kivel, Paul. *Uprooting Racism: How White People Can Work for Racial Justice*. 3rd ed., New Society Publishers, 2011.
  - ○ Schweizer, Tom. *Understanding What It Means to Be White and Privileged: Journal*. JPMC Press, 2016.
  - ○ Tochluk, Shelly. *Witnessing Whiteness: The Need to Talk About Race and How to Do It*. 2nd ed., Rowman & Littlefield, 2010.
- For those new to examining whiteness, consider the following:
  - ○ Peggy McIntosh's work can be a helpful place to begin, and it works well within the context of group activity and discussion. See "White Privilege: Unpacking the Invisible Knapsack" available in many anthologies and locations, including here: nationalseedproject.org/white-privilege-unpacking-the-invisible-knapsack.

- ○ Tim Wise's blog, books, and film *White Like Me*
- ○ Robin DiAngelo's work on "white fragility"
- ○ Chris Crass's books and presentations
- ○ Cook, Jeff. "Why I'm a Racist." *Huffington Post*, 15 July 2016, www.huffingtonpost.com/entry/why-im-a-racist_us_ 57893b9ee4b0e7c873500382.
- ○ Strauss, Valerie. "Teacher: A student told me I 'couldn't understand because I was a white lady.' Here's what I did then." *Washington Post*, 24 November 2015, www.washingtonpost.com/ news/answer-sheet/wp/2015/11/24/teacher-a-student-told-me-i-couldnt-understand-because-i-was-a-white-lady-heres-what-i-did-then/?utm_term=.c9c47ba9d94a.
- ○ Kapp, Jamie. "White Privilege, Explained in One Simple Comic." *Everyday Feminism*, 21 September 2014, everydayfem inism.com/2014/09/white-privilege-explained/.

- Recognize and learn more about the invention of whiteness. Learn how and why it was constructed in the first place, its placement at the top of the racial hierarchy, how it has been normalized through the law, and how it has been idealized in its association with beauty, intelligence, and reason. There are many Recommended Resources throughout this book to follow up on, especially these:
  - ○ Harris, Cheryl I. "Whiteness as Property." *Harvard Law Review*, vol. 106, no. 8, June 1993, pp. 1707–1791. JSTOR, www.jstor.org/stable/1341787.
  - ○ Painter, Nell Irvin. *The History of White People*. W.W. Norton & Company, 2010.
  - ○ López, Ian F. Haney. *White by Law: The Legal Construction of Race*. New York University Press, 1996.
  - ○ Lipsitz, George. *The Possessive Investment in Whiteness: How White People Profit from Identity Politics*. Temple University Press, 1998.
  - ○ Feagin, Joe R. *Racist America: Roots, Current Realities, and Future Reparations*. 3rd., Routledge, 2014.
  - ○ Jacobson, Matthew Frye. *Whiteness of a Different Color: European Immigrants and the Alchemy of Race*. Harvard University Press, 1998.
  - ○ Roediger, David R. *The Wages of Whiteness*. Revised ed., Verso, 1999.

- Delgado, Richard and Jean Stefancic, editors. *Critical White Studies: Looking Behind the Mirror.* Temple University Press, 1997.
- Recognize the history of the word "Caucasian," which Step 1 explains briefly. This word was invented in the 1700s to perpetuate the false belief that race is biological and that white people are superior. Does continuing to use this word today perpetuate these false ideas? Let's reconsider the continued use of this term.
- Recognize that the language of being an "ally" can be problematic because it implies that one can opt in and opt out at any point. Some use the language of being an "accomplice" instead.
- Participate in training for nonviolent direct action and civil disobedience.
- Participate in bystander intervention training.

5. Actions for Specific Audiences: Educators

There are many opportunities to engage students at various levels in action assignments associated with the ideas presented in this manual. Many of the suggestions already identified in Step 5 could be adapted for a classroom setting, but the suggestions that follow are aimed specifically at educators (K–12 and college). Note that there was a previous section (#3D) to support liberation-based education, and that was aimed more broadly to include parents, community members, and students, but it certainly applies to educators.

Professional Development

- Strengthen your understanding about the relationship between race, education, and justice. Join the Critical Race Studies in Education Association and consider attending their annual conference (see www.crsea.org/). Work on your own or with colleagues to explore recent work in this field:
  - Andrews, Dorinda J. Carter and Franklin Tuitt, editors. *Contesting the Myth of a "Post Racial" Era: The Continued Significance of Race in U.S. Education.* Peter Lang, 2013.
  - Emdin, Christopher. *For White Folks Who Teach in the Hood . . . and the Rest of Y'All Too.* Beacon Press, 2016.
  - hooks, bell. *Teaching to Transgress: Education as the Practice of Freedom.* Routledge, 1994.

- ○ Jiménez, Ileana. *Feminist Teacher.* 2017, feministteacher.com/. Also find her work on Twitter at @feministteacher.
- ○ Matias, Cheryl E. *Feeling White: Whiteness, Emotionality, and Education.* Sense Publishers, 2016.
- ○ Michael, Ali. *Raising Race Questions: Whiteness & Inquiry in Education.* Teachers College Press, 2015.
- ○ Picower, Bree and Edwin Mayorga, editors. *What's Race Got To Do With It?: How Current School Reform Policy Maintains Racial and Economic Inequality.* Peter Lang, 2015.
- ○ Picower, Bree and Rita Kohli, editors. *Confronting Racism in Teacher Education: Counternarratives of Critical Practice.* Routledge, 2017.
- ○ Staples, Brent. "Where Did All the Black Teachers Go?" *New York Times*, 20 April 2017, nyti.ms/2pFj74o.
- ○ Taylor, Edward, et al., editors. *Foundations of Critical Race Theory in Education.* 2nd ed., Routledge, 2016.
- ○ Tough, Paul. "Who Gets to Graduate?" *New York Times Magazine*, 15 May 2014, nyti.ms/2k6sruq.
- ○ Tuitt, Frank, et al., editors. *Race, Equity, and the Learning Environment: The Global Relevance of Critical and Inclusive Pedagogies in Higher Education.* Stylus Publishing, 2016.
- ○ Vilson, José Luis. *This Is Not a Test: A New Narrative on Race, Class, and Education.* Haymarket Books, 2014.
- Consider a specific part of this book that gets your attention. Perhaps it is a concept or an event that you have not learned much about or didn't learn more about until recently. Reflect on why that particular concept or event is not often taught. Follow up on the Recommended Resources to learn more. Educate your colleagues about this issue, and create strategies for raising awareness about this issue within your school, in your district, and at conferences. Develop strategies for integrating this issue into your classroom, and support other educators in doing the same.
- Follow educational activist-scholars like Edwin Mayorga, Yohuru Williams, and Bree Picower. Follow the Critical Education Policy Studies Group at Swarthmore.

- Create strategies for learning all of your students' names (the names by which the students want to be called) and pronouncing them correctly. From preschool to college, this is a clear action an educator can take that has a significant impact on a student. Find out what name the student wants used in class, use it, and check your pronunciation of the student's name with the student if needed. See, for example:
  - McLaughlin, Clare. "The Lasting Impact of Mispronouncing Students' Names." *NEA Today*, National Education Association, 1 September 2016, neatoday.org/2016/09/01/pronouncing-students-names/.
- Be careful about the assumptions you make regarding whether you think students did their own work. See, for example:
  - Martínez, Tiffany. "Academia, Love Me Back." *Tiffany Martínez: A Journal*, 27 October 2016, vivatiffany.wordpress.com/2016/10/27/academia-love-me-back/.

Educators Working With Other Educators

- In addition to organizing informal reading groups as described earlier, consider the coalitions you can develop with your colleagues to work together to redesign curriculum, plan events, advise clubs, and change or create policy, all with an intersectional approach to racial justice.
  - End the school-to-prison pipeline (see action #3D).
  - Attend a conference or workshop together (possibly with students) so you can take what you learn back to your school and address change together.
  - Bring racial justice training to your school. Consider, for example, Race Forward, Rootstrong, Crossroads Antiracism Organizing & Training, Anti-Oppression Resource and Training Alliance (AORTA), and Courageous Conversations.
  - Watch and discuss the videos on "Principals Share Advice on Addressing Racial Bias in Schools" (see www.edweek.org/ew/section/multimedia/principals-share-advice-on-addressing-racial-bias.html?cmp=SOC-SHR-TW).

Educators of Future Educators

- As you design curricula to teach students who will be future educators, do so with a racial justice, intersectional framework. The earlier future teachers develop an approach through which they reflect on pedagogy, curriculum, and policy in the context of race and power, the stronger their approach will become. Some of the resources suggested here could be integrated into education courses.

Supporting Students Outside of the Classroom

- Encourage students to use this book to help them create the racial justice education that they want to experience. Help students find out how they can participate in national organizations for students like the Youth Action Project and the Mikva Challenge. Encourage students to use their artistic talent and/or tech skills to raise awareness about racial justice in their school and community. Encourage students to work with the school librarian or local librarian to order books about racial justice and organize events that will raise awareness. Encourage students to run for student government with a racial justice platform.

Classroom Activities and Assignments (All Levels)

- The following websites provide a comprehensive selection of specific classroom activities, readings, and assignments for a wide range of levels (and note that they can also be helpful resources for parents):
  - *Rethinking Schools.* 2017, http://rethinkingschools.org/.
  - *Teaching a People's History.* The Zinn Education Project, 2017, zinnedproject.org/.
  - *Teaching for Change.* 2017, www.teachingforchange.org/.
  - *Teaching Tolerance.* Southern Poverty Law Center, 2017, www.tolerance.org/.
- Consider how you might integrate the Broadway musical *Hamilton* into your teaching. There are already many initiatives related to the use of the cast recording and the show (see #EduHam).

Lin-Manuel Miranda and Jeremy McCarter published an annotated libretto, *Hamilton: The Revolution.* The show prompts important questions about race and American history: what does it mean
for actors of color to portray the Founding Fathers? What does it
mean for hip-hop and its history to play such a significant role in
the show's music?

Classroom Activities and Assignments (College and High School)

- If students are reading this book as a required or optional
assignment, there are a variety of assignments that can be
developed to support their engagement with this text. Students
can select one issue from Steps 1 through 4 that catches their
attention and determine how to educate their peers about this
issue. They could create a presentation for the class, develop a
creative project, use social media, write a research paper, or create an exhibit. These could be part of a showcase, conference, or
other school event.

- Students can use any of the actions suggested in Step 5 to generate
an action plan that addresses a specific racial justice concern. They
could then write a letter to an elected official, find out how to support a local racial justice community organization, meet with the
school administration, propose an event or new club at the school,
develop a social media campaign, present a proposal to the school
board or local town council or other governing body, meet with a
state-wide elected official, senator, or member of Congress, have
a conversation (or series of conversations) with a family member
or friend to raise awareness, or carry out direct action. For inspir-
ing examples of high school students carrying out several of these
actions, watch the documentary *Precious Knowledge* (see action
#3D as well as Step 4). (This film works very well in the class-
room.) There could be time set aside for students to present their
actions to the class, perhaps before the action is taken to get feedback as well as after the action is taken to reflect on it. There could
be a showcase of presentations about these actions to further raise
awareness with other students, educators, and the community.

- Focus on how Representation Matters (see action #3C). You can provide some background reading for students regarding why representation matters (examples are included in action #3C). For high school students, consider polling them on what popular culture they are already consuming, and pick a few of those examples as ways to begin what could be watched and analyzed together. It's important to do some practice together, even if students are ultimately going to choose their own popular culture to research and analyze. When students in my college course on race do what I call the Media Social Action Assignment (the details of which are included on my blog dividednolonger.com), I've already provided them with ample tools for analyzing popular culture (including many of the articles listed in action #3C). Students pick a current piece of popular culture (a film, TV show, song, music video, video game, advertisement, etc.), submit a proposal about what they would like to focus on, receive feedback from me, do research, and receive feedback from their peers. Their final project includes two documents, the first of which is a five-page paper they write for me that creates a clear argument about their analysis of the pop culture. This argument responds to the assignment question: do they think the pop culture moves us closer to or further away from racial justice, and why? They also submit a copy of a letter/email that they are sending to the producer or someone responsible for the release of the popular culture, and here, the student requests a particular action that connects to the argument they're making in their paper. For example, if the student believes the popular culture reinforces a damaging stereotype, the action the student recommends might focus on the network no longer supporting this work and instead supporting more work featuring fully human, three-dimensional characters of color. The paper the student writes for me explains why the student is recommending this action. Students also share their conclusions with the class at the end of the semester. You can adapt this type of assignment in a variety of ways. Students could work together on the same popular culture. Students could start a social media campaign to draw attention to problematic stereotypes and/or support empowering work. Students could present their analysis to the class with clips of the popular culture. This work could be featured in a showcase class activity or something bigger. Students could take collective action together if they are working on the same popular culture and strategize together about an action plan.

- For any of these assignments in which students are working independently to do research and create something, it can be helpful to create a timeline with repeated check-ins. Students could begin by submitting a proposal and getting feedback. When students identify the action they want to take, they can be asked to reflect on why and how that action is relevant and appropriate for addressing the problem they're focusing on. The action plan they develop also needs a timeline. If they are meeting with a school official or elected official, for example, how is that meeting getting scheduled? If they are organizing an event, what process needs to occur to make those arrangements? Finally, after the action occurs, it's important to have an opportunity to reflect. This could be in the form of a paper the student submits, which summarizes the problem the student was trying to address, explains why the student chose the action to address it, and reports how the action went. If the student considers the action unsuccessful (for example, if an official rejects a proposal), it's important to encourage the student not to give up. What next step can the student take to pursue the issue? Likewise, even if a student considers the action successful, it's important to encourage the student to continue the work. What next step can the student take?

- The "Racism Machine" is one of many possible metaphors that can be used to represent and analyze systemic racism, and, as this book explains, it's one I find particularly helpful. Once students develop a foundation of the history of race and racism in this country, ask students to create their own metaphor. They could write a traditional paper about it, write a creative work about it, draw it, represent it through graphic design, or through other written, visual, or creative communication. There could be a showcase of student presentations/performances to teach other students, educators, and community members.

- Share and discuss any number of episodes of MTV's web series *Decoded* (see action #2C).
- Share and discuss the video *Unequal Opportunity Race* created by the African American Policy Forum (AAPF) (available at www. youtube.com/watch?v=eBb5TgOXgNY). Share and discuss background context about how the video was banned by a school board in Virginia. This website includes the AAPF's statement about the ban, as well as additional resources for educators (see www.aapf. org/2016/statement-from-aapf-and-naes).
- Share and discuss the *New York Times* info-graphic that shows "The Faces of American Power, Nearly as White as the Oscar Nominees" (see www.nytimes.com/interactive/2016/02/26/us/race-of-american-power.html?smid=fb-nytimes&smtyp=cur&_r=0). It's a powerful visual example that shows (as of February 2016) less than 10% of top decision makers in the areas of government, popular culture, book publishing, university education, music, news media, military, and sports are people of color.
- Share and discuss the *New York Times* short video op-doc "A Conversation With Latinos on Race" (see nyti.ms/2jT1q0y).
- Share and discuss the *New York Times* short video Op-Doc "A Conversation With Asian-Americans on Race" (see nyti.ms/2jZSnZo).

Classroom Activities and Assignments (K–8)

- The Representation Matters section (see action #3C) can be adapted for kids. For example, the music video for the song "Soy Yo" [That's Me] by the band Bomba Estéreo can be appropriate for many ages. It features an eleven-year-old Latina girl, Sarai Gonzalez, who is directly engaging with what it means to be a Latina girl (see www.youtube.com/watch?v=bxWxXncl53U). This article gives some context: Correaloct, Annie. "Declaring 'That's Me,' and Empowering Latinas." *New York Times*, 21 October 2016, nyti. ms/2jEW9qA. Consider showing it in class and facilitating a discussion about what the video means.
- The Representation Matters section (see action #3C) can also be adapted in relation to children's books. For example, in 2016,

eleven-year-old black girl Marley Dias was concerned that kids' books didn't have many characters who looked like her, so she created the campaign #1000blackgirlbooks. She's since collected many thousands of books and has been a source of inspiration to kids across the country. She's a great example that kids care about representation, that representation matters, and that kids can be effective activists. Here are a few related resources:

- Marley is working with the organization GrassRoots Community Foundation, which has a database and resource guide to support her campaign (see grassrootscommunityfoundation. org/1000-black-girl-books-resource-guide/).
- Marley also has a blog at *Elle* magazine, which you can find here: www.elle.com/marleymag/.
- The Cooperative Children Books Center at the School of Education at University of Wisconsin–Madison keeps annual statistics on "Children's Books By and About People of Color and First/Native Nations." They also include other related analysis (see ccbc.education.wisc.edu/books/pcstats.asp).
- Consider these recommendations
  - Russo, Maria. "Children's Books That Tackle Race and Ethnicity." *New York Times*, 23 September 2016, nyti. ms/2jYi7aQ.
  - "Where to Find Diverse Books." *We Need Diverse Books*. weneeddiversebooks.org/where-to-find-diverse-books/.

• The website for the textbook *Race: Are We So Different?* includes a section "For Kids (10 to 13)" available at www.understandingrace. org/kids.html.

• See Cowhey, Mary. *Black Ants and Buddhists: Thinking Critically and Teaching Differently in the Primary Grades.* Stenhouse Publishers, 2006.

Note: I will continue to update the blog I created in 2014, *Divided No Longer* (see dividednolonger.com), with additional resources and recommendations, so please check it out and email me suggestions (DismantlingTheRacismMachine@gmail.com). Educators, I would love for my blog to include sample assignments, so please email me.

Reflection Questions

1. What aspect of the Racism Machine do you want to learn more about, and why?
2. How will you reflect on your learning process?
3. What action do you want to begin with, and why?
4. How will you keep track of your progress on your action plan? Who will you share your plan with, and who will hold you accountable?
5. Do you know the racial history of your neighborhood, your profession, your religious organization, or another system you are close to? How might becoming more aware of this history (if you aren't already) inform your current relationship with this system and possibly what action you might take?

Recommended Resources

Note that these resources are broad-based and can relate to any aspect of Step 5. Other more specific resources are included within the relevant section of Step 5.

Websites

Race: Are We So Different? American Anthropological Association, 2016, www.understandingrace.org/.

Race: The Power of an Illusion. California Newsreel, www.pbs.org/race.

"Racial Equity Resource Guide." W.K. Kellogg Foundation, www.racialequityresourceguide.org/.

Southern Poverty Law Center. www.splcenter.org/.

Books

Cutting, Hunter and Makani Themba-Nixon. *Talking the Walk: A Communications Guide for Racial Justice.* AK Press, 2006.

Jobin-Leeds, Greg and AgitArte. *When We Fight We Win: Twenty-First-Century Social Movements and the Activists That Are Transforming Our World.* The New Press, 2016.

Liu, Eric. *You're More Powerful Than You Think: A Citizen's Guide to Making Change Happen.* Public Affairs, 2017.

Parker, Robin and Pamela Smith Chambers. *The Anti-Racist Cookbook: A Recipe Guide for Conversations About Race That Goes Beyond Covered Dishes and "Kum-Bah-Ya".* Crandall, Dostie & Douglass Books, Inc., 2005.

Sen, Rinku. *Stir It Up: Lessons in Community Organizing and Advocacy.* Jossey-Bass, 2003.

Smucker, Jonathan Matthew. *Hegemony How-to: A Roadmap for Radicals.* AK Press, 2017.

INDEX